Fundamentals of
Computer Programming

Fundamentals of Computer Programming

Emily Jones

www.statesacademicpress.com

Fundamentals of Computer Programming
Emily Jones
ISBN: 978-1-63989-224-2 (Hardback)

Published by States Academic Press,
109 South 5th Street,
Brooklyn, NY 11249, USA

Cataloging-in-Publication Data

Fundamentals of computer programming / Emily Jones.
    p. cm.
Includes bibliographical references and index.
ISBN 978-1-63989-224-2
1. Computer programming. 2. Coding theory. 3. Electronic data processing. I. Jones, Emily.
QA76.6 .F86 2022
001.642--dc23

For more information regarding States Academic Press and its products, please visit the publisher's website www.statesacademicpress.com

Table of Contents

Permissions

Index

Preface

This book is a culmination of my many years of practice in this field. I attribute the success of this book to my support group. I would like to thank my parents who have showered me with unconditional love and support and my peers and professors for their constant guidance.

The process of formulating and designing an executable computer program to establish a computing result is known as computer programming. It involves analysis, forming algorithms, profiling algorithms accuracy and resource consumption along with the use of algorithms in a particular programming language. The goal of the discipline is to identify a sequence of instructions that will lead to the performance of a particular task. Source code maintenance, management of derived artifacts, testing and debugging are some of the areas of study within this discipline. Robustness, portability, usability, efficiency and performance, reliability and maintainability are some of the fundamental requirements of computer programming. It uses techniques like object-oriented analysis and design, unified modelling language and model-driven architecture for the development of different software. This book provides comprehensive insights into the field of computer programming. Also included herein is a detailed explanation of the various concepts and applications of this discipline. It will serve as a valuable source of reference for those interested in this field.

The details of chapters are provided below for a progressive learning:

Chapter – Introduction

A set of instructions executed by a computer for performing specific tasks is termed as a computer program. The process of building and designing a computer program for achieving a specific computing result with the use of programming algorithms and codes is called computer programming. This chapter sheds light on computer programming for a thorough understanding of the subject.

Chapter – Computer Programming Languages

There are various languages that are used under the domain of computer programming. Some of them are C, C++, Java, Python, Perl, Ruby, HTML, etc. This chapter closely examines these various computer programming languages for a thorough understanding of the subject.

Chapter – Data Types and Structures

Data type is an attribute of data which tells the interpreter how the programmer wishes to use data. Data structure is an organization, storage and management format for systematic access and modification. Composite data type, abstract data type, variant type, object type, decision tree, binary tree, etc. are some of its types. This chapter discusses the subject of data types and structures in detail.

Chapter – Arrays, Strings and Variables

Arrays consist of a set of like variables stored at contiguous memory locations. Strings refer to series of characters either as a literal constant or some kind of variable. Variable is the storage address assigned to a storage area that stores value. This chapter has been carefully written to provide an easy understanding of arrays, strings and variables.

Chapter – Programming Tools

Different types of tools are used in computer programming namely compilers, linkers, assemblers, disassemblers, load testers, performance analysts, GUI development tool, debuggers, PyScripter, etc. This chapter closely examines these programming tools to provide an extensive understanding of the subject.

Emily Jones

1
Introduction

A set of instructions executed by a computer for performing specific tasks is termed as a computer program. The process of building and designing a computer program for achieving a specific computing result with the use of programming algorithms and codes is called computer programming. This chapter sheds light on computer programming for a thorough understanding of the subject.

Computer Program

Computer program is a detailed plan or procedure for solving a problem with a computer; more specifically, an unambiguous, ordered sequence of computational instructions necessary to achieve such a solution. The distinction between computer programs and equipment is often made by referring to the former as software and the latter as hardware.

Programs stored in the memory of a computer enable the computer to perform a variety of tasks in sequence or even intermittently. The idea of an internally stored program was introduced in the late 1940s by the Hungarian-born mathematician John von Neumann. The first digital computer designed with internal programming capacity was the EDVAC (acronym for Electronic Discrete Variable Automatic Computer), constructed in 1949.

A program is prepared by first formulating a task and then expressing it in an appropriate computer language, presumably one suited to the application. The specification thus rendered is translated, commonly in several stages, into a coded program directly executable by the computer on which the task is to be run. The coded program is said to be in machine language, while languages suitable for original formulation are called problem-oriented languages. A wide array of problem-oriented languages has been developed, some of the principal ones being COBOL (Common Business-Oriented Language), FORTRAN (Formula Translation), BASIC (Beginner's All-Purpose Symbolic Instruction Code), and Pascal.

Computers are supplied with various programs designed primarily to assist the user to run jobs or optimize system performance. This collection of programs, called the operating system, is as important to the operation of a computer system as its hardware.

Current technology makes it possible to build in some operating characteristics as fixed programs (introduced by customer orders) into a computer's central processing unit at the time of manufacture. Relative to user programs, the operating system may be in control during execution, as when a time-sharing (q.v.) monitor suspends one program and activates another, or at the time a user program is initiated or terminated, as when a scheduling program determines which user program is to be executed next. Certain operating-system programs, however, may operate as independent units to facilitate the programming process. These include translators (either assemblers or compilers), which transform an entire program from one language to another; interpreters, which execute a program sequentially, translating at each step; and debuggers, which execute a program piecemeal and monitor various circumstances, enabling the programmer to check whether the operation of the program is correct or not.

Computer Programming

Computer programming is defined as a process of developing and implementing various set of instructions given to the computer to perform a certain predefined task. Computer Programming is easy if it is appropriately managed. There are many computer programming languages available so finalizing the right language is not an easy task.

Basics of Programming

English is the most popular and well-known Human Language. The English language has its own set of grammar rules, which has to be followed to write in the English language correctly.Just like human languages, programming languages also follow grammar called syntax. There are certain basic program code elements which are common for all the programming languages.

Most important basic elements for programming languages are:

- Programming Environment.
- Data Types.
- Variables.
- Keywords.
- Logical and Arithmetical Operators.
- If else conditions.
- Loops.

- Numbers, Characters and Arrays.

- Functions.

- Input and Output Operations.

Applications of Computer Programming Languages

- Python: Web and Internet Development, Scientific and Numeric applications, Desktop GUIs, Business applications. It is widely used in AI and Machine Learning space.

- Java: Mostly used for developing Android apps, web apps, and Big data.

- R: Data Science projects, Statistical computing, Machine learning.

- Javascript: JavaScript usage include web/mobile app development, game development, and desktop app development.

- Swift: Swift is a specially designed language which works with Apple's Cocoa and Cocoa Touch frameworks to create all types of iOS apps.

- C++: C++ is widely used in Game Development, Advance Computations, and Graphics Compilers.

- C#: Widely used in Enterprise Cross-Applications Development, Web Applications.

- PHP: Web Development, Content Management Systems, eCommerce Applications.

- SQL: Used in Any Database.

- Go: Console utilities, GUI applications, and web applications.

Computer programming is a set of written instructions that the computer follows. These instructions can be written in various languages. Each programming languages have their unique ways of organizing the commands which are called syntax.

Multiple programming languages can help you solve the same programming problem. However, you need to select a language that you feel is relevant to perform your task. If you decide that a language does not suit your business requirement, you can always move on to a new language. Your skill in the chosen language will also be a deciding factor. Expected software system response time, a number of simultaneous users, security, maintains, compatibility with web, mobile, devices are few other factors to consider while choosing a language.

Principles of Programming

Learning some programming principles and using them in your code makes you a better developer. It improves the quality of code and later adding other functionality or making changes in it becomes easier for everyone.

KISS: Nobody in programming love to debug, maintain or make changes in complex code. "Keep It Simple, Stupid (KISS)" states that most systems work best if they are kept simple rather than making it complex, so when you are writing code your solution should not be complicated that takes a lot of time and effort to understand. If your code is simple then other developers won't face any problem understanding the code logic and they can easily proceed further with your code. So always try to simplify your code using different approaches like breaking a complex problem into smaller chunks or taking out some unnecessary code you have written.

DRY: Duplication of data, logic or function in code not only makes your code lengthy but also wastes a lot of time when it comes to maintain, debug or modify the code. If you need to make a small change in your code then you need to do it at several places. "Don't Repeat Yourself (DRY)" principal goal is to reduce the repetition of code. It states that a piece of code should be implemented in just one place in the source code. The opposite of the DRY principle is WET ("write everything twice" or "waste everyone's time") which breaks the DRY principle if you are writing the same logic at several places. You can create a common function or abstract your code to avoid the repetition in your code.

YAGNI: Your software or program can become larger and complex if you are writing some code which you may need in future but not at the moment. "You Aren't Gonna Need It (YAGNI)" principle states that "don't implement something until it is necessary" because in most of the cases you are not going to use that piece of code in future. Most of the programmers while implementing software think about the future possibility and add some code or logic for some other features which they don't need at present. They add all the unnecessary class and functionality which maybe they never use in the future. Doing this is completely wrong and you will eventually end up in writing bloated code also your project becomes complicated and difficult to maintain. We recommend all the programmers to avoid this mistake to save a lot of time and effort.

SOLID: The SOLID principle stands for five principles which are Single responsibility, Open-closed, Liskov substitution, Interface Segregation, and Dependency inversion.

Separation of Concerns (SoC): Separation of Concerns Principle partition a complicated application into different sections or domains. Each section or domain addresses a separate concern or has a specific job. Each section is independent of each other and that's why each section can be tackled independently also it becomes easier to maintain, update and reuse the code.

For example business logic (the content of the webpage) in an application is a different concern and user interface is a different concern in a web application program. One of the good examples of SoC is the MVC pattern where data ("model"), the logic ("controller"), and what the end-user sees ("view") divided into three different sections and each part is handled independently. Saving of data to a database has nothing to do with rendering the data on the web.

Avoid Premature Optimization: It is true that optimization helps in speeding up the program or algorithm but according to this principle you don't need to optimize your algorithm at an early stage of development. If you do premature optimization you won't be able to know where a program's bottlenecks will be and maintenance will become harder for you. If you optimize your code in the beginning and in case if the requirement may change than your efforts will be wasted and your code will go to the garbage. So it's better to optimize the algorithm at the right time to get the right benefit of it.

Law of Demeter: It is also known as the principle of least knowledge. This principle divides the responsibility between classes or different units and it can be summarized in three points.

- Each unit should have only limited knowledge about other units: only units "closely" related to the current unit.

- Each unit should only talk to its friends; don't talk to strangers.

- Only talk to your immediate friends.

The Law of Demeter helps in maintaining independent classes and makes your code less coupled which is very important in software development to make your application flexible, stable, maintainable and understandable.

Paradigms of Programming

There are also different types of programming paradigms: different ways to express logic, and different functionalities for each programming language that at an aggregate level, can be summed up into categorical differences.

- Declarative: Declarative programming is very simple and plain. It expresses the logic of a particular computation without specifying its flow. The easiest way to think about it is a programming language that declares what task is being done rather than how it should be done. Examples of this include programming languages like SQL, whose syntax is focused on explicitly specifying exactly what you want as opposed to specifying how it's done (ex: the SELECT command which selects data). The underlying steps behind the SELECT query do not have to be explicitly defined for the machine to act upon its underlying logic.

- Imperative:Imperative programming focuses on how a task is being done rather than what is being done, unlike the declarative model. Much like how in the imperative mode of language where commands are given, the imperative programming paradigm describes to machines how they should carry out a task. Imperative languages include languages such as Java, JavaScript, and Ruby, though all of them also have object-oriented logic as well — and most of them are multi-paradigm languages that are compatible with a variety of programming paradigms.

- Functional: Functional programming is based on mathematical functions. While here too, commands are meant to specify how routines are carried out rather than what routines are carried out, unlike in the imperative paradigm, the state of a current program cannot be affected incidentally: What this means in practice is that you can have functions without return calls, since the program state will remain constant. Functional programming is emphasized in academia with languages such as Lisp and Clojure prominently supporting functional programming as a paradigm.

- Object-oriented: The dominant programming paradigm since the 1980s, object-oriented programming involves building objects with data attributes and programming subroutines known as methods which can then, in turn, be invoked or modified. Languages such as Java, Python, C, C++, PHP, and Ruby are all principally object-oriented. Critically, unlike imperative or functional programming, the concept of inheritance and code reusability are firmly entrenched in programming objects which can persist either as classes (the definition of how a set of objects is defined, and what data they can carry) or objects themselves (which often correspond to real-world objects and a collection of attributes associated with them).

2
Computer Programming Languages

There are various languages that are used under the domain of computer programming. Some of them are C, C++, Java, Python, Perl, Ruby, HTML, etc. This chapter closely examines these various computer programming languages for a thorough understanding of the subject.

Computer programming languages allow us to give instructions to a computer in a language the computer understands. Just as many human-based languages exist, there are arrays of computer programming languages that programmers can use to communicate with a computer. The portion of the language that a computer can understand is called a "binary." Translating programming language into binary is known as "compiling." Each language, from C Language to Python, has its own distinct features, though many times there are commonalities between programming languages. These languages allow computers to quickly and efficiently process large and complex swaths of information. For example, if a person is given a list of randomized numbers ranging from one to ten thousand and is asked to place them in ascending order, chances are that it will take a sizable amount of time and include some errors.

Although many languages share similarities, each has its own syntax. Once a programmer learns the languages rules, syntax, and structure, they write the source code in a text editor or IDE. Then, the programmer often compiles the code into machine language that can be understood by the computer. Scripting languages, which do not require a compiler, use an interpreter to execute the script.

Types of Programming Languages

Each of the different programming languages can be broken into one or more of the following types (paradigms) of languages:

- High-level (most common)/low-level.

- Declarative/imperative/procedural.

- General-purpose/domain-specific.

- Object-oriented / concurrent.

- Command/Compiled/Script language.

- Answer set.

Applications and Program Development

Application and program development involves programs you work with on a daily basis. For example, the Internet browser you are using is considered a program.

Artificial Intelligence Development

Artificial intelligence or related fields involve creating the character interactions in computer games, portions of programs that make decisions, chatbots, and more. If you're interested in developing an AI, consider the following languages:

- AIML.

- C.

- C#.

- C++.

- Prolog.

- Python.

Database Development

Database developers create and maintain databases. If you're interested in creating or maintaining a database, consider any of the following languages:

- DBASE.

- FoxPro.

- MySQL.

- SQL.

- Visual FoxPro.

- Game development.

Game development involves creating computer games or other entertainment software. If you're interested in developing a game, consider the following languages:

- C.
- C#.
- C++.
- DarkBASIC.
- Java.

Computer Drivers or other Hardware Development

Computer drivers and programming hardware interface support are a necessity for hardware functionality. If you're interested in developing drivers or software interfaces for hardware devices, consider the following languages:

- Assembly.
- C.

Internet and Web Page Development

Internet and web page development are the essence of the Internet. Without developers, the Internet would not exist. If you're interested in creating web pages, Internet applications, or other Internet-related tasks, consider the following languages:

- HDML.
- HTML.
- Java.
- JavaScript.
- Perl.
- PHP.
- Python.
- XML.

Script Development

Although it is not likely to become a career, knowing how to create and develop scripts can increase productivity for you or your company, saving you countless hours. If you're interested in developing scripts, consider the following languages:

- AutoHotkey.

- Awk.

- Bash.

- Batch file.

- Perl.

- Python.

- Tcl.

Language Types

Machine and Assembly Languages

A machine language consists of the numeric codes for the operations that a particular computer can execute directly. The codes are strings of 0s and 1s, or binary digits ("bits"), which are frequently converted both from and to hexadecimal (base 16) for human viewing and modification. Machine language instructions typically use some bits to represent operations, such as addition, and some to represent operands, or perhaps the location of the next instruction. Machine language is difficult to read and write, since it does not resemble conventional mathematical notation or human language, and its codes vary from computer to computer.

Assembly language is one level above machine language. It uses short mnemonic codes for instructions and allows the programmer to introduce names for blocks of memory that hold data. One might thus write "add pay, total" instead of "0110101100101000" for an instruction that adds two numbers.

Assembly language is designed to be easily translated into machine language. Although blocks of data may be referred to by name instead of by their machine addresses, assembly language does not provide more sophisticated means of organizing complex information. Like machine language, assembly language requires detailed knowledge of internal computer architecture. It is useful when such details are important, as in programming a computer to interact with input/output devices (printers, scanners, storage devices, and so forth).

Algorithmic Languages

Algorithmic languages are designed to express mathematical or symbolic computations. They can express algebraic operations in notation similar to mathematics and allow the use of subprograms that package commonly used operations for reuse. They were the first high-level languages.

Fortran

The first important algorithmic language was FORTRAN (formula translation), designed in 1957 by an IBM team led by John Backus. It was intended for scientific computations with real numbers and collections of them organized as one- or multidimensional arrays. Its control structures included conditional IF statements, repetitive loops (so-called DO loops), and a GOTO statement that allowed nonsequential execution of program code. FORTRAN made it convenient to have subprograms for common mathematical operations, and built libraries of them. FORTRAN was also designed to translate into efficient machine language. It was immediately successful and continues to evolve.

Algol

ALGOL (algorithmic language) was designed by a committee of American and European computer scientists during 1958–60 for publishing algorithms, as well as for doing computations. Like LISP, ALGOL had recursive subprograms—procedures that could invoke themselves to solve a problem by reducing it to a smaller problem of the same kind. ALGOL introduced block structure, in which a program is composed of blocks that might contain both data and instructions and have the same structure as an entire program. Block structure became a powerful tool for building large programs out of small components.

ALGOL contributed a notation for describing the structure of a programming language, Backus–Naur Form, which in some variation became the standard tool for stating the syntax (grammar) of programming languages. ALGOL was widely used in Europe, and for many years it remained the language in which computer algorithms were published. Many important languages, such as Pascal and Ada, are its descendants.

Lisp

LISP (list processing) was developed about 1960 by John McCarthy at the Massachusetts Institute of Technology (MIT) and was founded on the mathematical theory of recursive functions (in which a function appears in its own definition). A LISP program is a function applied to data, rather than being a sequence of procedural steps as in FORTRAN and ALGOL. LISP uses a very simple notation in which operations and their operands are given in a parenthesized list. For example, (+ a (* b c)) stands for a + b*c. Although this appears awkward, the notation works well for computers. LISP also uses the list structure to represent data, and, because programs and data use the same structure, it is easy for a LISP program to operate on other programs as data.

LISP became a common language for artificial intelligence (AI) programming, partly owing to the confluence of LISP and AI work at MIT and partly because AI programs capable of "learning" could be written in LISP as self-modifying programs. LISP has evolved through numerous dialects, such as Scheme and Common LISP.

Business-oriented Languages

Sql

SQL (structured query language) is a language for specifying the organization of databases (collections of records). Databases organized with SQL are called relational because SQL provides the ability to query a database for information that falls in a given relation. For example, a query might be "find all records with both last_name Smith and city New York." Commercial database programs commonly use a SQL-like language for their queries.

Education-oriented Languages

Basic

BASIC (beginner's all-purpose symbolic instruction code) was designed in the mid-1960s by John Kemeny and Thomas Kurtz. It was intended to be easy to learn by novices, particularly non-computer science majors, and to run well on a time-sharing computer with many users. It had simple data structures and notation and it was interpreted: a BASIC program was translated line-by-line and executed as it was translated, which made it easy to locate programming errors.

Its small size and simplicity also made BASIC a popular language for early personal computers. Its recent forms have adopted many of the data and control structures of other contemporary languages, which makes it more powerful but less convenient for beginners.

Logo

Logo originated in the late 1960s as a simplified LISP dialect for education; Seymour Papert and others used it at MIT to teach mathematical thinking to schoolchildren. It had a more conventional syntax than LISP and featured "turtle graphics," a simple method for generating computer graphics. (The name came from an early project to program a turtlelike robot). Turtle graphics used body-centred instructions, in which an object was moved around a screen by commands, such as "left 90" and "forward," that specified actions relative to the current position and orientation of the object rather than in terms of a fixed framework. Together with recursive routines, this technique made it easy to program intricate and attractive patterns.

Hypertalk

Hypertalk was designed as "programming for the rest of us" by Bill Atkinson for Apple's Macintosh. Using a simple English-like syntax, Hypertalk enabled anyone to combine text, graphics, and audio quickly into "linked stacks" that could be navigated by clicking with a mouse on standard buttons supplied by the program. Hypertalk was particularly popular among educators in the 1980s and early '90s for classroom multimedia presentations. Although Hypertalk had many features of object-oriented languages, Apple did not develop it for other computer platforms and let it languish; as Apple's market share declined in the 1990s, a new cross-platform way of displaying multimedia left Hypertalk all but obsolete.

C++

The C++ language, developed by Bjarne Stroustrup at AT&T in the mid-1980s, extended C by adding objects to it while preserving the efficiency of C programs. It has been one of the most important languages for both education and industrial programming. Large parts of many operating systems, such as the Microsoft Corporation's Windows 98, were written in C++.

Ada

Ada was named for Augusta Ada King, countess of Lovelace, who was an assistant to the 19th-century English inventor Charles Babbage, and is sometimes called the first computer programmer. Ada, the language, was developed in the early 1980s for large-scale programming. It combined Pascal-like notation with the ability to package operations and data into independent modules. Its first form, Ada 83, was not fully object-oriented, but the subsequent Ada 95 provided objects and the ability to construct hierarchies of them. While no longer mandated for use in work for the Department of Defense, Ada remains an effective language for engineering large programs.

Java

In the early 1990s, Java was designed as a programming language for the World Wide Web (WWW). Although it resembled C++ in appearance, it was fully object-oriented. In particular, Java dispensed with lower-level features, including the ability to manipulate data addresses, a capability that is neither desirable nor useful in programs for distributed systems. In order to be portable, Java programs are translated by a Java Virtual Machine specific to each computer platform, which then executes the Java program. In addition to adding interactive capabilities to the Internet through Web "applets," Java has been widely used for programming small and portable devices, such as mobile telephones.

Visual Basic

Visual Basic was developed by Microsoft to extend the capabilities of BASIC by adding objects and "event-driven" programming: buttons, menus, and other elements of graphical user interfaces (GUIs). Visual Basic can also be used within other Microsoft software to program small routines.

Declarative Languages

Declarative languages, also called nonprocedural or very high level, are programming languages in which (ideally) a program specifies what is to be done rather than how to do it. In such languages there is less difference between the specification of a program and its implementation than in the procedural languages. The two common kinds of declarative languages are logic and functional languages.

Logic programming languages, of which PROLOG (programming in logic) is the best known, state a program as a set of logical relations (e.g., a grandparent is the parent of a parent of someone). Such languages are similar to the SQL database language. A program is executed by an "inference engine" that answers a query by searching these relations systematically to make inferences that will answer a query. PROLOG has been used extensively in natural language processing and other AI programs.

Functional languages have a mathematical style. A functional program is constructed by applying functions to arguments. Functional languages, such as LISP, ML, and Haskell, are used as research tools in language development, in automated mathematical theorem provers, and in some commercial projects.

Scripting Languages

Scripting languages are sometimes called little languages. They are intended to solve relatively small programming problems that do not require the overhead of data declarations and other features needed to make large programs manageable. Scripting languages are used for writing operating system utilities, for special-purpose file-manipulation programs, and, because they are easy to learn, sometimes for considerably larger programs.

PERL (practical extraction and report language) was developed in the late 1980s, originally for use with the UNIX operating system. It was intended to have all the capabilities of earlier scripting languages. PERL provided many ways to state common operations and thereby allowed a programmer to adopt any convenient style. In the 1990s it became popular as a system-programming tool, both for small utility programs and for prototypes of larger ones. Together with other languages, it also became popular for programming computer Web "servers."

Document Formatting Languages

Document formatting languages specify the organization of printed text and graphics. They fall into several classes: text formatting notation that can serve the same functions as a word processing program, page description languages that are interpreted by a printing device, and, most generally, markup languages that describe the intended function of portions of a document.

TeX

TeX was developed during 1977–86 as a text formatting language by Donald Knuth, to improve the quality of mathematical notation in his books. Text formatting systems, unlike WYSIWYG ("What You See Is What You Get") word processors, embed plain text formatting commands in a document, which are then interpreted by the language processor to produce a formatted document for display or printing. TeX marks italic text, for example, as {\it this is italicized}, which is then displayed as this is italicized.

TeX largely replaced earlier text formatting languages. Its powerful and flexible abilities gave an expert precise control over such things as the choice of fonts, layout of tables, mathematical notation, and the inclusion of graphics within a document. It is generally used with the aid of "macro" packages that define simple commands for common operations, such as starting a new paragraph; LaTeX is a widely used package. TeX contains numerous standard "style sheets" for different types of documents, and these may be further adapted by each user. There are also related programs such as BibTeX, which manages bibliographies and has style sheets for all of the common bibliography styles, and versions of TeX for languages with various alphabets.

PostScript

PostScript is a page-description language developed in the early 1980s by Adobe Systems Incorporated on the basis of work at Xerox PARC . Such languages describe documents in terms that can be interpreted by a personal computer to display the document on its screen or by a microprocessor in a printer or a typesetting device.

PostScript commands can, for example, precisely position text, in various fonts and sizes, draw images that are mathematically described, and specify colour or shading. PostScript uses postfix, also called reverse Polish notation, in which an operation name follows its arguments. Thus, "300 600 20 270 arc stroke" means: Draw ("stroke") a 270-degree arc with radius 20 at location (300, 600). Although PostScript can be read and written by a programmer, it is normally produced by text formatting programs, word processors, or graphic display tools.

The success of PostScript is due to its specification's being in the public domain and to its being a good match for high-resolution laser printers. It has influenced the development of printing fonts, and manufacturers produce a large variety of PostScript fonts.

SGML

SGML (standard generalized markup language) is an international standard for the definition of markup languages; that is, it is a metalanguage. Markup consists of notations called tags that specify the function of a piece of text or how it is to be displayed. SGML emphasizes descriptive markup, in which a tag might be "<emphasis>." Such a markup denotes the document function, and it could be interpreted as reverse video on a computer screen, underlining by a typewriter, or italics in typeset text.

SGML is used to specify DTDs (document type definitions). A DTD defines a kind of document, such as a report, by specifying what elements must appear in the document—e.g., <Title>—and giving rules for the use of document elements, such as that a paragraph may appear within a table entry but a table may not appear within a paragraph. A marked-up text may be analyzed by a parsing program to determine if it conforms to a DTD. Another program may read the markups to prepare an index or to translate the document into PostScript for printing. Yet another might generate large type or audio for readers with visual or hearing disabilities.

World Wide Web Display Languages

HTML

The World Wide Web is a system for displaying text, graphics, and audio retrieved over the Internet on a computer monitor. Each retrieval unit is known as a Web page, and such pages frequently contain "links" that allow related pages to be retrieved. HTML (hypertext markup language) is the markup language for encoding Web pages. It was designed by Tim Berners-Lee at the CERN nuclear physics laboratory in Switzerland during the 1980s and is defined by an SGML DTD. HTML markup tags specify document elements such as headings, paragraphs, and tables. They mark up a document for display by a computer program known as a Web browser.

The browser interprets the tags, displaying the headings, paragraphs, and tables in a layout that is adapted to the screen size and fonts available to it. HTML documents also contain anchors, which are tags that specify links to other Web pages.

XML

HTML does not allow one to define new text elements; that is, it is not extensible. XML (extensible markup language) is a simplified form of SGML intended for documents that are published on the Web. Like SGML, XML uses DTDs to define document types and the meanings of tags used in them. XML adopts conventions that make it easy to parse, such as that document entities are marked by both a beginning and an ending tag, such as <BEGIN>...</BEGIN>. XML provides more kinds of hypertext links than HTML, such as bidirectional links and links relative to a document subsection.

Because an author may define new tags, an XML DTD must also contain rules that instruct a Web browser how to interpret them—how an entity is to be displayed or how it is to generate an action such as preparing an e-mail message.

Web Scripting

Web pages marked up with HTML or XML are largely static documents. Web scripting can add information to a page as a reader uses it or let the reader enter information that may, for example, be passed on to the order department of an online business. CGI (common gateway interface) provides one mechanism; it transmits requests and responses between the reader's Web browser and the Web server that provides the page. The CGI component on the server contains small programs called scripts that take information from the browser system or provide it for display. A simple script might ask the reader's name, determine the Internet address of the system that the reader uses, and print a greeting. Scripts may be written in any programming language, but, because they are generally simple text-processing routines, scripting languages like PERL are particularly appropriate.

Another approach is to use a language designed for Web scripts to be executed by the browser. JavaScript is one such language, designed by the Netscape Communications Corp., which may be used with both Netscape's and Microsoft's browsers. JavaScript is a simple language, quite different from Java. A JavaScript program may be embedded in a Web page with the HTML tag <script language="JavaScript">. JavaScript instructions following that tag will be executed by the browser when the page is selected. In order to speed up display of dynamic (interactive) pages, JavaScript is often combined with XML or some other language for exchanging information between the server and the client's browser. In particular, the XMLHttpRequest command enables asynchronous data requests from the server without requiring the server to resend the entire Web page. This approach, or "philosophy," of programming is called Ajax (asynchronous JavaScript and XML).

VB Script is a subset of Visual Basic. Originally developed for Microsoft's Office suite of programs, it was later used for Web scripting as well. Its capabilities are similar to those of JavaScript, and it may be embedded in HTML in the same fashion.

Behind the use of such scripting languages for Web programming lies the idea of component programming, in which programs are constructed by combining independent previously written components without any further language processing. JavaScript and VB Script programs were designed as components that may be attached to Web browsers to control how they display information.

Elements of Programming

Despite notational differences, contemporary computer languages provide many of the same programming structures. These include basic control structures and data structures. The former provide the means to express algorithms, and the latter provide ways to organize information.

Control Structures

Programs written in procedural languages, the most common kind, are like recipes, having lists of ingredients and step-by-step instructions for using them. The three basic control structures in virtually every procedural language are:

- Sequence: Combine the liquid ingredients, and next add the dry ones.

- Conditional: If the tomatoes are fresh then simmer them, but if canned, skip this step.

- Iterative: Beat the egg whites until they form soft peaks.

Sequence is the default control structure; instructions are executed one after another. They might, for example, carry out a series of arithmetic operations, assigning results to variables, to find the roots of a quadratic equation $ax^2 + bx + c = 0$. The conditional IF-THEN or IF-THEN-ELSE control structure allows a program to follow alternative paths of execution. Iteration, or looping, gives computers much of their power. They can repeat a sequence of steps as often as necessary, and appropriate repetitions of quite simple steps can solve complex problems.

These control structures can be combined. A sequence may contain several loops; a loop may contain a loop nested within it, or the two branches of a conditional may each contain sequences with loops and more conditionals. In the "pseudocode" "*" indicates multiplication and "←" is used to assign values to variables. The following programming fragment employs the IF-THEN structure for finding one root of the quadratic equation, using the quadratic formula:

$$x = \frac{-b \pm \sqrt{b^2 - 4ac}}{2a}.$$

The quadratic formula assumes that a is nonzero and that the discriminant (the portion within the square root sign) is not negative (in order to obtain a real number root). Conditionals check those assumptions:

- IF a = 0 THEN.

- ROOT ← −c/b.

- ELSE.

- DISCRIMINANT ← b*b − 4*a*c.

- IF DISCRIMINANT ≥ 0 THEN.

- ROOT ← (−b + SQUARE_ROOT(DISCRIMINANT))/2*a.

- ENDIF.

- ENDIF.

The SQUARE_ROOT function used in the above fragment is an example of a subprogram (also called a procedure, subroutine, or function). A subprogram is like a sauce recipe given once and used as part of many other recipes. Subprograms take inputs (the quantity needed) and produce results (the sauce). Commonly used subprograms are generally in a collection or library provided with a language. Subprograms may call other subprograms in their definitions, as shown by the following routine (where ABS is the absolute-value function). SQUARE_ROOT is implemented by using a WHILE (indefinite) loop that produces a good approximation for the square root of real numbers unless x is very small or very large. A subprogram is written by declaring its name, the type of input data, and the output:

- FUNCTION SQUARE_ROOT(REAL x) RETURNS REAL.

- ROOT ← 1.0.

- WHILE ABS(ROOT*ROOT − x) ≥ 0.000001.

- AND WHILE ROOT ← (x/ROOT + ROOT)/2.

- RETURN ROOT.

Subprograms can break a problem into smaller, more tractable subproblems. Sometimes a problem may be solved by reducing it to a subproblem that is a smaller version of the original. In that case the routine is known as a recursive subprogram because it solves the problem by repeatedly calling itself. For example, the factorial function in mathematics ($n! = n·(n−1)···3·2·1$—i.e., the product of the first n integers), can be programmed as a recursive routine:

- FUNCTION FACTORIAL(INTEGER n) RETURNS INTEGER.

- IF n = 0 THEN RETURN 1.

- ELSE RETURN n * FACTORIAL(n−1).

At the machine-language level, loops and conditionals are implemented with branch instructions that say "jump to" a new point in the program. The "goto" statement in higher-level languages expresses the same operation but is rarely used because it makes it difficult for humans to follow the "flow" of a program. Some languages, such as Java and Ada, do not allow it.

Data Structures

Whereas control structures organize algorithms, data structures organize information. In particular, data structures specify types of data, and thus which operations can be performed on them, while eliminating the need for a programmer to keep track of memory addresses. Simple data structures include integers, real numbers, Booleans (true/false), and characters or character strings. Compound data structures are formed by combining one or more data types.

The most important compound data structures are the array, a homogeneous collection of data, and the record, a heterogeneous collection. An array may represent a vector of numbers, a list of strings, or a collection of vectors (an array of arrays, or mathematical matrix). A record might store employee information—name, title, and salary. An array of records, such as a table of employees, is a collection of elements, each of which is heterogeneous. Conversely, a record might contain a vector—i.e., an array.

Record components, or fields, are selected by name; for example, E.SALARY might represent the salary field of record E. An array element is selected by its position or index; A is the element at position 10 in array A. A FOR loop (definite iteration) can thus run through an array with index limits (FIRST TO LAST in the following example) in order to sum its elements:

- FOR i ← FIRST TO LAST

- SUM ← SUM + A[i]

Arrays and records have fixed sizes. Structures that can grow are built with dynamic allocation, which provides new storage as required. These data structures have components, each containing data and references to further components (in machine terms, their addresses). Such self-referential structures have recursive definitions. A bintree (binary tree) for example, either is empty or contains a root component with data and left and right bintree "children." Such bintrees implement tables of information efficiently. Subroutines to operate on them are naturally recursive; the following routine prints out all the elements of a bintree (each is the root of some subtree):

- PROCEDURE TRAVERSE(ROOT: BINTREE).

- IF NOT(EMPTY(ROOT)).

- TRAVERSE(ROOT.LEFT).

- PRINT ROOT.DATA.

- TRAVERSE(ROOT.RIGHT).

- ENDIF.

Abstract data types (ADTs) are important for large-scale programming. They package data structures and operations on them, hiding internal details. For example, an ADT table provides insertion and lookup operations to users while keeping the underlying structure, whether an array, list, or binary tree, invisible. In object-oriented languages, classes are ADTs and objects are instances of them. The following object-oriented pseudocode example assumes that there is an ADT bintree and a "superclass" COMPARABLE, characterizing data for which there is a comparison operation (such as "<" for integers). It defines a new ADT, TABLE, that hides its data-representation and provides operations appropriate to tables. This class is polymorphic—defined in terms of an element-type parameter of the COMPARABLE class. Any instance of it must specify that type, here a class with employee data (the COMPARABLE declaration means that PERS_REC must provide a comparison operation to sort records). Implementation details are omitted.

- CLASS TABLE OF <COMPARABLE T>.

- PRIVATE DATA: BINTREE OF <T>.

- PUBLIC INSERT(ITEM: T).

- PUBLIC LOOKUP(ITEM: T) RETURNS BOOLEAN.

- END.

- CLASS PERS_REC: COMPARABLE.

- PRIVATE NAME: STRING.

- PRIVATE POSITION: {STAFF, SUPERVISOR, MANAGER}.

- PRIVATE SALARY: REAL.

- PUBLIC COMPARE (R: PERS_REC) RETURNS BOOLEAN.

- END.

- EMPLOYEES: TABLE <PERS_REC>.

TABLE makes public only its own operations; thus, if it is modified to use an array or list rather than a bintree, programs that use it cannot detect the change. This information hiding is essential to managing complexity in large programs. It divides them into small parts, with "contracts" between the parts; here the TABLE class contracts to provide lookup and insertion operations, and its users contract to use only the operations so publicized.

C Language

C is a general-purpose, procedural computer programming language supporting structured programming, lexical variable scope, and recursion, while a static type system prevents unintended operations. By design, C provides constructs that map efficiently to typical machine instructions and has found lasting use in applications previously coded in assembly language. Such applications include operating systems and various application software for computers, from supercomputers to embedded systems.

C was originally developed at Bell Labs by Dennis Ritchie between 1972 and 1973 to make utilities running on Unix. Later, it was applied to re-implementing the kernel of the Unix operating system. During the 1980s, C gradually gained popularity. It has become one of the most widely used programming languages, with C compilers from various vendors available for the majority of existing computer architectures and operating systems.

C is an imperative procedural language. It was designed to be compiled using a relatively straightforward compiler to provide low-level access to memory and language constructs that map efficiently to machine instructions, all with minimal runtime support. Despite its low-level capabilities, the language was designed to encourage cross-platform programming. A standards-compliant C program written with portability in mind can be compiled for a wide variety of computer platforms and operating systems with few changes to its source code. The language is available on various platforms, from embedded microcontrollers to supercomputers.

Dennis Ritchie (right), the inventor of the C programming language, with Ken Thompson.

Like most procedural languages in the ALGOL tradition, C has facilities for structured programming and allows lexical variable scope and recursion. Its static type system prevents unintended operations. In C, all executable code is contained within subroutines (also called "functions", though not strictly in the sense of functional programming). Function parameters are always passed by value. Pass-by-reference is simulated in C by explicitly passing pointer values. C program source text is free-format, using the semicolon as a statement terminator and curly braces for grouping blocks of statements.

The C language also exhibits the following characteristics:

- The language has a small, fixed number of keywords, including a full set of control flow primitives: `if`/`else`, `for`, `do`/`while`, `while`, and `switch`. User-defined names are not distinguished from keywords by any kind of sigil.

- It has a large number of arithmetic, bitwise, and logic operators: `+`, `+=`, `++`, `&`, `||`, etc.

- More than one assignment may be performed in a single statement.

- Functions:

  ○ Function return values can be ignored, when not needed.

  ○ Function and data pointers permit ad hoc run-time polymorphism.

  ○ Functions may not be defined within the lexical scope of other functions.

- Data typing is static, but weakly enforced; all data has a type, but implicit conversions are possible.

- Declaration syntax mimics usage context. C has no "define" keyword; instead, a statement beginning with the name of a type is taken as a declaration. There is no "function" keyword; instead, a function is indicated by the presence of a parenthesized argument list.

- User-defined (typedef) and compound types are possible.

  ○ Heterogeneous aggregate data types (`struct`) allow related data elements to be accessed and assigned as a unit.

  ○ Union is a structure with overlapping members; only the last member stored is valid.

  ○ Array indexing is a secondary notation, defined in terms of pointer arithmetic. Unlike structs, arrays are not first-class objects: they cannot be assigned or compared using single built-in operators. There is no "array" keyword in use or definition; instead, square brackets indicate arrays syntactically, for example `month`.

  ○ Enumerated types are possible with the `enum` keyword. They are freely interconvertible with integers.

  ○ Strings are not a distinct data type, but are conventionally implemented as null-terminated character arrays.

- Low-level access to computer memory is possible by converting machine addresses to typed pointers.

- Procedures (subroutines not returning values) are a special case of function, with an untyped return type `void`.

- A preprocessor performs macro definition, source code file inclusion, and conditional compilation.

- There is a basic form of modularity: files can be compiled separately and linked together, with control over which functions and data objects are visible to other files via `static` and `extern` attributes.

- Complex functionality such as I/O, string manipulation, and mathematical functions are consistently delegated to library routines.

While C does not include certain features found in other languages (such as object orientation and garbage collection), these can be implemented or emulated, often through the use of external libraries (e.g., the GLib Object System or the Boehm garbage collector).

Relations to Other Languages

Many later languages have borrowed directly or indirectly from C, including C++, C#, Unix's C shell, D, Go, Java, JavaScript (including transpilers), Limbo, LPC, Objective-C, Perl, PHP, Python, Rust, Swift, Verilog and SystemVerilog (hardware description languages). These languages have drawn many of their control structures and other basic features from C. Most of them (Python being a dramatic exception) also express highly similar syntax to C, and they tend to combine the recognizable expression and statement syntax of C with underlying type systems, data models, and semantics that can be radically different.

"Hello, World" Example

The program prints "hello, world" to the standard output, which is usually a terminal or screen display.

The original version was:

```
main()

{

    printf("hello, world\n");

}
```

A standard-conforming "hello, world" program is:

```
#include <stdio.h>


int main(void)

{

    printf("hello, world\n");

}
```

The first line of the program contains a preprocessing directive, indicated by #include. This causes the compiler to replace that line with the entire text of the stdio.h standard header, which contains declarations for standard input and output functions such as printf and scanf. The angle brackets surrounding stdio.h indicate that stdio.h is located using a search strategy that prefers headers provided with the compiler to other headers having the same name, as opposed to double quotes which typically include local or project-specific header files.

The next line indicates that a function named main is being defined. The main function serves a special purpose in C programs; the run-time environment calls the main function to begin program execution. The type specifier int indicates that the value that is returned to the invoker (in this case the run-time environment) as a result of evaluating the main function, is an integer. The keyword void as a parameter list indicates that this function takes no arguments. The opening curly brace indicates the beginning of the definition of the main function.

The next line calls (diverts execution to) a function named printf, which in this case is supplied from a system library. In this call, the printf function is passed (provided with) a single argument, the address of the first character in the string literal "hello, world\n". The string literal is an unnamed array with elements of type char, set up automatically by the compiler with a final 0-valued character to mark the end of the array (printf needs to know this). The \n is an escape sequence that C translates to a newline character, which on output signifies the end of the current line. The return value of the printf function is of type int, but it is silently discarded since it is not used. (A more careful program might test the return value to determine whether or not the printf function succeeded). The semicolon (;) terminates the statement.

The closing curly brace indicates the end of the code for the main function. According to the C99 specification and newer, the main function, unlike any other function, will implicitly return a value of 0 upon reaching the } that terminates the function. (Formerly an explicit return 0; statement was required). This is interpreted by the run-time system as an exit code indicating successful execution.

Data Types

The type system in C is static and weakly typed, which makes it similar to the type system of ALGOL descendants such as Pascal. There are built-in types for integers of various sizes, both signed and unsigned, floating-point numbers, and enumerated types (enum). Integer type char is often used for single-byte characters. C99 added a boolean datatype. There are also derived types including arrays, pointers, records (struct), and unions (union).

C is often used in low-level systems programming where escapes from the type system may be necessary. The compiler attempts to ensure type correctness of most expressions, but the programmer can override the checks in various ways, either by using a type cast to explicitly convert a value from one type to another, or by using pointers or unions to reinterpret the underlying bits of a data object in some other way.

Some find C's declaration syntax unintuitive, particularly for function pointers. C's usual arithmetic conversions allow for efficient code to be generated, but can sometimes produce unexpected results. For example, a comparison of signed and unsigned integers of equal width requires a conversion of the signed value to unsigned. This can generate unexpected results if the signed value is negative.

Pointers

C supports the use of pointers, a type of reference that records the address or location of an object or function in memory. Pointers can be dereferenced to access data stored at the address pointed to, or to invoke a pointed-to function. Pointers can be manipulated using assignment or pointer arithmetic. The run-time representation of a pointer value is typically a raw memory address (perhaps augmented by an offset-within-word field), but since a pointer's type includes the type of the thing pointed to, expressions including pointers can be type-checked at compile time. Pointer arithmetic is automatically scaled by the size of the pointed-to data type. Pointers are used for many purposes in C. Text strings are commonly manipulated using pointers into arrays of characters. Dynamic memory allocation is performed using pointers. Many data types, such as trees, are commonly implemented as dynamically allocated `struct` objects linked together using pointers. Pointers to functions are useful for passing functions as arguments to higher-order functions (such as qsort or bsearch) or as callbacks to be invoked by event handlers.

A null pointer value explicitly points to no valid location. Dereferencing a null pointer value is undefined, often resulting in a segmentation fault. Null pointer values are useful for indicating special cases such as no "next" pointer in the final node of a linked list, or as an error indication from functions returning pointers. In appropriate contexts in source code, such as for assigning to a pointer variable, a null pointer constant can be written as 0, with or without explicit casting to a pointer type, or as the NULL macro defined by several standard headers. In conditional contexts, null pointer values evaluate to false, while all other pointer values evaluate to true.

Void pointers (`void *`) point to objects of unspecified type, and can therefore be used as "generic" data pointers. Since the size and type of the pointed-to object is not known, void pointers cannot be dereferenced, nor is pointer arithmetic on them allowed, although they can easily be (and in many contexts implicitly are) converted to and from any other object pointer type.

Careless use of pointers is potentially dangerous. Because they are typically unchecked, a pointer variable can be made to point to any arbitrary location, which can cause undesirable effects. Although properly used pointers point to safe places, they can be made to point to unsafe places by using invalid pointer arithmetic; the objects they point to may continue to be used after deallocation (dangling pointers); they may be used without having been initialized (wild pointers); or they may be directly assigned an unsafe value using a cast, union, or through another corrupt pointer. In general, C is permissive in allowing manipulation of and conversion between pointer types, although compilers typically provide options for various levels of checking. Some other programming languages address these problems by using more restrictive reference types.

Arrays

Array types in C are traditionally of a fixed, static size specified at compile time. (The more recent C99 standard also allows a form of variable-length arrays). However, it is also possible to allocate a block of memory (of arbitrary size) at run-time, using the standard library's `malloc` function, and treat it as an array. C's unification of arrays and pointers means that declared arrays and these dynamically allocated simulated arrays are virtually interchangeable.

Since arrays are always accessed (in effect) via pointers, array accesses are typically not checked against the underlying array size, although some compilers may provide bounds checking as an option. Array bounds violations are therefore possible and rather common in carelessly written code, and can lead to various repercussions, including illegal memory accesses, corruption of data, buffer overruns, and run-time exceptions. If bounds checking is desired, it must be done manually.

C does not have a special provision for declaring multi-dimensional arrays, but rather relies on recursion within the type system to declare arrays of arrays, which effectively accomplishes the same thing. The index values of the resulting "multi-dimensional array" can be thought of as increasing in row-major order.

Multi-dimensional arrays are commonly used in numerical algorithms (mainly from applied linear algebra) to store matrices. The structure of the C array is well suited to this particular task. However, since arrays are passed merely as pointers, the bounds of the array must be known fixed values or else explicitly passed to any subroutine that requires them, and dynamically sized arrays of arrays cannot be accessed using double indexing. (A workaround for this is to allocate the array with an additional "row vector" of pointers to the columns). C99 introduced "variable-length arrays" which address some, but not all, of the issues with ordinary C arrays.

Array–pointer Interchangeability

The subscript notation `x[i]` (where `x` designates a pointer) is syntactic sugar for `*(x+i)`. Taking advantage of the compiler's knowledge of the pointer type, the address that `x + i` points to is not the base address (pointed to by `x`) incremented by `i` bytes, but rather is defined to be the base address incremented by i multiplied by the size of an element that x points to. Thus, x[i] designates the i+1th element of the array.

Furthermore, in most expression contexts (a notable exception is as operand of sizeof), the name of an array is automatically converted to a pointer to the array's first element. This implies that an array is never copied as a whole when named as an argument to a function, but rather only the address of its first element is passed. Therefore, although function calls in C use pass-by-value semantics, arrays are in effect passed by reference.

The size of an element can be determined by applying the operator sizeof to any dereferenced element of x, as in n = sizeof *x or n = sizeof x, and the number of elements in a declared array A can be determined as sizeof A / sizeof A. The latter only applies to array names: variables declared with subscripts (int A). Due to the semantics of C, it is not possible to determine the entire size of arrays through pointers to arrays or those created by dynamic allocation (malloc); code such as sizeof arr / sizeof arr (where arr designates a pointer) will not work since the compiler assumes the size of the pointer itself is being requested. Since array name arguments to sizeof are not converted to pointers, they do not exhibit such ambiguity. However, arrays created by dynamic allocation are accessed by pointers rather than true array variables, so they suffer from the same sizeof issues as array pointers.

Thus, despite this apparent equivalence between array and pointer variables, there is still a distinction to be made between them. Even though the name of an array is, in most expression contexts, converted into a pointer (to its first element), this pointer does not itself occupy any storage; the array name is not an l-value, and its address is a constant, unlike a pointer variable. Consequently, what an array "points to" cannot be changed, and it is impossible to assign a new address to an array name. Array contents may be copied, however, by using the memcpy function, or by accessing the individual elements.

Memory Management

One of the most important functions of a programming language is to provide facilities for managing memory and the objects that are stored in memory. C provides three distinct ways to allocate memory for objects:

- Static memory allocation: Space for the object is provided in the binary at compile-time; these objects have an extent (or lifetime) as long as the binary which contains them is loaded into memory.

- Automatic memory allocation: Temporary objects can be stored on the stack, and this space is automatically freed and reusable after the block in which they are declared is exited.

- Dynamic memory allocation: Blocks of memory of arbitrary size can be requested at run-time using library functions such as `malloc` from a region of memory called the heap; these blocks persist until subsequently freed for reuse by calling the library function `realloc` or `free`.

These three approaches are appropriate in different situations and have various trade-offs. For example, static memory allocation has little allocation overhead, automatic allocation may involve slightly more overhead, and dynamic memory allocation can potentially have a great deal of overhead for both allocation and deallocation. The persistent nature of static objects is useful for maintaining state information across function calls, automatic allocation is easy to use but stack space is typically much more limited and transient than either static memory or heap space, and dynamic memory allocation allows convenient allocation of objects whose size is known only at run-time. Most C programs make extensive use of all three.

Where possible, automatic or static allocation is usually simplest because the storage is managed by the compiler, freeing the programmer of the potentially error-prone chore of manually allocating and releasing storage. However, many data structures can change in size at runtime, and since static allocations (and automatic allocations before C99) must have a fixed size at compile-time, there are many situations in which dynamic allocation is necessary. Prior to the C99 standard, variable-sized arrays were a common example of this. Unlike automatic allocation, which can fail at run time with uncontrolled consequences, the dynamic allocation functions return an indication (in the form of a null pointer value) when the required storage cannot be allocated. (Static allocation that is too large is usually detected by the linker or loader, before the program can even begin execution).

Unless otherwise specified, static objects contain zero or null pointer values upon program startup. Automatically and dynamically allocated objects are initialized only if an initial value is explicitly specified; otherwise they initially have indeterminate values (typically, whatever bit pattern happens to be present in the storage, which might not even represent a valid value for that type). If the program attempts to access an uninitialized value, the results are undefined. Many modern compilers try to detect and warn about this problem, but both false positives and false negatives can occur.

Another issue is that heap memory allocation has to be synchronized with its actual usage in any program in order for it to be reused as much as possible. For example, if the only pointer to a heap memory allocation goes out of scope or has its value overwritten before `free()` is called, then that memory cannot be recovered for later reuse and is essentially lost to the program, a phenomenon known as a memory leak. Conversely, it is possible for memory to be freed but continue to be referenced, leading to unpredictable results. Typically, the symptoms will appear in a portion of the program far removed from the actual error, making it difficult to track down the problem. (Such issues are ameliorated in languages with automatic garbage collection).

Libraries

The C programming language uses libraries as its primary method of extension. In C, a library is a set of functions contained within a single "archive" file. Each library typically has a header file, which contains the prototypes of the functions contained within the library that may be used by a program, and declarations of special data types and macro symbols used with these functions. In order for a program to use a library, it must include the library's header file, and the library must be linked with the program, which in many cases requires compiler flags (e.g., -lm, shorthand for "link the math library").

The most common C library is the C standard library, which is specified by the ISO and ANSI C standards and comes with every C implementation (implementations which target limited environments such as embedded systems may provide only a subset of the standard library). This library supports stream input and output, memory allocation, mathematics, character strings, and time values. Several separate standard headers (for example, stdio.h) specify the interfaces for these and other standard library facilities.

Another common set of C library functions are those used by applications specifically targeted for Unix and Unix-like systems, especially functions which provide an interface to the kernel. These functions are detailed in various standards such as POSIX and the Single UNIX Specification.

Since many programs have been written in C, there are a wide variety of other libraries available. Libraries are often written in C because C compilers generate efficient object code; programmers then create interfaces to the library so that the routines can be used from higher-level languages like Java, Perl, and Python.

File Handling and Streams

File input and output (I/O) is not part of the C language itself but instead is handled by libraries (such as the C standard library) and their associated header files (e.g. stdio.h). File handling is generally implemented through high-level I/O which works through streams. A stream is from this perspective a data flow that is independent of devices, while a file is a concrete device. The high level I/O is done through the association of a stream to a file. In the C standard library, a buffer (a memory area or queue) is temporarily used to store data before it's sent to the final destination. This reduces the time spent waiting for slower devices, for example a hard drive or solid state drive. Low-level I/O functions are not part of the standard C library but are generally part of "bare metal" programming (programming that's independent of any operating system such as most but not all embedded programming). With few exceptions, implementations include low-level I/O.

Language Tools

A number of tools have been developed to help C programmers find and fix statements with undefined behavior or possibly erroneous expressions, with greater rigor than that provided by the compiler. The tool lint was the first such, leading to many others.

Automated source code checking and auditing are beneficial in any language, and for C many such tools exist, such as Lint. A common practice is to use Lint to detect questionable code when a program is first written. Once a program passes Lint, it is then compiled using the C compiler. Also, many compilers can optionally warn about syntactically valid constructs that are likely to actually be errors. MISRA C is a proprietary set of guidelines to avoid such questionable code, developed for embedded systems.

There are also compilers, libraries, and operating system level mechanisms for performing actions that are not a standard part of C, such as bounds checking for arrays, detection of buffer overflow, serialization, dynamic memory tracking, and automatic garbage collection. Tools such as Purify or Valgrind and linking with libraries containing special versions of the memory allocation functions can help uncover runtime errors in memory usage.

Uses

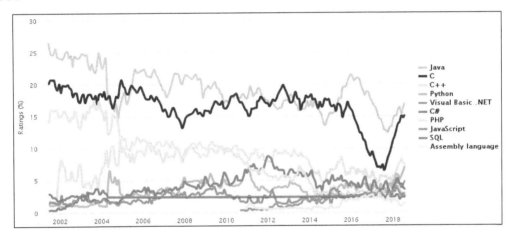

The TIOBE index graph, showing a comparison of the popularity of various programming languages.

C is widely used for systems programming in implementing operating systems and embedded system applications, because C code, when written for portability, can be used for most purposes, yet when needed, system-specific code can be used to access specific hardware addresses and to perform type punning to match externally imposed interface requirements, with a low run-time demand on system resources.

C can also be used for website programming using CGI as a "gateway" for information between the Web application, the server, and the browser. C is often chosen over interpreted languages because of its speed, stability, and near-universal availability. One consequence of C's wide availability and efficiency is that compilers, libraries and interpreters of other programming languages are often implemented in C. The reference implementations of Python, Perl and PHP, for example, are all written in C.

Because the layer of abstraction is thin and the overhead is low, C enables programmers to create efficient implementations of algorithms and data structures, useful for computationally intense programs. For example, the GNU Multiple Precision Arithmetic Library, the GNU Scientific Library, Mathematica, and MATLAB are completely or partially written in C.

C is sometimes used as an intermediate language by implementations of other languages. This approach may be used for portability or convenience; by using C as an intermediate language, additional machine-specific code generators are not necessary. C has some features, such as line-number preprocessor directives and optional superfluous commas at the end of initializer lists, that support compilation of generated code. However, some of C's shortcomings have prompted the development of other C-based languages specifically designed for use as intermediate languages, such as C--.

C has also been widely used to implement end-user applications. However, such applications can also be written in newer, higher-level languages.

C++ Language

C++ is a high-level, general-purpose programming language created by Bjarne Stroustrup as an extension of the C programming language, or "C with Classes". The language has expanded significantly over time, and modern C++ has object-oriented, generic, and functional features in addition to facilities for low-level memory manipulation. It is almost always implemented as a compiled language, and many vendors provide C++ compilers, including the Free Software Foundation, LLVM, Microsoft, Intel, Oracle, and IBM, so it is available on many platforms.

A programmer writing a C++ main() function in 2018.

C++ was designed with a bias toward system programming and embedded, resource-constrained software and large systems, with performance, efficiency, and flexibility of use as its design highlights. C++ has also been found useful in many other contexts, with key strengths being software infrastructure and resource-constrained applications, including desktop applications, video games, servers (e.g. e-commerce, Web search, or SQL servers), and performance-critical applications (e.g. telephone switches or space probes).

The C++ language has two main components: a direct mapping of hardware features provided primarily by the C subset, and zero-overhead abstractions based on those mappings. Stroustrup describes C++ as "a light-weight abstraction programming language [designed] for building and using efficient and elegant abstractions"; and "offering both hardware access and abstraction is the basis of C++. Doing it efficiently is what distinguishes it from other languages."

C++ inherits most of C's syntax. The following is Bjarne Stroustrup's version of the Hello world program that uses the C++ Standard Library stream facility to write a message to standard output:

```
1 #include <iostream>

2

3 int main()

4 {

5     std::cout << "Hello, world!\n";

6 }
```

Object Storage

As in C, C++ supports four types of memory management: static storage duration objects, thread storage duration objects, automatic storage duration objects, and dynamic storage duration objects.

Static Storage Duration Objects

Static storage duration objects are created before main() is entered and destroyed in reverse order of creation after main() exits. The exact order of creation is not specified by the standard to allow implementations some freedom in how to organize their implementation. More formally, objects of this type have a lifespan that "shall last for the duration of the program".

Static storage duration objects are initialized in two phases. First, "static initialization" is performed, and only after all static initialization is performed, "dynamic initialization" is performed. In static initialization, all objects are first initialized with zeros; after that, all objects that have a constant initialization phase are initialized with the constant expression (i.e. variables initialized with a literal or constexpr). Though it is not specified in the standard, the static initialization phase can be completed at compile time and saved in the data partition of the executable. Dynamic initialization involves all object initialization done via a constructor or function call (unless the function is marked with `constexpr`, in C++11). The dynamic initialization order is defined as the order of declaration within the compilation unit (i.e. the same file). No guarantees are provided about the order of initialization between compilation units.

Thread Storage Duration Objects

Variables of this type are very similar to static storage duration objects. The main difference is the creation time is just prior to thread creation and destruction is done after the thread has been joined.

Automatic Storage Duration Objects

The most common variable types in C++ are local variables inside a function or block, and temporary variables. The common feature about automatic variables is that they have a lifetime that is limited to the scope of the variable. They are created and potentially initialized at the point of declaration and destroyed in the reverse order of creation when the scope is left. This is implemented by allocation on the stack.

Local variables are created as the point of execution passes the declaration point. If the variable has a constructor or initializer this is used to define the initial state of the object. Local variables are destroyed when the local block or function that they are declared in is closed. C++ destructors for local variables are called at the end of the object lifetime, allowing a discipline for automatic resource management termed RAII, which is widely used in C++.

Member variables are created when the parent object is created. Array members are initialized from 0 to the last member of the array in order. Member variables are destroyed when the parent object is destroyed in the reverse order of creation. i.e. If the parent is an "automatic object" then it will be destroyed when it goes out of scope which triggers the destruction of all its members.

Temporary variables are created as the result of expression evaluation and are destroyed when the statement containing the expression has been fully evaluated (usually at the `;` at the end of a statement).

Dynamic Storage Duration Objects

These objects have a dynamic lifespan and can be created directly with a call to `new` and destroyed explicitly with a call to `delete`. C++ also supports `malloc` and `free`, from C, but these are not compatible with `new` and `delete`. Use of `new` returns an address to the allocated memory. The C++ Core Guidelines advise against using `new` directly for creating dynamic objects in favor of smart pointers through `make_unique<T>` for single ownership and `make_shared<T>` for reference-counted multiple ownership, which were introduced in C++11.

Templates

C++ templates enable generic programming. C++ supports function, class, alias, and variable templates. Templates may be parameterized by types, compile-time constants, and other templates. Templates are implemented by instantiation at compile-time. To instantiate a template, compilers substitute specific arguments for a template's parameters to generate a concrete function or class instance. Some substitutions are not possible; these are eliminated by an overload resolution policy described by the phrase "Substitution failure is not an error" (SFINAE). Templates are a powerful tool that can be used for generic programming, template metaprogramming, and code optimization, but this power implies a cost. Template use may increase code size, because each template instantiation produces a copy of the template code: one for each set of template arguments, however, this is the same or smaller amount of code that would be generated if the code was written by hand. This is in contrast to run-time generics seen in other languages (e.g., Java) where at compile-time the type is erased and a single template body is preserved.

Templates are different from macros: while both of these compile-time language features enable conditional compilation, templates are not restricted to lexical substitution. Templates are aware of the semantics and type system of their companion language, as well as all compile-time type definitions, and can perform high-level operations including programmatic flow control based on evaluation of strictly type-checked parameters. Macros are capable of conditional control over compilation based on predetermined criteria, but cannot instantiate new types, recurse, or perform type evaluation and in effect are limited to pre-compilation text-substitution and text-inclusion/exclusion. In other words, macros can control compilation flow based on pre-defined symbols but cannot, unlike templates, independently instantiate new symbols. Templates are a tool for static polymorphism and generic programming.

In addition, templates are a compile time mechanism in C++ that is Turing-complete, meaning that any computation expressible by a computer program can be computed, in some form, by a template metaprogram prior to runtime.

A template is a compile-time parameterized function or class written without knowledge of the specific arguments used to instantiate it. After instantiation, the resulting code is equivalent to code written specifically for the passed arguments. In this manner, templates provide a way to decouple generic, broadly applicable aspects of functions and classes (encoded in templates) from specific aspects (encoded in template parameters) without sacrificing performance due to abstraction.

Objects

C++ introduces object-oriented programming (OOP) features to C. It offers classes, which provide the four features commonly present in OOP (and some non-OOP) languages: abstraction, encapsulation, inheritance, and polymorphism. One distinguishing feature of C++ classes compared to classes in other programming languages is support for deterministic destructors, which in turn provide support for the Resource Acquisition is Initialization (RAII) concept.

Encapsulation

Encapsulation is the hiding of information to ensure that data structures and operators are used as intended and to make the usage model more obvious to the developer. C++ provides the ability to define classes and functions as its primary encapsulation mechanisms. Within a class, members can be declared as either public, protected, or private to explicitly enforce encapsulation. A public member of the class is accessible to any function. A private member is accessible only to functions that are members of that class and to functions and classes explicitly granted access permission by the class ("friends"). A protected member is accessible to members of classes that inherit from the class in addition to the class itself and any friends.

The object-oriented principle ensures the encapsulation of all and only the functions that access the internal representation of a type. C++ supports this principle via member functions and friend functions, but it does not enforce it. Programmers can declare parts or all of the representation of a type to be public, and they are allowed to make public entities not part of the representation of a type. Therefore, C++ supports not just object-oriented programming, but other decomposition paradigms such as modular programming.

It is generally considered good practice to make all data private or protected, and to make public only those functions that are part of a minimal interface for users of the class. This can hide the details of data implementation, allowing the designer to later fundamentally change the implementation without changing the interface in any way.

Inheritance

Inheritance allows one data type to acquire properties of other data types. Inheritance from a base class may be declared as public, protected, or private. This access specifier determines whether unrelated and derived classes can access the inherited public and protected members of the base class. Only public inheritance corresponds to what is usually meant by "inheritance". The other two forms are much less frequently used. If the access specifier is omitted, a "class" inherits privately, while a "struct" inherits publicly. Base classes may be declared as virtual; this is called virtual inheritance. Virtual inheritance ensures that only one instance of a base class exists in the inheritance graph, avoiding some of the ambiguity problems of multiple inheritance.

Multiple inheritance is a C++ feature not found in most other languages, allowing a class to be derived from more than one base class; this allows for more elaborate inheritance relationships. For example, a "Flying Cat" class can inherit from both "Cat" and "Flying

Mammal". Some other languages, such as C# or Java, accomplish something similar (although more limited) by allowing inheritance of multiple interfaces while restricting the number of base classes to one (interfaces, unlike classes, provide only declarations of member functions, no implementation or member data). An interface as in C# and Java can be defined in C++ as a class containing only pure virtual functions, often known as an abstract base class or "ABC". The member functions of such an abstract base class are normally explicitly defined in the derived class, not inherited implicitly. C++ virtual inheritance exhibits an ambiguity resolution feature called dominance.

Operators and Operator Overloading

Table: Operators that cannot be overloaded.

Operator	Symbol
Scope resolution operator	`::`
Conditional operator	`?:`
dot operator	`.`
Member selection operator	`.*`
"sizeof" operator	`sizeof`
"typeid" operator	`typeid`

C++ provides more than 35 operators, covering basic arithmetic, bit manipulation, indirection, comparisons, logical operations and others. Almost all operators can be overloaded for user-defined types, with a few notable exceptions such as member access (`.` and `.*`) as well as the conditional operator. The rich set of overloadable operators is central to making user-defined types in C++ seem like built-in types.

Overloadable operators are also an essential part of many advanced C++ programming techniques, such as smart pointers. Overloading an operator does not change the precedence of calculations involving the operator, nor does it change the number of operands that the operator uses (any operand may however be ignored by the operator, though it will be evaluated prior to execution). Overloaded "`&&`" and "`||`" operators lose their short-circuit evaluation property.

Polymorphism

Polymorphism enables one common interface for many implementations, and for objects to act differently under different circumstances. C++ supports several kinds of static (resolved at compile-time) and dynamic (resolved at run-time) polymorphisms, supported by the language features Compile-time polymorphism does not allow for certain run-time decisions, while runtime polymorphism typically incurs a performance penalty.

Static Polymorphism

Function overloading allows programs to declare multiple functions having the same name but with different arguments (i.e. ad hoc polymorphism). The functions are distinguished by the number or types of their formal parameters. Thus, the same function name can refer to different functions depending on the context in which it is used. The type returned by the function is not used to distinguish overloaded functions and would result in a compile-time error message.

When declaring a function, a programmer can specify for one or more parameters a default value. Doing so allows the parameters with defaults to optionally be omitted when the function is called, in which case the default arguments will be used. When a function is called with fewer arguments than there are declared parameters, explicit arguments are matched to parameters in left-to-right order, with any unmatched parameters at the end of the parameter list being assigned their default arguments. In many cases, specifying default arguments in a single function declaration is preferable to providing overloaded function definitions with different numbers of parameters.

Templates in C++ provide a sophisticated mechanism for writing generic, polymorphic code (i.e. parametric polymorphism). In particular, through the curiously recurring template pattern, it's possible to implement a form of static polymorphism that closely mimics the syntax for overriding virtual functions. Because C++ templates are type-aware and Turing-complete, they can also be used to let the compiler resolve recursive conditionals and generate substantial programs through template metaprogramming. Contrary to some opinion, template code will not generate a bulk code after compilation with the proper compiler settings.

Dynamic Polymorphism

Inheritance

Variable pointers and references to a base class type in C++ can also refer to objects of any derived classes of that type. This allows arrays and other kinds of containers to hold pointers to objects of differing types (references cannot be directly held in containers). This enables dynamic (run-time) polymorphism, where the referred objects can behave differently, depending on their (actual, derived) types. C++ also provides the `dynamic_cast` operator, which allows code to safely attempt conversion of an object, via a base reference/pointer, to a more derived type: downcasting.

The attempt is necessary as often one does not know which derived type is referenced. (Upcasting, conversion to a more general type, can always be checked/performed at compile-time via `static_cast`, as ancestral classes are specified in the derived class's interface, visible to all callers.) `dynamic_cast` relies on run-time type information (RTTI), metadata in the program that enables differentiating types and their relationships. If a `dynamic_cast` to a pointer fails, the result is the `nullptr` constant, whereas if the destination is a reference (which cannot be null), the cast throws an exception. Objects known to be of a certain derived type can be cast to that with `static_cast`, bypassing RTTI and the safe runtime type-checking of `dynamic_cast`, so this should be used only if the programmer is very confident the cast is, and will always be, valid.

Virtual Member Functions

Ordinarily, when a function in a derived class overrides a function in a base class, the function to call is determined by the type of the object. A given function is overridden when there exists no difference in the number or type of parameters between two or more definitions of that function. Hence, at compile time, it may not be possible to determine the type of the object and therefore the correct function to call, given only a base class pointer; the decision is therefore put off until runtime. This is called dynamic dispatch. Virtual member functions or methods allow the most specific implementation of the function to be called, according to the actual run-time type of the object. In C++ implementations, this is commonly done using virtual function tables. If the object type is known, this may be bypassed by prepending a fully qualified class name before the function call, but in general calls to virtual functions are resolved at run time.

In addition to standard member functions, operator overloads and destructors can be virtual. As a rule of thumb, if any function in the class is virtual, the destructor should be as well. As the type of an object at its creation is known at compile time, constructors, and by extension copy constructors, cannot be virtual. Nonetheless a situation may arise where a copy of an object needs to be created when a pointer to a derived object is passed as a pointer to a base object. In such a case, a common solution is to create a `clone()` (or similar) virtual function that creates and returns a copy of the derived class when called.

A member function can also be made "pure virtual" by appending it with = 0 after the closing parenthesis and before the semicolon. A class containing a pure virtual function is called an abstract class. Objects cannot be created from an abstract class; they can only be derived from. Any derived class inherits the virtual function as pure and must provide a non-pure definition of it (and all other pure virtual functions) before objects of the derived class can be created. A program that attempts to create an object of a class with a pure virtual member function or inherited pure virtual member function is ill-formed.

Lambda Expressions

C++ provides support for anonymous functions, also known as lambda expressions, with the following form:

```
[capture](parameters) -> return_type { function_body }
```

The return type of a lambda expression can also be automatically inferred, if possible, e.g.:

```
[] (int x, int y) { return x - y; } // inferred

[] (int x, int y) -> int { return x + y; } // explicit
```

The [capture] list supports the definition of closures. Such lambda expressions are defined in the standard as syntactic sugar for an unnamed function object.

Exception Handling

Exception handling is used to communicate the existence of a runtime problem or error from where it was detected to where the issue can be handled. It permits this to be done in a uniform manner and separately from the main code, while detecting all errors. Should an error occur, an exception is thrown (raised), which is then caught by the nearest suitable exception handler. The exception causes the current scope to be exited, and also each outer scope (propagation) until a suitable handler is found, calling in turn the destructors of any objects in these exited scopes. At the same time, an exception is presented as an object carrying the data about the detected problem.

Some C++ style guides, such as Google's, LLVM's, and Qt's forbid the usage of exceptions. The exception-causing code is placed inside a try block. The exceptions are handled in separate catch blocks (the handlers); each try block can have multiple exception handlers,

```
1 #include <iostream>

2 #include <vector>

3 #include <stdexcept>

4

5 int main() {

6     try {

7         std::vector<int> vec{3, 4, 3, 1};

8         int i{vec.at(4)}; // Throws an exception, std::out_of_range
(indexing for vec is from 0-3 not 1-4)

9     }

10    // An exception handler, catches std::out_of_range, which is
thrown by vec.at(4)

11    catch (std::out_of_range &e) {

12        std::cerr << "Accessing a non-existent element: " << e.what()
```

```
    << '\n';

13      }

14      // To catch any other standard library exceptions (they derive
from std::exception)

15      catch (std::exception &e) {

16          std::cerr << "Exception thrown: " << e.what() << '\n';

17      }

18      // Catch any unrecognised exceptions (i.e. those which don't
derive from std::exception)

19      catch (...) {

20          std::cerr << "Some fatal error\n";

21      }

22  }
```

It is also possible to raise exceptions purposefully, using the `throw` keyword; these exceptions are handled in the usual way. In some cases, exceptions cannot be used due to technical reasons. One such example is a critical component of an embedded system, where every operation must be guaranteed to complete within a specified amount of time. This cannot be determined with exceptions as no tools exist to determine the maximum time required for an exception to be handled.

Unlike signal handling, in which the handling function is called from the point of failure, exception handling exits the current scope before the catch block is entered, which may be located in the current function or any of the previous function calls currently on the stack.

Standard Library

The C++ standard consists of two parts: the core language and the standard library. C++ programmers expect the latter on every major implementation of C++; it includes aggregate types (vectors, lists, maps, sets, queues, stacks, arrays, tuples), algorithms (find, for_each, binary_search, random_shuffle, etc.), input/output facilities (iostream, for reading from and writing to the console and files), filesystem library, localisation support, smart pointers for automatic memory management, regular expression support, multi-threading library, atomics support (allowing a variable to be read or written to by at most one thread at a time without any external synchronisation), time utilities (measurement, getting current time, etc.), a system for converting error reporting that doesn't use C++ exceptions into C++ exceptions, a random number generator and a slightly modified version of the C standard library (to make it comply with the C++ type system).

A large part of the C++ library is based on the Standard Template Library (STL). Useful tools provided by the STL include containers as the collections of objects (such as vectors and lists), iterators that provide array-like access to containers, and algorithms that perform operations such as searching and sorting.

The draft "Working Paper" standard that became approved as C++98;
half of its size was devoted to the C++ Standard Library.

Furthermore, (multi)maps (associative arrays) and (multi)sets are provided, all of which export compatible interfaces. Therefore, using templates it is possible to write generic algorithms that work with any container or on any sequence defined by iterators. As in C, the features of the library are accessed by using the #include directive to include a standard header. The C++ Standard Library provides 105 standard headers, of which 27 are deprecated.

The standard incorporates the STL that was originally designed by Alexander Stepanov, who experimented with generic algorithms and containers for many years. When he started with C++, he finally found a language where it was possible to create generic algorithms (e.g., STL sort) that perform even better than, for example, the C standard library qsort, thanks to C++ features like using inlining and compile-time binding instead of function pointers. The standard does not refer to it as "STL", as it is merely a part of the standard library, but the term is still widely used to distinguish it from the rest of the standard library (input/output streams, internationalization, diagnostics, the C library subset, etc.).

Most C++ compilers, and all major ones, provide a standards-conforming implementation of the C++ standard library.

Compatibility

To give compiler vendors greater freedom, the C++ standards committee decided not to dictate the implementation of name mangling, exception handling, and other implementation-specific features. The downside of this decision is that object code produced by different compilers is expected to be incompatible. There were, however, attempts to standardize compilers for particular machines or operating systems (for example C++ ABI), though they seem to be largely abandoned now.

With C

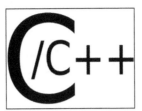

The relationship of C++ to C has always been a bit problematic.

C++ is often considered to be a superset of C but this is not strictly true. Most C code can easily be made to compile correctly in C++ but there are a few differences that cause some valid C code to be invalid or behave differently in C++. For example, C allows implicit conversion from void* to other pointer types but C++ does not (for type safety reasons). Also, C++ defines many new keywords, such as new and class, which may be used as identifiers (for example, variable names) in a C program.

Some incompatibilities have been removed by the 1999 revision of the C standard (C99), which now supports C++ features such as line comments (//) and declarations mixed with code. On the other hand, C99 introduced a number of new features that C++ did not support that were incompatible or redundant in C++, such as variable-length arrays, native complex-number types (however, the std::complex class in the C++ standard library provides similar functionality, although not code-compatible), designated initializers, compound literals, and the restrict keyword. Some of the C99-introduced features were included in the subsequent version of the C++ standard, C++11 (out of those which were not redundant). However, the C++11 standard introduces new incompatibilities, such as disallowing assignment of a string literal to a character pointer, which remains valid C.

To intermix C and C++ code, any function declaration or definition that is to be called from/used both in C and C++ must be declared with C linkage by placing it within an extern "C" {/*...*/} block. Such a function may not rely on features depending on name mangling (i.e., function overloading).

Java Language

Java is a general-purpose programming language that is class-based, object-oriented, and designed to have as few implementation dependencies as possible. It is intended to let application developers write once, run anywhere (WORA), meaning that compiled Java code can run on all platforms that support Java without the need for recompilation. Java applications are typically compiled to bytecode that can run on any Java virtual machine (JVM) regardless of the underlying computer architecture. The syntax of Java is similar to C and C++, but it has fewer low-level facilities than either of them.

As of 2019, Java was one of the most popular programming languages in use according to GitHub, particularly for client-server web applications, with a reported 9 million developers.

Java was originally developed by James Gosling at Sun Microsystems (which has since been acquired by Oracle) and released in 1995 as a core component of Sun Microsystems' Java platform. The original and reference implementation Java compilers, virtual machines, and class libraries were originally released by Sun under proprietary licenses. As of May 2007, in compliance with the specifications of the Java Community Process, Sun had relicensed most of its Java technologies under the GNU General Public License. Meanwhile, others have developed alternative implementations of these Sun technologies, such as the GNU Compiler for Java (bytecode compiler), GNU Classpath (standard libraries), and IcedTea-Web (browser plugin for applets).

The latest versions are Java 13, released in September 2019, and Java 11, a currently supported long-term support (LTS) version, released on September 25, 2018; Oracle released for the legacy Java 8 LTS the last free public update in January 2019 for commercial use, while it will otherwise still support Java 8 with public updates for personal use up to at least December 2020. Oracle (and others) highly recommend uninstalling older versions of Java because of serious risks due to unresolved security issues. Since Java 9 (and 10 and 12) is no longer supported, Oracle advises its users to immediately transition to the latest version (currently Java 13) or an LTS release.

Execution System

Java JVM and Bytecode

One design goal of Java is portability, which means that programs written for the Java platform must run similarly on any combination of hardware and operating system with adequate run time support. This is achieved by compiling the Java language code to an intermediate representation called Java bytecode, instead of directly to architecture-specific machine code. Java bytecode instructions are analogous to machine code, but they are intended to be executed by a virtual machine (VM) written specifically for the host hardware. End users commonly use a Java Runtime Environment (JRE) installed on their machine for standalone Java applications, or in a web browser for Java applets.

Standard libraries provide a generic way to access host-specific features such as graphics, threading, and networking. The use of universal bytecode makes porting simple. However, the overhead of interpreting bytecode into machine instructions made interpreted programs almost always run more slowly than native executables. Just-in-time (JIT) compilers that compile byte-codes to machine code during runtime were introduced from an early stage. Java itself is platform-independent and is adapted to the particular platform it is to run on by a Java virtual machine for it, which translates the Java bytecode into the platform's machine language.

Non-JVM

Some platforms offer direct hardware support for Java; there are micro controllers that can run Java bytecode in hardware instead of a software Java virtual machine, and some ARM-based processors could have hardware support for executing Java bytecode through their Jazelle option, though support has mostly been dropped in current implementations of ARM.

Automatic Memory Management

Java uses an automatic garbage collector to manage memory in the object lifecycle. The programmer determines when objects are created, and the Java runtime is responsible for recovering the memory once objects are no longer in use. Once no references to an object remain, the unreachable memory becomes eligible to be freed automatically by the garbage collector. Something similar to a memory leak may still occur if a programmer's code holds a reference to an object that is no longer needed, typically when objects that are no longer needed are stored in containers that are still in use. If methods for a non-existent object are called, a null pointer exception is thrown.

One of the ideas behind Java's automatic memory management model is that programmers can be spared the burden of having to perform manual memory management. In some languages, memory for the creation of objects is implicitly allocated on the stack or explicitly allocated and deallocated from the heap. In the latter case, the responsibility of managing memory resides with the programmer. If the program does not deallocate an object, a memory leak occurs. If the program attempts to access or deallocate memory that has already been deallocated, the result is undefined and difficult to predict, and the program is likely to become unstable or crash. This can be partially remedied by the use of smart pointers, but these add overhead and complexity. Note that garbage collection does not prevent logical memory leaks, i.e. those where the memory is still referenced but never used.

Garbage collection may happen at any time. Ideally, it will occur when a program is idle. It is guaranteed to be triggered if there is insufficient free memory on the heap to allocate a new object; this can cause a program to stall momentarily. Explicit memory management is not possible in Java.

Java does not support C/C++ style pointer arithmetic, where object addresses can be arithmetically manipulated (e.g. by adding or subtracting an offset). This allows the garbage collector to relocate referenced objects and ensures type safety and security.

As in C++ and some other object-oriented languages, variables of Java's primitive data types are either stored directly in fields (for objects) or on the stack (for methods) rather than on the heap, as is commonly true for non-primitive data types (but see escape analysis). This was a conscious decision by Java's designers for performance reasons.

Java contains multiple types of garbage collectors. By default, HotSpot uses the parallel scavenge garbage collector. However, there are also several other garbage collectors that can be used to manage the heap. For 90% of applications in Java, the Concurrent Mark-Sweep (CMS) garbage collector is sufficient. Oracle aims to replace CMS with the Garbage-First Collector (G1).

Having solved the memory management problem does not relieve the programmer of the burden of handling properly other kind of resources, like network or database connections, file handles, etc., especially in the presence of exceptions. Paradoxically, the presence of a garbage collector has faded the necessity of having an explicit destructor method in the classes, thus rendering the management of these other resources more difficult.

Syntax

The syntax of Java is largely influenced by C++. Unlike C++, which combines the syntax for structured, generic, and object-oriented programming, Java was built almost exclusively as an object-oriented language. All code is written inside classes, and every data item is an object, with the exception of the primitive data types, (i.e. integers, floating-point numbers, boolean values, and characters), which are not objects for performance reasons. Java reuses some popular aspects of C++ (such as the `printf` method).

Dependency graph of the Java Core classes.

Unlike C++, Java does not support operator overloading or multiple inheritance for classes, though multiple inheritance is supported for interfaces. Java uses comments similar to those of C++. There are three different styles of comments: a single line style marked with two slashes (//), a multiple line style opened with /* and closed with */, and the Javadoc commenting style opened with /** and closed with */. The Javadoc style of commenting allows the user to run the Javadoc executable to create documentation for the program and can be read by some integrated development environments (IDEs) such as Eclipse to allow developers to access documentation within the IDE.

Hello World Example

The traditional Hello world program can be written in Java as:

```
public class HelloWorldApp {

    public static void main(String[] args) {

        System.out.println("Hello World!"); // Prints the string to the
console.

    }

}
```

Source files must be named after the public class they contain, appending the suffix .java, for example, HelloWorldApp.java. It must first be compiled into bytecode, using a Java compiler, producing a file with the .class suffix (HelloWorldApp.class, in this case). Only then can it be executed, or launched. The Java source file may only contain one public class, but it can contain multiple classes with a non-public access modifier and any number of public inner classes. When the source file contains multiple classes, it is necessary to make one class (introduced by the class keyword) public (preceded by the public keyword) and name the source file with that public class name.

A class that is not declared public may be stored in any .java file. The compiler will generate a class file for each class defined in the source file. The name of the class file is the name of the class, with .class appended. For class file generation, anonymous classes are treated as if their name were the concatenation of the name of their enclosing class, a $, and an integer.

The keyword public denotes that a method can be called from code in other classes, or that a class may be used by classes outside the class hierarchy. The class hierarchy is related to the name of the directory in which the .java file is located. This is called an access level modifier. Other access level modifiers include the keywords private and protected.

The keyword static in front of a method indicates a static method, which is associated only with the class and not with any specific instance of that class. Only static methods can be invoked without a reference to an object. Static methods cannot access any class members that are not also static. Methods that are not designated static are instance methods and require a specific instance of a class to operate. The keyword void indicates that the main method does not return any value to the caller. If a Java program is to exit with an error code, it must call System.exit() explicitly.

The method name main is not a keyword in the Java language. It is simply the name of the method the Java launcher calls to pass control to the program. Java classes that run in managed environments such as applets and Enterprise JavaBeans do not use or need a `main()` method. A Java program may contain multiple classes that have `main` methods, which means that the VM needs to be explicitly told which class to launch from.

The main method must accept an array of String objects. By convention, it is referenced as args although any other legal identifier name can be used. Since Java 5, the main method can also use variable arguments, in the form of `public static void main(String... args)`, allowing the main method to be invoked with an arbitrary number of `String` arguments. The effect of this alternate declaration is semantically identical (to the `args` parameter which is still an array of `String` objects), but it allows an alternative syntax for creating and passing the array.

The Java launcher launches Java by loading a given class (specified on the command line or as an attribute in a JAR) and starting its `public static void main(String[])` method. Stand-alone programs must declare this method explicitly. The `String[]` `args` parameter is an array of `String` objects containing any arguments passed to the class. The parameters to `main` are often passed by means of a command line.

Printing is part of a Java standard library: The System class defines a public static field called out. The `out` object is an instance of the `PrintStream` class and provides many methods for printing data to standard out, including println(String) which also appends a new line to the passed string. The string `"Hello World!"` is automatically converted to a String object by the compiler.

Example with Methods

```
// This is an example of a single line comment using two slashes


/*

 * This is an example of a multiple line comment using the slash and
asterisk.

 * This type of comment can be used to hold a lot of information or
deactivate

 * code, but it is very important to remember to close the comment.

 */


package fibsandlies;

import java.util.HashMap;


/**
```

```
 * This is an example of a Javadoc comment; Javadoc can compile docu-
mentation

 * from this text. Javadoc comments must immediately precede the class,
method,

 * or field being documented.

 */
public class FibCalculator extends Fibonacci implements Calculator {

    private static Map<Integer, Integer> memoized = new HashMap<>();


    /*

     * The main method written as follows is used by the JVM as a start-
ing point

     * for the program.

     */
    public static void main(String[] args) {

        memoized.put(1, 1);

        memoized.put(2, 1);

        System.out.println(fibonacci(12)); // Get the 12th Fibonacci
number and print to console

    }
    /**

     * An example of a method written in Java, wrapped in a class.

     * Given a non-negative number FIBINDEX, returns

     * the Nth Fibonacci number, where N equals FIBINDEX.

     *

     * @param fibIndex The index of the Fibonacci number

     * @return the Fibonacci number

     */
    public static int fibonacci(int fibIndex) {

        if (memoized.containsKey(fibIndex)) return memoized.get(fibIn-
dex);

        else {

            int answer = fibonacci(fibIndex - 1) + fibonacci(fibIndex - 2);
```

```
                memoized.put(fibIndex, answer);

                return answer;

        }

    }

}
```

Special Classes

Applet

Java applets were programs that were embedded in other applications, typically in a Web page displayed in a web browser. The Java applet API is now deprecated since Java 8 in 2017.

Servlet

Java servlet technology provides Web developers with a simple, consistent mechanism for extending the functionality of a Web server and for accessing existing business systems. Servlets are server-side Java EE components that generate responses (typically HTML pages) to requests (typically HTTP requests) from clients.

The Java servlet API has to some extent been superseded by two standard Java technologies for web services:

- The java api for restful web services (jax-rs 2.0) useful for ajax, json and rest services.

- The java api for xml web services (jax-ws) useful for soap web services.

JavaServer Pages

JavaServer Pages (JSP) are server-side Java EE components that generate responses, typically HTML pages, to HTTP requests from clients. JSPs embed Java code in an HTML page by using the special delimiters <% and %>. A JSP is compiled to a Java servlet, a Java application in its own right, the first time it is accessed. After that, the generated servlet creates the response.

Swing Application

Swing is a graphical user interface library for the Java SE platform. It is possible to specify a different look and feel through the pluggable look and feel system of Swing. Clones of Windows, GTK+, and Motif are supplied by Sun. Apple also provides an Aqua look and feel for macOS. Where prior implementations of these looks and feels may have been considered lacking, Swing in Java SE 6 addresses this problem by using more native GUI widget drawing routines of the underlying platforms.

JavaFX Application

JavaFX is a software platform for creating and delivering desktop applications, as well as rich Internet applications (RIAs) that can run across a wide variety of devices. JavaFX is intended to replace Swing as the standard GUI library for Java SE, but both will be included for the foreseeable future. JavaFX has support for desktop computers and web browsers on Microsoft Windows, Linux, and macOS. JavaFX does not have support for native OS look and feels.

Class Libraries

The Java Class Library is the standard library, developed to support application development in Java. It is controlled by Oracle in cooperation with others through the Java Community Process program. Companies or individuals participating in this process can influence the design and development of the APIs. The class library contains features such as:

- The core libraries, which include:

    ○ IO/NIO.

    ○ Networking.

    ○ Reflection.

    ○ Concurrency.

    ○ Generics.

    ○ Scripting/Compiler.

    ○ Functional programming (Lambda, Streaming).

    ○ Collection libraries that implement data structures such as lists, dictionaries, trees, sets, queues and double-ended queue, or stacks.

    ○ XML Processing (Parsing, Transforming, Validating) libraries.

    ○ Security.

    ○ Internationalization and localization libraries.

- The integration libraries, which allow the application writer to communicate with external systems. These libraries include:

    ○ The Java Database Connectivity (JDBC) API for database access.

- ◦ Java Naming and Directory Interface (JNDI) for lookup and discovery.

- ◦ RMI and CORBA for distributed application development.

- ◦ JMX for managing and monitoring applications.

- User interface libraries, which include:

  - ◦ The (heavyweight, or native) Abstract Window Toolkit (AWT), which provides GUI components, the means for laying out those components and the means for handling events from those components.

  - ◦ The (lightweight) Swing libraries, which are built on AWT but provide (non-native) implementations of the AWT widgetry.

  - ◦ APIs for audio capture, processing, and playback.

  - ◦ JavaFX.

- A platform dependent implementation of the Java virtual machine that is the means by which the bytecodes of the Java libraries and third party applications are executed.

- Plugins, which enable applets to be run in web browsers.

- Java Web Start, which allows Java applications to be efficiently distributed to end users across the Internet.

- Licensing and documentation.

Python Language

Python is an interpreted, high-level, general-purpose programming language. Created by Guido van Rossum and first released in 1991, Python's design philosophy emphasizes code readability with its notable use of significant whitespace. Its language constructs and object-oriented approach aim to help programmers write clear, logical code for small and large-scale projects.

Python is dynamically typed and garbage-collected. It supports multiple programming paradigms, including procedural, object-oriented, and functional programming. Python is often described as a "batteries included" language due to its comprehensive standard library.

Python was conceived in the late 1980s as a successor to the ABC language. Python 2.0, released in 2000, introduced features like list comprehensions and a garbage collection system capable of collecting reference cycles. Python 3.0, released in 2008, was a major revision of the language that is not completely backward-compatible, and much Python 2 code does not run unmodified on Python 3.

Python interpreters are available for many operating systems. A global community of programmers develops and maintains CPython, an open source reference implementation. A non-profit organization, the Python Software Foundation, manages and directs resources for Python and CPython development.

Syntax and Semantics

Python is meant to be an easily readable language. Its formatting is visually uncluttered, and it often uses English keywords where other languages use punctuation. Unlike many other languages, it does not use curly brackets to delimit blocks, and semicolons after statements are optional. It has fewer syntactic exceptions and special cases than C or Pascal.

Indentation

Python uses whitespace indentation, rather than curly brackets or keywords, to delimit blocks. An increase in indentation comes after certain statements; a decrease in indentation signifies the end of the current block. Thus, the program's visual structure accurately represents the program's semantic structure. This feature is sometimes termed the off-side rule, which some other languages share, but in most languages indentation doesn't have any semantic meaning.

Statements and Control Flow

Python's statements include (among others):

- The assignment statement (token '=', the equals sign). This operates differently than in traditional imperative programming languages, and this fundamental mechanism (including the nature of Python's version of variables) illuminates many other features of the language. Assignment in C, e.g., x = 2, translates to "typed variable name x receives a copy of numeric value 2". The (right-hand) value is copied into an allocated storage location for which the (left-hand) variable name is the symbolic address. The memory allocated to the variable is large enough (potentially quite large) for the declared type. In the simplest case of Python assignment, using the same example, x = 2, translates to "(generic) name x receives a reference to a separate, dynamically allocated object of numeric (int) type of value 2." This is termed binding the name to the object. Since the name's storage location doesn't contain the indicated value, it is improper to call it a variable. Names may be subsequently rebound at any time to objects of greatly varying types, including strings, procedures, complex objects with data and methods, etc. Successive assignments of a common value to multiple names, e.g., x = 2; y = 2; z = 2 result in allocating storage to (at most) three names and one numeric object, to which all three names are bound. Since a name is a generic reference holder it is unreasonable to associate a fixed data type with it. However at a given time a name will be bound to some object, which will have a type; thus there is dynamic typing.

- The `if` statement, which conditionally executes a block of code, along with `else` and `elif` (a contraction of else-if).

- The `for` statement, which iterates over an iterable object, capturing each element to a local variable for use by the attached block.

- The `while` statement, which executes a block of code as long as its condition is true.

- The `try` statement, which allows exceptions raised in its attached code block to be caught and handled by `except` clauses; it also ensures that clean-up code in a `finally` block will always be run regardless of how the block exits.

- The `raise` statement, used to raise a specified exception or re-raise a caught exception.

- The `class` statement, which executes a block of code and attaches its local namespace to a class, for use in object-oriented programming.

- The `def` statement, which defines a function or method.

- The `with` statement, from Python 2.5 released in September 2006, which encloses a code block within a context manager (for example, acquiring a lock before the block of code is run and releasing the lock afterwards, or opening a file and then closing it), allowing Resource Acquisition Is Initialization (RAII)-like behavior and replaces a common try/finally idiom.

- The `break` statement, exits from the loop.

- The `continue` statement, skips this iteration and continues with the next item.

- The `pass` statement, which serves as a NOP. It is syntactically needed to create an empty code block.

- The `assert` statement, used during debugging to check for conditions that ought to apply.

- The `yield` statement, which returns a value from a generator function. From Python 2.5, `yield` is also an operator. This form is used to implement coroutines.

- The `import` statement, which is used to import modules whose functions or variables can be used in the current program. There are three ways of using

import: `import <module name> [as <alias>]` or `from <module name> im-port * ` or `from <module name> import <definition 1> [as <alias 1>],  <definition 2> [as <alias 2>], ....`

- The `print` statement was changed to the `print()` function in Python 3.

Python does not support tail call optimization or first-class continuations, and, according to Guido van Rossum, it never will. However, better support for coroutine-like functionality is provided in 2.5, by extending Python's generators. Before 2.5, generators were lazy iterators; information was passed unidirectionally out of the generator. From Python 2.5, it is possible to pass information back into a generator function, and from Python 3.3, the information can be passed through multiple stack levels.

Expressions

Some Python expressions are similar to languages such as C and Java, while some are not:

- Addition, subtraction, and multiplication are the same, but the behavior of division differs. There are two types of divisions in Python. They are floor division (or integer division) `//` and floating point/division. Python also added the `**` operator for exponentiation.

- From Python 3.5, the new `@` infix operator was introduced. It is intended to be used by libraries such as NumPy for matrix multiplication.

- From Python 3.8, the syntax `:=`, called the 'walrus operator' was introduced. It assigns values to variables as part of a larger expression.

- In Python, `==` compares by value, versus Java, which compares numerics by value and objects by reference. (Value comparisons in Java on objects can be performed with the `equals()` method.) Python's `is` operator may be used to compare object identities (comparison by reference). In Python, comparisons may be chained, for example `a <= b <= c`.

- Python uses the words `and`, `or`, `not` for its boolean operators rather than the symbolic `&&`, `||`, `!` used in Java and C.

- Python has a type of expression termed a list comprehension. Python 2.4 extended list comprehensions into a more general expression termed a generator expression.

- Anonymous functions are implemented using lambda expressions; however, these are limited in that the body can only be one expression.

- Conditional expressions in Python are written as `x if c else y` (different in order of operands from the `c ? x : y` operator common to many other languages).

- Python makes a distinction between lists and tuples. Lists are written as `[1, 2, 3]`, are mutable, and cannot be used as the keys of dictionaries (dictionary keys must be immutable in Python). Tuples are written as `(1, 2, 3)`, are immutable and thus can be used as the keys of dictionaries, provided all elements of the tuple are immutable. The + operator can be used to concatenate two tuples, which does not directly modify their contents, but rather produces a new tuple containing the elements of both provided tuples. Thus, given the variable `t` initially equal to `(1, 2, 3)`, executing `t = t + (4, 5)` first evaluates `t + (4, 5)`, which yields `(1, 2, 3, 4, 5)`, which is then assigned back to `t`, thereby effectively "modifying the contents" of `t`, while conforming to the immutable nature of tuple objects. Parentheses are optional for tuples in unambiguous contexts.

- Python features sequence unpacking wherein multiple expressions, each evaluating to anything that can be assigned to (a variable, a writable property, etc.), are associated in the identical manner to that forming tuple literals and, as a whole, are put on the left hand side of the equal sign in an assignment statement. The statement expects an iterable object on the right hand side of the equal sign that produces the same number of values as the provided writable expressions when iterated through, and will iterate through it, assigning each of the produced values to the corresponding expression on the left.

- Python has a "string format" operator `%`. This functions analogous to `printf` format strings in C, e.g. `"spam=%s eggs=%d" % ("blah", 2)` evaluates to `"spam=blah eggs=2"`. In Python 3 and 2.6+, this was supplemented by the `format()` method of the `str` class, e.g. `"spam={0} eggs={1}".format("blah", 2)`. Python 3.6 added "f-strings": `blah = "blah"; eggs = 2; f'spam={blah} eggs={eggs}'`.

- Python has various kinds of string literals:

  - Strings delimited by single or double quote marks. Unlike in Unix shells, Perl and Perl-influenced languages, single quote marks and double quote marks function identically. Both kinds of string use the backslash (\) as an escape character. String interpolation became available in Python 3.6 as "formatted string literals".

  - Triple-quoted strings, which begin and end with a series of three single or double quote marks. They may span multiple lines and function like here documents in shells, Perl and Ruby.

  - Raw string varieties, denoted by prefixing the string literal with an `r`. Escape sequences are not interpreted; hence raw strings are useful where literal backslashes are common, such as regular expressions and Windows-style paths. Compare "@-quoting" in C#.

- Python has array index and array slicing expressions on lists, denoted as `a[key]`, `a[start:stop]` or `a[start:stop:step]`. Indexes are zero-based, and negative indexes are relative to the end. Slices take elements from the start index up to, but not including, the stop index. The third slice parameter, called step or stride, allows elements to be skipped and reversed. Slice indexes may be omitted, for example `a[:]` returns a copy of the entire list. Each element of a slice is a shallow copy.

In Python, a distinction between expressions and statements is rigidly enforced, in contrast to languages such as Common Lisp, Scheme, or Ruby. This leads to duplicating some functionality. For example:

- List comprehensions vs. `for`-loops.

- Conditional expressions vs. `if` blocks.

- The `eval()` vs. `exec()` built-in functions (in Python 2, `exec` is a statement); the former is for expressions, the latter is for statements.

Statements cannot be a part of an expression, so list and other comprehensions or lambda expressions, all being expressions, cannot contain statements. A particular case of this is that an assignment statement such as `a = 1` cannot form part of the conditional expression of a conditional statement. This has the advantage of avoiding a classic C error of mistaking an assignment operator = for an equality operator == in conditions: `if (c = 1) { ... }` is syntactically valid (but probably unintended) C code but `if c = 1: ...` causes a syntax error in Python.

Methods

Methods on objects are functions attached to the object's class; the syntax `instance.method(argument)` is, for normal methods and functions, syntactic sugar for `Class.method(instance, argument)`. Python methods have an explicit `self` parameter to access instance data, in contrast to the implicit `self` (or `this`) in some other object-oriented programming languages (e.g., C++, Java, Objective-C, or Ruby).

Typing

Python uses duck typing and has typed objects but untyped variable names. Type constraints are not checked at compile time; rather, operations on an object may fail, signifying that the given object is not of a suitable type. Despite being dynamically typed, Python is strongly typed, forbidding operations that are not well-defined (for example, adding a number to a string) rather than silently attempting to make sense of them.

Python allows programmers to define their own types using classes, which are most often used for object-oriented programming. New instances of classes are constructed by calling the class (for example, `SpamClass()` or `EggsClass()`), and the classes are instances of the metaclass `type` (itself an instance of itself), allowing metaprogramming and reflection.

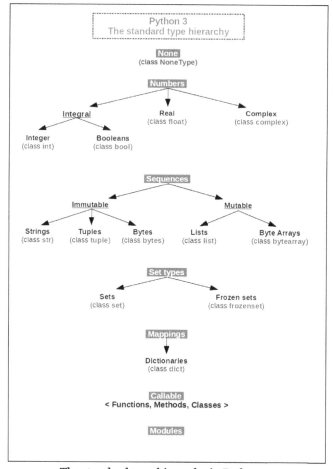

The standard type hierarchy in Python 3.

Before version 3.0, Python had two kinds of classes: old-style and new-style. The syntax of both styles is the same, the difference being whether the class `object` is inherited from, directly or indirectly (all new-style classes inherit from `object` and are instances of `type`). In versions of Python 2 from Python 2.2 onwards, both kinds of classes can be used. Old-style classes were eliminated in Python 3.0.

The long term plan is to support gradual typing and from Python 3.5, the syntax of the language allows specifying static types but they are not checked in the default implementation, CPython. An experimental optional static type checker named mypy supports compile-time type checking.

Mathematics

Python has the usual symbols for arithmetic operators (+, -, *, /), and the remainder operator % (where the remainder can be negative, e.g. 4 % -3 == -2). It also has ** for exponentiation, e.g. `5**3 == 125` and `9**0.5 == 3.0`, and a matrix multiply `@` opera-tor. These operators work like in traditional math; with the same precedence rules, the operators infix (`+` and `-` can also be unary to represent positive and negative numbers respectively). Additionally, it has a unary operator (`~`), which essentially inverts all the bits of its one argument. For integers, this means `~x=-x-1`. Other operators include bitwise shift operators `x << y`, which shifts `x` to the left `y` places, the same as `x*(2**y)`, and `x >> y`, which shifts `x` to the right `y` places, the same as `x//(2**y)`.

The behavior of division has changed significantly over time so that division between integers produces floating point results:

- Python 2.1 and earlier used C's division behavior. The `/` operator is integer divi-sion if both operands are integers, and floating-point division otherwise. Inte-ger division rounds towards 0, e.g. `7/3 == 2` and `-7/3 == -2`.

- Python 2.2 changed integer division to round towards negative infinity, e.g. `7/3 == 2` and `-7/3 == -3`. The floor division `//` operator was introduced. So `7//3 == 2, -7//3 == -3, 7.5//3 == 2.0` and `-7.5//3 == -3.0`. Adding `from __future__ import division` causes a module to use Python 3.0 rules for division.

- Python 3.0 changed `/` to always be floating-point division, e.g. `5/2 == 2.5`.

In Python terms, `/` before version 3.0 is classic division, `/` in versions 3.0 and higher is true division, and `//` is floor division. Rounding towards negative infinity, though dif-ferent from most languages, adds consistency. For instance, it means that the equation `(a + b)//b == a//b + 1` is always true. It also means that the equation `b*(a//b) + a%b == a` is valid for both positive and negative values of `a`. However, maintaining the validity of this equation means that while the result of `a%b` is, as expected, in the half-open interval [0, b), where `b` is a positive integer, it has to lie in the interval (b, 0] when `b` is negative.

Python provides a `round` function for rounding a float to the nearest integer. For tie-breaking, versions before 3 use round-away-from-zero: `round(0.5)` is 1.0, `round(-0.5)` is −1.0. Python 3 uses round to even: `round(1.5)` is 2, `round(2.5)` is 2.

Python allows boolean expressions with multiple equality relations in a manner that is consistent with general use in mathematics. For example, the expression `a < b < c` tests whether `a` is less than `b` and `b` is less than `c`. C-derived languages interpret this expression differently: in C, the expression would first evaluate `a < b`, resulting in 0 or 1, and that result would then be compared with `c`.

Python has extensive built-in support for arbitrary-precision arithmetic. Integers are transparently switched from the machine-supported maximum fixed-precision (usu-ally 32 or 64 bits), belonging to the python type `int`, to arbitrary precision, belonging to the Python type `long`, where needed. The latter have an "L" suffix in their textual representation. (In Python 3, the distinction between the `int` and `long` types was eliminated; this behavior is now entirely contained by the `int` class.) The `Decimal` type/class in module `decimal` (since version 2.4) provides decimal floating point numbers to arbitrary precision and several rounding modes. The `Fraction` type in module `fractions` (since version 2.6) provides arbitrary precision for rational numbers.

Due to Python's extensive mathematics library, and the third-party library NumPy that further extends the native capabilities, it is frequently used as a scientific scripting language to aid in problems such as numerical data processing and manipulation.

Python Programming Examples

Hello world program:

```
print('Hello, world!')
```

Program to calculate the factorial of a positive integer:

```
n = int(input('Type a number, then its factorial will be printed: '))


if n < 0:
    raise ValueError('You must enter a positive number')


fact = 1
i = 2
while i <= n:
    fact = fact * i
    i += 1


print(fact)
```

Libraries

Python's large standard library, commonly cited as one of its greatest strengths, provides tools suited to many tasks. For Internet-facing applications, many standard formats and protocols such as MIME and HTTP are supported. It includes modules for creating graphical user interfaces, connecting to relational databases, generating pseudorandom numbers, arithmetic with arbitrary-precision decimals, manipulating regular expressions, and unit testing.

Some parts of the standard library are covered by specifications (for example, the Web Server Gateway Interface (WSGI) implementation `wsgiref` follows PEP 333), but most modules are not. They are specified by their code, internal documentation, and test suites (if supplied). However, because most of the standard library is cross-platform Python code, only a few modules need altering or rewriting for variant implementations.

As of November 2019, the Python Package Index (PyPI), the official repository for third-party Python software, contains over 200,000 packages with a wide range of functionality, including:

- Graphical user interfaces.

- Web frameworks.

- Multimedia.

- Databases.

- Networking.

- Test frameworks.

- Automation.

- Web scraping.

- Documentation.

- System administration.

- Scientific computing.

- Text processing.

- Image processing.

- Machine learning.

- Data analytics.

Development Environments

Most Python implementations (including CPython) include a read–eval–print loop (REPL), permitting them to function as a command line interpreter for which the user enters statements sequentially and receives results immediately. Other shells, including IDLE and IPython, add further abilities such as auto-completion, session state retention and syntax highlighting.

As well as standard desktop integrated development environments, there are Web browser-based IDEs; SageMath (intended for developing science and math-related Python programs); PythonAnywhere, a browser-based IDE and hosting environment; and Canopy IDE, a commercial Python IDE emphasizing scientific computing.

Development

Python's development is conducted largely through the Python Enhancement Proposal (PEP) process, the primary mechanism for proposing major new features, collecting community input on issues and documenting Python design decisions. Python coding style is covered in PEP 8. Outstanding PEPs are reviewed and commented on by the Python community and the steering council.

Enhancement of the language corresponds with development of the CPython reference implementation. The mailing list python-dev is the primary forum for the language's development. Development originally took place on a self-hosted source-code repository running Mercurial, until Python moved to GitHub in January 2017.

CPython's public releases come in three types, distinguished by which part of the version number is incremented:

- Backward-incompatible versions, where code is expected to break and need to be manually ported. The first part of the version number is incremented. These releases happen infrequently—for example, version 3.0 was released 8 years after 2.0.

- Major or "feature" releases, about every 18 months, are largely compatible but introduce new features. The second part of the version number is incremented. Each major version is supported by bugfixes for several years after its release.

- Bugfix releases, which introduce no new features, occur about every 3 months and are made when a sufficient number of bugs have been fixed upstream since the last release. Security vulnerabilities are also patched in these releases. The third and final part of the version number is incremented.

Python 3.9 alpha1 was announced in November 2019, but the release date for the final version depends on what new proposal for release dates are adopted with three draft proposals under discussion, and a yearly cadence is one option.

Many alpha, beta, and release-candidates are also released as previews and for testing before final releases. Although there is a rough schedule for each release, they are often delayed if the code is not ready. Python's development team monitors the state of the code by running the large unit test suite during development, and using the BuildBot continuous integration system.

The community of Python developers has also contributed over 206,000 software modules to the Python Package Index (PyPI), the official repository of third-party Python libraries. The major academic conference on Python is PyCon. There are also special Python mentoring programmes, such as Pyladies.

API Documentation Generators

Python API documentation generators include:

- Sphinx.

- Epydoc.

- HeaderDoc.

- pydoc.

Uses

An empirical study found that scripting languages, such as Python, are more productive than conventional languages, such as C and Java, for programming problems involving string manipulation and search in a dictionary, and determined that memory consumption was often "better than Java and not much worse than C or C++".

Large organizations that use Python include Wikipedia, Google, Yahoo!, CERN, NASA, Facebook, Amazon, Instagram, Spotify and some smaller entities like ILM and ITA. The social news networking site Reddit is written entirely in Python.

Python can serve as a scripting language for web applications, e.g., via mod_wsgi for the Apache web server. With Web Server Gateway Interface, a standard API has evolved to facilitate these applications. Web frameworks like Django, Pylons, Pyramid, Turbo-Gears, web2py, Tornado, Flask, Bottle and Zope support developers in the design and maintenance of complex applications. Pyjs and IronPython can be used to develop the client-side of Ajax-based applications. SQLAlchemy can be used as data mapper to a relational database. Twisted is a framework to program communications between computers, and is used (for example) by Dropbox.

Libraries such as NumPy, SciPy and Matplotlib allow the effective use of Python in scientific computing, with specialized libraries such as Biopython and Astropy providing domain-specific functionality. SageMath is a mathematical software with a notebook interface programmable in Python: its library covers many aspects of mathematics, including algebra, combinatorics, numerical mathematics, number theory, and calculus.

Python has been successfully embedded in many software products as a scripting language, including in finite element method software such as Abaqus, 3D parametric modeler like FreeCAD, 3D animation packages such as 3ds Max, Blender, Cinema 4D, Lightwave, Houdini, Maya, modo, MotionBuilder, Softimage, the visual effects compositor Nuke, 2D imaging programs like GIMP, Inkscape, Scribus and Paint Shop Pro, and musical notation programs like scorewriter and capella. GNU Debugger uses Python as a pretty printer to show complex structures such as C++ containers. Esri promotes Python as the best choice for writing scripts in ArcGIS. It has also been used in several video games, and has been adopted as first of the three available programming languages in Google App Engine, the other two being Java and Go.

Python is commonly used in artificial intelligence projects with the help of libraries like TensorFlow, Keras and Scikit-learn. As a scripting language with modular architecture, simple syntax and rich text processing tools, Python is often used for natural language processing.

Many operating systems include Python as a standard component. It ships with most Linux distributions, AmigaOS 4, FreeBSD (as a package), NetBSD, OpenBSD (as a package) and macOS and can be used from the command line (terminal). Many Linux distributions use installers written in Python: Ubuntu uses the Ubiquity installer, while Red Hat Linux and Fedora use the Anaconda installer. Gentoo Linux uses Python in its package management system, Portage.

Python is used extensively in the information security industry, including in exploit development.

Most of the Sugar software for the One Laptop per Child XO, now developed at Sugar Labs, is written in Python. The Raspberry Pi single-board computer project has adopted Python as its main user-programming language.

Pascal

Pascal is an imperative and procedural programming language, designed by Niklaus Wirth as a small, efficient language intended to encourage good programming practices using structured programming and data structuring. It is named in honour of the French mathematician, philosopher and physicist Blaise Pascal.

Pascal was developed on the pattern of the ALGOL 60 language. Wirth was involved in the process to improve the language as part of the ALGOL X efforts and proposed a version known as ALGOL W. This was not accepted, and the ALGOL X process bogged down. In 1968, Wirth decided to abandon the ALGOL X process and further improve ALGOL W, releasing this as Pascal in 1970.

On top of ALGOL's scalars and arrays, Pascal enabled defining complex datatypes and building dynamic and recursive data structures such as lists, trees and graphs. Pascal has strong typing on all objects, which means that one type of data cannot be converted or interpreted as another without explicit conversions. Unlike most languages in the C-family, Pascal allows nested procedure definitions to any level of depth, and also allows most kinds of definitions and declarations inside subroutines (procedures and functions). A program is thus syntactically similar to a single procedure or function.

Pascal became very successful in the 1970s, notably on the burgeoning minicomputer market. Compilers were also available for many microcomputers as the field emerged in the late 1970s. It was widely used as a teaching language in university-level programming courses in the 1980s, and also used in production settings for writing commercial software during the same period. It was displaced by the C programming language during the late 1980s and early 1990s as UNIX-based systems became popular, and especially with the release of C++.

Language Constructs

Pascal, in its original form, is a purely procedural language and includes the traditional array of ALGOL-like control structures with reserved words such as if, then, else, while, for, and case ranging on a single statement or a begin-end statements block. Pascal also has data structuring constructs not included in the original ALGOL 60 types, like records, variants, pointers, enumerations, and sets and procedure/pointers. Such constructs were in part inherited or inspired from Simula 67, ALGOL 68, Niklaus Wirth's own ALGOL W and suggestions by C. A. R. Hoare.

Pascal programs start with the program keyword with a list of external file descriptors as parameters (not required in Turbo Pascal etc.); then follows the main block bracketed by the begin and end keywords. Semicolons separate statements, and the full stop (i.e., a period) ends the whole program (or unit). Letter case is ignored in Pascal source. Here is an example of the source code in use for a very simple "Hello, World!" program:

```
program HelloWorld(output);

begin

    Write('Hello, World!')

    {No ";" is required after the last statement of a block -

         adding one adds a "null statement" to the program, which is
ignored by the compiler.}

end.
```

Data Types

A type in Pascal, and in several other popular programming languages, defines a variable in such a way that it defines a range of values which the variable is capable of storing, and it also defines a set of operations that are permissible to be performed on variables of that type. The predefined types are:

Data type	Type of values which the variable is capable of storing
integer	integer (whole) numbers
real	floating-point numbers
boolean	the values True or False
char	a single character from an ordered character set
string	a sequence or "string" of characters
set	equivalent to an array of boolean values

The range of values allowed for each (except boolean) is implementation defined. Functions are provided for some data conversions. For conversion of `real` to `integer`, the following functions are available: `round` (which rounds to integer using banker's rounding) and `trunc` (rounds towards zero).

The programmer has the freedom to define other commonly used data types (e.g. byte, string, etc.) in terms of the predefined types using Pascal's type declaration facility, for example:

```
type
    byte         = 0..255;
    signed_byte = -128..127;
    string       = packed array[1..255] of char;
```

(Often-used types like byte and string are already defined in many implementations).

Subrange Types

Subranges of any ordinal data type (any simple type except real) can also be made:

```
var
    x : 1..10;
    y : 'a'..'z';
```

Set Types

In contrast with other programming languages from its time, Pascal supports a set type:

```
var
```

```
Set1 : set of 1..10;

Set2 : set of 'a'..'z';
```

A set is a fundamental concept for modern mathematics, and they may be used in many algorithms. Such a feature is useful and may be faster than an equivalent construct in a language that does not support sets. For example, for many Pascal compilers:

```
if i in [5..10] then ...
```

executes faster than:

```
if (i > 4) and (i < 11) then ...
```

Sets of non-contiguous values can be particularly useful, in terms of both performance and readability:

```
if i in [0..3, 7, 9, 12..15] then ...
```

For these examples, which involve sets over small domains, the improved performance is usually achieved by the compiler representing set variables as bit vectors. The set operators can then be implemented efficiently as bitwise machine code operations.

Type Declarations

Types can be defined from other types using type declarations:

```
type

    x = integer;

    y = x;

...
```

Further, complex types can be constructed from simple types:

```
type

    a = array[1..10] of integer;

    b = record

        x : integer;

        y : char   {extra semicolon not strictly required}

    end;

    c = file of a;
```

File Type

Pascal files are sequences of components. Every file has a buffer variable which is denoted by f^. The procedures get (for reading) and put (for writing) move the buffer variable to the next element. Read is introduced such that read(f, x) is the same as x := f^; get(f);. Write is introduced such that write(f, x) is the same as f^ := x; put(f); The type text is predefined as file of char. While the buffer variable could be used for inspecting the next character to be used (check for a digit before reading an integer), this leads to serious problems with interactive programs in early implementations, but was solved later with the "lazy I/O" concept.

Pointer Types

Pascal supports the use of pointers:

```
type
     pNode = ^Node;
     Node  = record
          a : integer;
          b : char;
          c : pNode
     end;
var
     NodePtr : pNode;
     IntPtr  : ^integer;
```

Here the variable NodePtr is a pointer to the data type Node, a record. Pointers can be used before they are declared. This is a forward declaration, an exception to the rule that things must be declared before they are used.

To create a new record and assign the value 10 and character A to the fields a and b in the record, and to initialise the pointer c to the null pointer ("NIL" in Pascal), the statements would be:

```
New(NodePtr);

...

NodePtr^.a := 10;

NodePtr^.b := 'A';

NodePtr^.c := NIL;

...
```

This could also be done using the with statement, as follows:

```
New(NodePtr);

...

with NodePtr^ do

begin

    a := 10;

    b := 'A';

    c := NIL

end;

...
```

Inside of the scope of the with statement, a and b refer to the subfields of the record pointer NodePtr and not to the record Node or the pointer type pNode. Linked lists, stacks and queues can be created by including a pointer type field (c) in the record.

Unlike many languages that feature pointers, Pascal only allows pointers to reference dynamically created variables that are anonymous, and does not allow them to reference standard static or local variables. Pointers also must have an associated type, and a pointer to one type is not compatible with a pointer to another type (e.g. a pointer to a char is not compatible with a pointer to an integer). This helps eliminate the type security issues inherent with other pointer implementations, particularly those used for PL/I or C.

It also removes some risks caused by dangling pointers, but the ability to dynamically deallocate referenced space by using the dispose function (which has the same effect as the free library function found in C) means that the risk of dangling pointers has not been entirely eliminated as it has in languages such as Java and C#, which provide automatic garbage collection (but which do not entirely eliminate the related problem of memory leaks). Some of these restrictions can be lifted in newer dialects.

Control Structures

Pascal is a structured programming language, meaning that the flow of control is structured into standard statements, usually without 'goto' commands.

```
while a <> b do  WriteLn('Waiting');


if a > b then WriteLn('Condition met')    {no semicolon allowed!}
```

```
     else WriteLn('Condition not met');


for i := 1 to 10 do   {no semicolon for single statements allowed!}
     WriteLn('Iteration: ', i);


repeat
     a := a + 1
until a = 10;


case i of
     0 : Write('zero');
     1 : Write('one');
     2 : Write('two');
     3,4,5,6,7,8,9,10: Write('?')
end;
```

Procedures and Functions

Pascal structures programs into procedures and functions.

```
program Printing;


var i : integer;


procedure Print(j : integer);
begin
    ...
end;
begin { main program }
    ...
    Print(i);
end.
```

Procedures and functions can be nested to any depth, and the 'program' construct is the logical outermost block. By default, parameters are passed by value. If 'var' precedes a parameter's name, it is passed by reference.

Each procedure or function can have its own declarations of goto labels, constants, types, variables, and other procedures and functions, which must all be in that order. This ordering requirement was originally intended to allow efficient single-pass compilation. However, in some dialects (such as Embarcadero Delphi) the strict ordering requirement of declaration sections has been relaxed.

Semicolons as Statement Separators

Pascal adopted many language syntax features from the ALGOL language, including the use of a semicolon as a statement separator. This is in contrast to other languages, such as PL/I, C etc. which use the semicolon as a statement terminator. No semicolon is needed before the end keyword of a record type declaration, a block, or a case statement; before the until keyword of a repeat statement; and before the else keyword of an if statement.

Perl Language

Perl is a general-purpose, high level interpreted and dynamic programming language. It was developed by Larry Wall, in 1987. There is no official Full form of the Perl, but still, the most used expansion is "Practical Extraction and Reporting Language". Some of the programmers also refer Perl as the "Pathologically Eclectic Rubbish Lister" Or "Practically Everything Really Likable". The acronym "Practical Extraction and Reporting Language" is used widely because Perl was originally developed for the text processing like extracting the required information from a specified text file and for converting the text file into a different form.

Perl supports both the procedural and Object-Oriented programming. Perl is a lot similar to C syntactically and is easy for the users who have knowledge of C, C++. It all started when Larry Wall was working on a task to generate the reports from a lot of text files which have cross-references. Then he started to use awk for this task but soon he found that it is not sufficient for this task. So instead of writing a utility for this task, he wrote a new language i.e. Perl and also wrote the interpreter for it. He wrote the language Perl in C and some of the concepts are taken from awk, sed, and LISP etc. At the beginning level, Perl was developed only for the system management and text handling but in later versions, Perl got the ability to handle regular expressions, and network sockets etc. In present Perl is popular for its ability to handling the Regex(Regular Expressions). The first version of Perl was 1.0 which released on December 18, 1987. The latest version of Perl is 5.28. Perl 6 is different from Perl 5 because it is a fully object-oriented reimplementation of Perl 5.

Why Perl?

Perl has many reasons for being popular and in demand. Few of the reasons are mentioned below:

- Easy to Start: Perl is a high-level language so it is closer to other popular programming languages like C, C++ and thus, becomes easy to learn for anyone.

- Text-Processing: As the acronym "Practical Extraction and Reporting Language" suggest that Perl has the high text manipulation abilities by which it can generate reports from different text files easily. Also, it can convert the files into some another form.

- Contained best Features: Perl contains the features of different languages like C, sed, awk, and sh etc. which makes the Perl more useful and productive.

- System Administration: Due to having the different scripting languages capabilities Perl make the task of system administration very easy. Instead of becoming dependent on many languages, just use Perl to complete out the whole task of system administration. In Spite of this Perl also used in web programming, web automation, GUI programming etc.

- Web and Perl: Perl can be embedded into web servers to increase its processing power and it has the DBI package, which makes web-database integration very easy.

Beginning with Perl Programming

- Finding a Interpreter: There are various online IDEs which can be used to run Perl programs without installing.

- Windows: There are various IDEs to run Perl programs or scripts: Padre, Eclipse with EPIC plugin etc.

Programming in Perl

Since the Perl is a lot similar to other widely used languages syntactically, it is easier to code and learn in Perl. Programs can be written in Perl in any of the widely used text editors like Notepad++, gedit etc. After writing the program save the file with the extension .pl or .PL To run the program use perl file_name.pl on the command line.

Example: A simple program to print Welcome to GFG!

```
# Perl program to print Welcome to GFG!

#!/usr/bin/perl

# Below line will print "Welcome to GFG!"

print "Welcome to GFG!\n";
```

Output:

```
Welcome to GFG!
```

Comments: Comments are used for enhancing the readability of the code. The interpreter will ignore the comment entries and does not execute them. Comments can be of the single line or multiple lines.

```
Single line Comment:
```

Syntax:

```
# Single line comment
```

Multi-line comment:

Syntax:

```
= Multi line comments

Line start from  = is interpreted as the

starting of multiline comment and =cut is

consider as the end of multiline comment

=cut
```

Print: It is a function in Perl to show the result or any specified output on the console.

Quotes: In Perl, you can use either single quotes(")or double quotes(""). Using single quotes will not interpolate any variable or special character but using double quotes will interpolates.

\n: It is used for the new line character which uses the backslash (\) character to escape any type of character.

/usr/bin/perl: It is actual Perl interpreter binary which always starts with #!. This is used in the Perl Script Mode Programming.

Advantages of Perl

- Perl Provides supports for cross platform and it is compatible with mark-up languages like HTML, XML etc.

- It is very efficient in text-manipulation i.e. Regular Expression. It also provides the socket capability.

- It is free and a Open Source software which is licensed under Artistic and GNU General Public License (GPL).

- It is an embeddable language that's why it can embed in web servers and database servers.

- It supports more than 25, 000 open source modules on CPAN(Comprehensive Perl Archive Network) which provide many powerful extensions to the standard library. For example, XML processing, GUI(Graphical User Interface) and DI(-Database Integration) etc.

Disadvantages of Perl

- Perl doesn't supports portability due to CPAN modules.

- Programs runs slowly and program needs to be interpreted each time when any changes are made.

- In Perl, the same result can be achieved in several different ways which make the code untidy as well as unreadable.

- Usability factor is lower when compared to other languages.

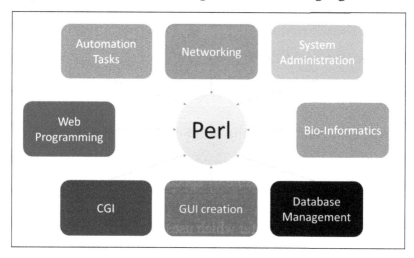

Applications

- One of the major application of Perl language is to processing of text files and analysis of the strings.

- Perl also used for CGI(Common Gateway Interface) scripts.

- Used in web development, GUI(Graphical User Interface) development.

- Perl's text-handling capabilities is also used for generating SQL queries.

References

- "Programming Language Popularity". 2009. Archived from the original on 13 December 2007. Retrieved 16 January 2009

- Computer-programming-language, technology: britannica.com, Retrieved 19 February, 2020

- Peter Seibel (16 September 2009). Coders at Work: Reflections on the Craft of Programming. Apress. pp. 475–476. ISBN 978-1-4302-1948-4

- Gosling, James; Joy, Bill; Steele, Guy L., Jr.; Bracha, Gilad (2005). The Java Language Specification (3rd ed.). Addison-Wesley. ISBN 0-321-24678-0

- Programming-language, jargon: computerhope.com: Retrieved 1 March, 2020

- Oliphant, Travis (2007). "Python for Scientific Computing". Computing in Science and Engineering. 9 (3): 10–20. Bibcode:2007CSE.....9c..10O. CiteSeerX 10.1.1.474.6460. doi:10.1109/MCSE.2007.58

3
Data Types and Structures

Data type is an attribute of data which tells the interpreter how the programmer wishes to use data. Data structure is an organization, storage and management format for systematic access and modification. Composite data type, abstract data type, variant type, object type, decision tree, binary tree, etc. are some of its types. This chapter discusses the subject of data types and structures in detail.

Data type is a data storage format that can contain a specific type or range of values. When computer programs store data in variables, each variable must be assigned a specific data type. Some common data types include integers, floating point numbers, characters, strings, and arrays. They may also be more specific types, such as dates, timestamps, boolean values, and varchar (variable character) formats.

Some programming languages require the programmer to define the data type of a variable before assigning it a value. Other languages can automatically assign a variable's data type when the initial data is entered into the variable. For example, if the variable "var1" is created with the value "1.25," the variable would be created as a floating point data type. If the variable is set to "Hello world!," the variable would be assigned a string data type. Most programming languages allow each variable to store a single data type. Therefore, if the variable's data type has already been set to an integer, assigning string data to the variable may cause the data to be converted to an integer format.

Data types are also used by database applications. The fields within a database of-ten require a specific type of data to be input. For example, a company's record for an employee may use a string data type for the employee's first and last name. The employee's date of hire would be stored in a date format, while his or her salary may be stored as an integer. By keeping the data types uniform across multiple re-cords, database applications can easily search, sort, and compare fields in different records.

Composite Data Type

In computer science, a composite data type or compound data type is any data type which can be constructed in a program using the programming language's primitive data types and other composite types. It is sometimes called a structure or aggregate data type, although the latter term may also refer to arrays, lists, etc. The act of constructing a composite type is known as composition. Composite data types are often contrasted with scalar variables.

C/C++ Structures and Classes

A struct is C's and C++'s notion of a composite type, a datatype that composes a fixed set of labeled fields or members. It is so called because of the struct keyword used in declaring them, which is short for structure or, more precisely, user-defined data structure.

In C++, the only difference between a struct and a class is the default access level, which is private for classes and public for structs. Note that while classes and the class keyword were completely new in C++, the C programming language already had a crude type of structs. For all intents and purposes, C++ structs form a superset of C structs: virtually all valid C structs are valid C++ structs with the same semantics.

Declaration

A struct declaration consists of a list of fields, each of which can have any type. The total storage required for a struct object is the sum of the storage requirements of all the fields, plus any internal padding.

For example:

```
struct Account {
    int account_number;
    char *first_name;
    char *last_name;
    float balance;
};
```

defines a type, referred to as struct Account. To create a new variable of this type, we can write struct Account myAccount; which has an integer component, accessed by myAccount.account_number, and a floating-point component, accessed by `myAccount.balance`, as well as the `first_name` and `last_name` components. The structure `myAccount` contains all four values, and all four fields may be changed independently.

Since writing struct Account repeatedly in code becomes cumbersome, it is not unusual to see a typedef statement in C code to provide a more convenient synonym for the struct.

For example:

```
typedef struct Account_ {
    int     account_number;
    char    *first_name;
    char    *last_name;
    float   balance;
} Account;
```

In C++ code, the `typedef` is not needed because types defined using `struct` are already part of the regular namespace, so the type can be referred to as either `struct Account` or simply `Account`.

As another example, a three-dimensional Vector composite type that uses the floating point data type could be created with:

```
struct Vector {
    float x;
    float y;
    float z;
};
```

A variable named `velocity` with a `Vector` composite type would be declared as `Vector velocity;` Members of the `velocity` would be accessed using a dot notation. For example, `velocity.x = 5;` would set the x component of `velocity` equal to 5.

Likewise, a color structure could be created using:

```
struct Color {
    unsigned int red;
    unsigned int green;
    unsigned int blue;
};
```

In 3D graphics, you usually must keep track of both the position and color of each vertex. One way to do this would be to create a Vertex composite type, using the previously created Vector and Color composite types:

```
struct Vertex {

    Vector position;

    Color color;

};
```

Instantiation

Create a variable of type `struct Vertex` using the same format as before: `Vertex v;`

Member Access

Assign values to the components of v like so:

```
v.position.x = 0.0;

v.position.y = 1.5;

v.position.z = 0.0;

v.color.red = 128;

v.color.green = 0;

v.color.blue = 255;
```

Primitive Subtype

The primary use of struct is for the construction of complex datatypes, but sometimes it is used to create primitive structural subtyping. For example, since Standard C requires that if two structs have the same initial fields, those fields will be represented in the same way, the code:

```
struct ifoo_old_stub {

    long x, y;

};

struct ifoo_version_42 {

    long x, y, z;

    char *name;

    long a, b, c;
```

```
};

void operate_on_ifoo(struct ifoo_old_stub *);

struct ifoo_version_42 s;

. . .

operate_on_ifoo(&s);
```

will work correctly.

Type Signature

Type signatures (or Function types) are constructed from primitive and composite types, and can serve as types themselves when constructing composite types:

```
typedef struct {

    int x;

    int y;

} Point;


typedef double (*Metric) (Point p1, Point p2);


typedef struct {

    Point centre;

    double radius;

    Metric metric;

} Circle;
```

Abstract Data Type

In computer science, an abstract data type (ADT) is a mathematical model for data types, where a data type is defined by its behavior (semantics) from the point of view of a *user* of the data, specifically in terms of possible values, possible operations on data of this type, and the behavior of these operations. This contrasts with data structures, which are concrete representations of data, and are the point of view of an implementer, not a user.

Formally, an ADT may be defined as a "class of objects whose logical behavior is defined by a set of values and a set of operations"; this is analogous to an algebraic structure in mathematics. What is meant by "behavior" varies by author, with the two main types of formal specifications for behavior being *axiomatic (algebraic) specification* and an *abstract model;* these correspond to axiomatic semantics and operational semantics of an abstract machine, respectively. the computational complexity ("cost"), both in terms of time (for computing operations) and space (for representing values). In practice many common data types are not ADTs, as the abstraction is not perfect, and users must be aware of issues like arithmetic overflow that are due to the representation. For example, integers are often stored as fixed width values (32-bit or 64-bit binary numbers), and thus experience integer overflow if the maximum value is exceeded.

ADTs are a theoretical concept in computer science, used in the design and analysis of algorithms, data structures, and software systems, and do not correspond to specific features of computer languages—mainstream computer languages do not directly support formally specified ADTs. However, various language features correspond to certain aspects of ADTs, and are easily confused with ADTs proper; these include abstract types, opaque data types, protocols, and design by contract. ADTs were first proposed by Barbara Liskov and Stephen N. Zilles in 1974, as part of the development of the CLU language.

Examples:

For example, integers are an ADT, defined as the values ..., −2, −1, 0, 1, 2, ..., and by the operations of addition, subtraction, multiplication, and division, together with greater than, less than, etc., which behave according to familiar mathematics (with care for integer division), independently of how the integers are represented by the computer. Explicitly, "behavior" includes obeying various axioms (associativity and commutativity of addition etc.), and preconditions on operations (cannot divide by zero). Typically integers are represented in a data structure as binary numbers, most often as two's complement, but might be binary-coded decimal or in ones' complement, but the user is abstracted from the concrete choice of representation, and can simply use the data as data types.

An ADT consists not only of operations, but also of values of the underlying data and of constraints on the operations. An "interface" typically refers only to the operations, and perhaps some of the constraints on the operations, notably pre-conditions and post-conditions, but not other constraints, such as relations between the operations.

For example, an abstract stack, which is a last-in-first-out structure, could be defined by three operations: `push`, that inserts a data item onto the stack; `pop`, that removes a data item from it; and `peek` or `top`, that accesses a data item on top of the stack without removal. An abstract queue, which is a first-in-first-out structure, would also have three operations: `enqueue`, that inserts a data item into the queue; `dequeue`, that removes the first data item from it; and `front`, that accesses and serves the first data item in the queue. There would be no way of differentiating these two data types, unless a mathematical constraint is introduced that for a stack specifies that each pop always returns the most recently pushed item that has not been popped yet. When analyzing the efficiency of algorithms that use stacks, one may also specify that all operations take the same time no matter how many data items have been pushed into the stack, and that the stack uses a constant amount of storage for each element.

Abstract data types are purely theoretical entities, used (among other things) to simplify the description of abstract algorithms, to classify and evaluate data structures, and to formally describe the type systems of programming languages. However, an ADT may be implemented by specific data types or data structures, in many ways and in many programming languages; or described in a formal specification language. ADTs are often implemented as modules: the module's interface declares procedures that correspond to the ADT operations, sometimes with comments that describe the constraints. This information hiding strategy allows the implementation of the module to be changed without disturbing the client programs.

The term abstract data type can also be regarded as a generalized approach of a number of algebraic structures, such as lattices, groups, and rings. The notion of abstract data types is related to the concept of data abstraction, important in object-oriented programming and design by contract methodologies for software development.

An abstract data type is defined as a mathematical model of the data objects that make up a data type as well as the functions that operate on these objects. There are no standard conventions for defining them. A broad division may be drawn between "imperative" and "functional" definition styles.

Imperative-style

An abstract data structure is conceived as an entity that is *mutable*—meaning that it may be in different *states* at different times. Some operations may change the state of the ADT; therefore, the order in which operations are evaluated is important, and the same operation on the same entities may have different effects if executed at different times—just like the instructions of a computer, or the commands and procedures of an imperative language. To underscore this view, it is customary to say that the operations are *executed* or *applied*, rather than *evaluated*. The imperative style is often used when describing abstract algorithms.

Abstract Variable

Imperative-style definitions of ADT often depend on the concept of an *abstract variable*, which may be regarded as the simplest non-trivial ADT. An abstract variable *V* is a mutable entity that admits two operations:

- store(V, x) where x is a value of unspecified nature.

- fetch(V), that yields a value.

with the constraint that,

- fetch(V) always returns the value x used in the most recent store(V, x) operation on the same variable V.

As in so many programming languages, the operation store(V, x) is often written V ← x (or some similar notation), and fetch(V) is implied whenever a variable V is used in a context where a value is required. Thus, for example, V ← V + 1 is commonly understood to be a shorthand for store(V,fetch(V) + 1).

In this definition, it is implicitly assumed that storing a value into a variable *U* has no effect on the state of a distinct variable *V*. To make this assumption explicit, one could add the constraint that:

- if U and V are distinct variables, the sequence { store(U, x); store(V, y) } is equivalent to { store(V, y); store(U, x) }.

More generally, ADT definitions often assume that any operation that changes the state of one ADT instance has no effect on the state of any other instance (including other instances of the same ADT) — unless the ADT axioms imply that the two instances are connected (aliased) in that sense. For example, when extending the definition of abstract variable to include abstract records, the operation that selects a field from a record variable *R* must yield a variable *V* that is aliased to that part of *R*.

The definition of an abstract variable *V* may also restrict the stored values *x* to members of a specific set *X*, called the *range* or *type* of *V*. As in programming languages, such restrictions may simplify the description and analysis of algorithms, and improve their readability.

This definition does not imply anything about the result of evaluating fetch(V) when V is un-initialized, that is, before performing any store operation on V. An algorithm that does so is usually considered invalid, because its effect is not defined. (However, there are some important algorithms whose efficiency strongly depends on the assumption that such a fetch is legal, and returns some arbitrary value in the variable's range).

Instance Creation

Some algorithms need to create new instances of some ADT (such as new variables, or new stacks). To describe such algorithms, one usually includes in the ADT definition a create() operation that yields an instance of the ADT, usually with axioms equivalent to:

- The result of create() is distinct from any instance in use by the algorithm.

This axiom may be strengthened to exclude also partial aliasing with other instances. On the other hand, this axiom still allows implementations of create() to yield a previously created instance that has become inaccessible to the program.

Abstract Stack (Imperative)

As another example, an imperative-style definition of an abstract stack could specify that the state of a stack S can be modified only by the operations:

- push(S, x), where x is some value of unspecified nature.

- pop(S), that yields a value as a result.

with the constraint that:

- For any value x and any abstract variable V, the sequence of operations { push(S, x); $V \leftarrow$ pop(S) } is equivalent to $V \leftarrow x$.

Since the assignment $V \leftarrow x$, by definition, cannot change the state of S, this condition implies that $V \leftarrow$ pop(S) restores S to the state it had before the push(S, x). From this condition and from the properties of abstract variables, it follows, for example, that the sequence:

{ push(S, x); push(S, y); U $\leftarrow$ pop(S); push(S, z); V $\leftarrow$ pop(S); W $\leftarrow$ pop(S) }

where x, y, and z are any values, and U, V, W are pairwise distinct variables, is equivalent to:

{ $U \leftarrow y$; $V \leftarrow z$; $W \leftarrow x$ }

Here it is implicitly assumed that operations on a stack instance do not modify the state of any other ADT instance, including other stacks; that is,

- For any values x, y, and any distinct stacks S and T, the sequence { push(S, x); push(T, y) } is equivalent to { push(T, y); push(S, x) }.

An abstract stack definition usually includes also a Boolean-valued function empty(S) and a create() operation that returns a stack instance, with axioms equivalent to:

- create() $\neq$ S for any prior stack S (a newly created stack is distinct from all previous stacks).

- empty(create()) (a newly created stack is empty).

- not empty(push(S, x)) (pushing something into a stack makes it non-empty).

Single-instance Style

Sometimes an ADT is defined as if only one instance of it existed during the execution of the algorithm, and all operations were applied to that instance, which is not explicitly notated. For example, the abstract stack above could have been defined with operations push(*x*) and pop(), that operate on *the* only existing stack. ADT definitions in this style can be easily rewritten to admit multiple coexisting instances of the ADT, by adding an explicit instance parameter (like *S*) to every operation that uses or modifies the implicit instance.

On the other hand, some ADTs cannot be meaningfully defined without assuming multiple instances. This is the case when a single operation takes two distinct instances of the ADT as parameters. For an example, consider augmenting the definition of the abstract stack with an operation compare(*S*, *T*) that checks whether the stacks *S* and *T* contain the same items in the same order.

Functional-style

Another way to define an ADT, closer to the spirit of functional programming, is to consider each state of the structure as a separate entity. In this view, any operation that modifies the ADT is modeled as a mathematical function that takes the old state as an argument, and returns the new state as part of the result. Unlike the imperative operations, these functions have no side effects. Therefore, the order in which they are evaluated is immaterial, and the same operation applied to the same arguments (including the same input states) will always return the same results (and output states).

In the functional view, in particular, there is no way (or need) to define an "abstract variable" with the semantics of imperative variables (namely, with `fetch` and `store` operations). Instead of storing values into variables, one passes them as arguments to functions.

Abstract Stack (Functional)

For example, a complete functional-style definition of an abstract stack could use the three operations:

- `push`: Takes a stack state and an arbitrary value, returns a stack state.

- `top`: Takes a stack state, returns a value.

- `pop`: Takes a stack state, returns a stack state.

In a functional-style definition there is no need for a `create` operation. Indeed, there is no notion of "stack instance". The stack states can be thought of as being potential states of a single stack structure, and two stack states that contain the same values in the same order are considered to be identical states. This view actually mirrors the behavior of some concrete implementations, such as linked lists with hash cons.

Instead of create(), a functional-style definition of an abstract stack may assume the existence of a special stack state, the empty stack, designated by a special symbol like Λ or "()"; or define a bottom() operation that takes no arguments and returns this special stack state. Note that the axioms imply that:

- push(Λ, x) $\neq \Lambda$.

In a functional-style definition of a stack one does not need an empty predicate: instead, one can test whether a stack is empty by testing whether it is equal to Λ.

These axioms do not define the effect of top s or pop s, unless s is a stack state returned by a push. Since push leaves the stack non-empty, those two operations are undefined (hence invalid) when s = Λ. On the other hand, the axioms (and the lack of side effects) imply that push(s, x) = push(t, y) if and only if x = y and s = t.

As in some other branches of mathematics, it is customary to assume also that the stack states are only those whose existence can be proved from the axioms in a finite number of steps. In the abstract stack example above, this rule means that every stack is a finite sequence of values, that becomes the empty stack (Λ) after a finite number of pops. By themselves, the axioms above do not exclude the existence of infinite stacks (that can be poped forever, each time yielding a different state) or circular stacks (that return to the same state after a finite number of pops). In particular, they do not exclude states s such that pop s = s or push(s, x) = s for some x. However, since one cannot obtain such stack states with the given operations, they are assumed "not to exist".

Whether to include Complexity

Aside from the behavior in terms of axioms, it is also possible to include, in the definition of an ADT operation, their algorithmic complexity. Alexander Stepanov, designer of the C++ Standard Template Library, included complexity guarantees in the STL specification, arguing:

> "The reason for introducing the notion of abstract data types was to allow interchangeable software modules. You cannot have interchangeable modules unless these modules share similar complexity behavior. If I replace one module with another module with the same functional behavior but with different complexity tradeoffs, the user of this code will be unpleasantly surprised. I could tell him anything I like about data abstraction, and he still would not want to use the code. Complexity assertions have to be part of the interface".

Advantages of Abstract Data Typing

Encapsulation

Abstraction provides a promise that any implementation of the ADT has certain properties and abilities; knowing these is all that is required to make use of an ADT object. The user does not need any technical knowledge of how the implementation works to use the ADT. In this way, the implementation may be complex but will be encapsulated in a simple interface when it is actually used.

Localization of Change

Code that uses an ADT object will not need to be edited if the implementation of the ADT is changed. Since any changes to the implementation must still comply with the interface, and since code using an ADT object may only refer to properties and abilities specified in the interface, changes may be made to the implementation without requiring any changes in code where the ADT is used.

Flexibility

Different implementations of the ADT, having all the same properties and abilities, are equivalent and may be used somewhat interchangeably in code that uses the ADT. This gives a great deal of flexibility when using ADT objects in different situations. For example, different implementations of the ADT may be more efficient in different situations; it is possible to use each in the situation where they are preferable, thus increasing overall efficiency.

Typical Operations

Some operations that are often specified for ADTs (possibly under other names) are:

- `compare`(s, t), that tests whether two instances' states are equivalent in some sense.

- `hash`s, that computes some standard hash function from the instance's state.

- `print`s or `show`s, that produces a human-readable representation of the instance's state.

In imperative-style ADT definitions, one often finds also:

- `create`(), that yields a new instance of the ADT.

- `initialize`s, that prepares a newly created instance s for further operations, or resets it to some "initial state".

- `copy`(s, t), that puts instance s in a state equivalent to that of t.

- `clone`(t), that performs s ← `create`(), `copy`(s, t), and returns s.

- `free`(s) or `destroy`(s), that reclaims the memory and other resources used by s.

The `free` operation is not normally relevant or meaningful, since ADTs are theoretical entities that do not "use memory". However, it may be necessary when one needs to analyze the storage used by an algorithm that uses the ADT. In that case one needs additional axioms that specify how much memory each ADT instance uses, as a function of its state, and how much of it is returned to the pool by `free`.

Examples:

Some common ADTs, which have proved useful in a great variety of applications, are:

- Container.

- List.

- Set.

- Multiset.

- Map.

- Multimap.

- Graph.

- Tree.

- Stack.

- Queue.

- Priority queue.

- Double-ended queue.

- Double-ended priority queue.

Each of these ADTs may be defined in many ways and variants, not necessarily equivalent. For example, an abstract stack may or may not have a `count` operation that tells how many items have been pushed and not yet popped. This choice makes a difference not only for its clients but also for the implementation.

Abstract Graphical Data Type

An extension of ADT for computer graphics was proposed in 1979: an abstract graphical data type (AGDT). It was introduced by Nadia Magnenat Thalmann, and Daniel

Thalmann. AGDTs provide the advantages of ADTs with facilities to build graphical objects in a structured way.

Primitive Data Type

Primitive data type is:

- A *basic type* is a data type provided by a programming language as a basic building block. Most languages allow more complicated *composite types* to be recursively constructed starting from basic types.

- A *built-in type* is a data type for which the programming language provides built-in support.

In most programming languages, all basic data types are built-in. In addition, many languages also provide a set of composite data types.

Depending on the language and its implementation, primitive data types may or may not have a one-to-one correspondence with objects in the computer's memory. However, one usually expects operations on basic primitive data types to be the fastest language constructs there are. Integer addition, for example, can be performed as a single machine instruction, and some processors offer specific instructions to process sequences of characters with a single instruction. In particular, the C standard mentions that "a 'plain' int object has the natural size suggested by the architecture of the execution environment". This means that int is likely to be 32 bits long on a 32-bit architecture. Basic primitive types are almost always value types.

Most languages do not allow the behavior or capabilities of primitive (either built-in or basic) data types to be modified by programs. Exceptions include Smalltalk, which permits all data types to be extended within a program, adding to the operations that can be performed on them or even redefining the built-in operations.

The actual range of primitive data types that is available is dependent upon the specific programming language that is being used. For example, in C#, strings are a composite but built-in data type, whereas in modern dialects of BASIC and in JavaScript, they are assimilated to a primitive data type that is both basic and built-in.

Classic basic primitive types may include:

- Character (`character`, `char`).

- Integer (`integer`, `int`, `short`, `long`, `byte`) with a variety of precisions.

- Floating-point number (`float`, `double`, `real`, `double precision`).

- Fixed-point number (fixed) with a variety of precisions and a programmer-selected scale.

- Boolean, logical values true and false.

- Reference (also called a *pointer* or *handle* or *descriptor*), a value referring to another object. The reference can be a memory address, or an index to a collection of values.

   The above primitives are generally supported more or less directly by computer hardware, except possibly for floating point, so operations on such primitives are usually fairly efficient. Some programming languages support text strings as a primitive (e.g. Basic) while others treat a text string as an array of characters (e.g. C). Some computer hardware (e.g. x86) has instructions which help in dealing with text strings, but complete hardware support for text strings is rare.

Strings could be any series of characters in the used encoding. To separate strings from code, most languages enclose them by single or double quotes. For example "Hello World" or 'Hello World'. "200" could be mistaken as an integer type but is actually string type because it contained in double quotes.

More sophisticated types which can be built-in include:

- Tuple in Standard ML, Python, Scala, Swift, Elixir.

- List in Common Lisp, Python, Scheme, Haskell.

- Complex number in C99, Fortran, Common Lisp, Python, D, Go.

- Rational number in Common Lisp, Haskell.

- Associative array in Perl, Python, Ruby, JavaScript, Lua, D, Go.

- First-class function, in all functional languages, JavaScript, Lua, D, Go, and in newer standards of C++, Java, C#, Perl.

Specific Primitive Data Types

Integer Numbers

An integer data type that represents some range of mathematical integers. Integers may be either signed (allowing negative values) or unsigned (non-negative integers only). Common ranges are:

Size (bytes)	Size (bits)	Names	Signed range (assuming two's complement for signed)	Unsigned range
1 byte	8 bits	Byte, octet, minimum size of char in C99	−128 to +127	0 to 255

2 bytes	16 bits	x86 word, minimum size of short and int in C	−32,768 to +32,767	0 to 65,535
4 bytes	32 bits	x86 double word, minimum size of long in C, actual size of int for most modern C compilers, pointer for IA-32-compatible processors	−2,147,483,648 to +2,147,483,647	0 to 4,294,967,295
8 bytes	64 bits	x86 quadruple word, minimum size of long long in C, actual size of long for most modern C compilers, pointer for x86-64-compatible processors	−9,223,372,036,854,775,808 to 9,223,372,036,854,775,807	0 to 8,446,744,073,709, 551,615
unlimited/8	un-limit-ed	Bignum	$-2^{\text{unlimited}}/2$ to $+(2^{\text{unlimited}}/2 - 1)$	0 to $2^{\text{unlimited}} - 1$

Literals for integers can be written as regular Arabic numerals, consisting of a sequence of digits and with negation indicated by a minus sign before the value. However, most programming languages disallow use of commas for or spaces digit grouping. Examples of integer literals are:

- `42`

- `10000`

- `-233000`

There are several alternate methods for writing integer literals in many programming languages:

- Most programming languages, especially those influenced by C, prefix an integer literal with `0X` or `0x` to represent a hexadecimal value, e.g. `0xDEADBEEF`. Other languages may use a different notation, e.g. some assembly languages append an `H` or `h` to the end of a hexadecimal value.

- Perl, Ruby, Java, Julia, D, Rust and Python (starting from version 3.6) allow embedded underscores for clarity, e.g. `10_000_000`, and fixed-form Fortran ignores embedded spaces in integer literals.

- In C and C++, a leading zero indicates an octal value, e.g. `0755`. This was primarily intended to be used with Unix modes; however, it has been criticized because normal integers may also lead with zero. As such, Python, Ruby, Haskell, and OCaml prefix octal values with `0O` or `0o`, following the layout used by hexadecimal values.

- Several languages, including Java, C#, Scala, Python, Ruby, and OCaml, can represent binary values by prefixing a number with `0B` or `0b`.

Booleans

A boolean type, typically denoted "bool" or "boolean", is typically a *logical type* that can be either "true" or "false". Although only one bit is necessary to accommodate the value set "true" and "false", programming languages typically implement boolean types as one or more bytes.

Many languages (e.g. Java, Pascal and Ada) implement booleans adhering to the concept of boolean as a distinct logical type. Languages, though, may implicitly convert booleans to numeric types at times to give extended semantics to booleans and boolean expressions or to achieve backwards compatibility with earlier versions of the language. For example, ANSI C and its former standards did not have a dedicated boolean type. Instead, numeric values of zero are interpreted as "false", and any other value is interpreted as "true". C99 adds a distinct boolean type that can be included with stdbool.h, and C++ supports `bool` as a built-in type and "true" and "false" as reserved words.

Floating-point Numbers

A floating-point number represents a limited-precision rational number that may have a fractional part. These numbers are stored internally in a format equivalent to scientific notation, typically in binary but sometimes in decimal. Because floating-point numbers have limited precision, only a subset of real or rational numbers are exactly representable; other numbers can be represented only approximately. Many languages have both a single precision (often called "float") and a double precision type.

Literals for floating point numbers include a decimal point, and typically use e or E to denote scientific notation. Examples of floating-point literals are:

- `20.0005.`
- `99.9.`
- `-5000.12.`
- `6.02e23.`

Some languages (e.g., Fortran, Python, D) also have a complex number type comprising two floating-point numbers: a real part and an imaginary part.

Fixed-point Numbers

A fixed-point number represents a limited-precision rational number that may have a fractional part. These numbers are stored internally in a scaled-integer form, typically in binary but sometimes in decimal. Because fixed-point numbers have limited precision, only a subset of real or rational numbers are exactly representable; other numbers can be represented only approximately. Fixed-point numbers also tend to have a more limited range of values than floating point, and so the programmer must be careful to avoid overflow in intermediate calculations as well as the final result.

Characters and Strings

A character type (typically called "char") may contain a single letter, digit, punctuation mark, symbol, formatting code, control code, or some other specialized code (e.g., a byte order mark). In C, `char` is defined as the smallest addressable unit of memory. On most systems, this is 8 bits; Several standards, such as POSIX, require it to be this size. Some languages have two or more character types, for example a single-byte type for ASCII characters and a multi-byte type for Unicode characters. The term "character type" is normally used even for types whose values more precisely represent code units, for example a UTF-16 code unit as in Java (support limited to 16-bit characters only) and JavaScript.

Characters may be combined into strings. The string data can include numbers and other numerical symbols but will be treated as text.

Strings are implemented in various ways, depending on the programming language. The simplest way to implement strings is to create them as an array of characters, followed by a delimiting character used to signal the end of the string, usually NUL. These are referred to as null-terminated strings, and are usually found in languages with a low amount of hardware abstraction, such as C and Assembly. While easy to implement, null terminated strings have been criticized for causing buffer overflows. Most high-level scripting languages, such as Python, Ruby, and many dialects of BASIC, have no separate character type; strings with a length of one are normally used to represent single characters. Some languages, such as C++ and Java, have the capability to use null-terminated strings (usually for backwards-compatibility measures), but additionally provide their own class for string handling (`std::string` and `java.lang.String`, respectively) in the standard library.

There is also a difference on whether or not strings are mutable or immutable in a language. Mutable strings may be altered after their creation, whereas immutable strings maintain a constant size and content. In the latter, the only way to alter strings are to create new ones. There are both advantages and disadvantages to each approach: although immutable strings are much less flexible, they are simpler and completely thread-safe. Some examples of languages that use mutable strings include C++, Perl and Ruby, whereas languages that do not include JavaScript, Lua, Python and Go. A few languages, such as Objective-C, provide different types for mutable and immutable strings.

Literals for characters and strings are usually surrounded by quotation marks: sometimes, single quotes (') are used for characters and double quotes (") are used for strings. Python accepts either variant for its string notation.

Examples of character literals in C syntax are:

- `'A'`.

- `'4'`.

- `'$'`.

- `'\t'` (tab character).

Examples of string literals in C syntax are:

- `"A"`.

- `"Hello World"`.

Numeric Data Type Ranges

Each numeric data type has its maximum and minimum value known as the range. Attempting to store a number outside the range may lead to compiler/runtime errors, or to incorrect calculations (due to truncation) depending on the language being used.

The range of a variable is based on the number of bytes used to save the value, and an integer data type is usually able to store 2n values (where n is the number of bits that contribute to the value). For other data types (e.g. floating-point values) the range is more complicated and will vary depending on the method used to store it. There are also some types that do not use entire bytes, e.g. a boolean that requires a single bit, and represents a binary value (although in practice a byte is often used, with the remaining 7 bits being redundant). Some programming languages (such as Ada and Pascal) also allow the opposite direction, that is, the programmer defines the range and precision needed to solve a given problem and the compiler chooses the most appropriate integer or floating-point type automatically.

Variant Type

Variant is a data type in certain programming languages, particularly Visual Basic, OCaml, Delphi and C++ when using the Component Object Model.

In Visual Basic (and Visual Basic for Applications) the Variant data type is a tagged union that can be used to represent any other data type (for example, integer, floating-point, single- and double-precision, object, etc.) except fixed-length string type and record types. In Visual Basic, any variable not declared explicitly or the type of which is not declared explicitly, is taken to be a variant.

While the use of not explicitly declared variants is not recommended, they can be of use when the needed data type can only be known at runtime, when the data type is expected to vary, or when optional parameters and parameter arrays are desired. In fact, languages with a dynamic type system often have variant as the *only* available type for variables.

Among the major changes in Visual Basic .NET, being a .NET language, the variant type was replaced with the .NET *object* type. There are similarities in concept, but also major differences, and no direct conversions exist between these two types. For conversions, as might be needed if Visual Basic .NET code is interacting with a Visual Basic 6 COM object, the normal methodology is to use .NET marshalling.

In unrelated usage, *variant type* is also used to refer to an algebraic data type (comparable to a tagged union), whose constructors are often called *variants*. In languages such as OCaml and Haskell, this kind of variant type is the standard language building block for representing many data structures.

Examples:

In Visual Basic, a variant named A can be explicitly declared as shown in either of these two examples:

```
Dim A
```

```
Dim A as Variant
```

In Delphi, a variant named A is declared in the following way:

```
var A: variant;
```

Format

A variable of variant type, for brevity called a "variant", as defined in Visual Basic, needs 16 bytes storage and its layout is as follows:

Offset	Size	Description
0	2	The value returned by VarType; specifies what kind of data the variant contains.
2	6	Reserved bytes; should be set to zero.
8	up to 8	The data the variant contains.

Common Uses

Collections

The `Collection` class in OLE Automation can store items of different data types. Since the data type of these items cannot be known at compile time, the methods to add items to and retrieve items from a collection use variants. If in Visual Basic the `For   Each` construct is used, the iterator variable must be of object type, or a variant.

Dispatch Method Calls

In OLE Automation the `IDispatch` interface is used when the class of an object cannot be known in advance. Hence when calling a method on such an object the types of the arguments and the return value is not known at compile time. The arguments are passed as an array of variants and when the call completes a variant is returned.

Optional Parameters

In Visual Basic a procedure argument can be declared to be optional by prefixing it with the `Optional` keyword.

```
Function GetText(Optional ByVal Index) As String

    If IsMissing(Index) Then

        GetText = Item(CurrentItem)

    Else

        GetText = Item(Index)

    End If

End Function
```

Similarly the keyword ParamArray can be used to pass all following arguments in a variant array.

Object Type

In computer science, an object type (a.k.a. wrapping object) is a datatype that is used in object-oriented programming to wrap a non-object type to make it look like a dynamic object.

Some object-oriented programming languages make a distinction between reference and value types, often referred to as objects and non-objects on platforms where complex value types don't exist, for reasons such as runtime efficiency and syntax or semantic issues. For example, Java has primitive wrapper classes corresponding to each primitive type: `Integer` and `int`, `Character` and `char`, `Float` and `float`, etc. Languages like C++ have little or no notion of reference type; thus, the use of object type is of little interest.

Boxing

Boxing, otherwise known as wrapping, is the process of placing a primitive type within an object so that the primitive can be used as a reference object. For example, in Java, a `LinkedList` can change its size, but an array must have a fixed size. One might desire to have a `LinkedList` of `int`, but the `LinkedList` class only lists references to dynamic objects—it cannot list primitive types, which are value types.

To circumvent this, `int` can be boxed into `Integer`, which are dynamic objects, and then added to a `LinkedList` of `Integer`. (Using generic parameterized types introduced in J2SE 5.0, this type is represented as `LinkedList<Integer>`). On the other hand, C# has no primitive wrapper classes, but allows boxing of any value type, returning a generic `Object` reference.

The boxed object is always a copy of the value object, and is usually immutable. Unboxing the object also returns a copy of the stored value. Repeated boxing and unboxing of objects can have a severe performance impact, because boxing dynamically allocates new objects and unboxing (if the boxed value is no longer used) then makes them eligible for garbage collection. However, modern garbage collectors such as the default Java HotSpot garbage collector can more efficiently collect short-lived objects, so if the boxed objects are short-lived, the performance impact may not be so bad.

There is a direct equivalence between an unboxed primitive type and a reference to an immutable, boxed object type. In fact, it is possible to substitute all the primitive types in a program with boxed object types. Whereas assignment from one primitive to another will copy its value, assignment from one reference to a boxed object to another will copy the reference value to refer to the same object as the first reference. However, this will not cause any problems, because the objects are immutable, so there is semantically no real difference between two references to the same object or to different objects (unless you look at physical equality). For all operations other than assignment, such as arithmetic, comparison, and logical operators, one can unbox the boxed type, perform the operation, and re-box the result as needed. Thus, it is possible to not store primitive types at all.

Autoboxing

Autoboxing is the term for getting a reference type out of a value type just through type conversion (either implicit or explicit). The compiler automatically supplies the extra source code that creates the object.

For example, in versions of Java prior to J2SE 5.0, the following code did not compile:

```
Integer i = new Integer(9);

Integer i = 9; // error in versions prior to 5.0!
```

Compilers prior to 5.0 would not accept the last line. `Integer` are reference objects, on the surface no different from `List`, `Object`, and so forth. To convert from an `int` to an

`Integer`, one had to "manually" instantiate the Integer object. As of J2SE 5.0, the compiler will accept the last line, and automatically transform it so that an Integer object is created to store the value 9. This means that, from J2SE 5.0 on, something like `Integer c = a + b`, where a and b are `Integer` themselves, will compile now - a and b are unboxed, the integer values summed up, and the result is autoboxed into a new `Integer`, which is finally stored inside variable c. The equality operators cannot be used this way, because the equality operators are already defined for reference types, for equality of the references; to test for equality of the value in a boxed type, one must still manually unbox them and compare the primitives, or use the `Objects.equals` method.

Another example: J2SE 5.0 allows the programmer to treat a collection (such as a `LinkedList`) as if it contained `int` values instead of `Integer` objects. This does not contradict what was said above: the collection still only contains references to dynamic objects, and it cannot list primitive types. It cannot be a `LinkedList<int>`, but it must be a `LinkedList<Integer>` instead. However, the compiler automatically transforms the code so that the list will "silently" receive objects, while the source code only mentions primitive values. For example, the programmer can now write `list.add(3)` and think as if the `int` 3 were added to the list; but, the compiler will have actually transformed the line into `list.add(new Integer(3))`.

Unboxing

Unboxing refers to getting the value that is associated to a given object, just through type conversion (either implicit or explicit). The compiler automatically supplies the extra source code that retrieves the value out of that object, either by invoking some method on that object, or by other means.

For example, in versions of Java prior to J2SE 5.0, the following code did not compile:

```
Integer k = new Integer(4);

int l = k.intValue();  // always okay

int m = k;             // would have been an error, but okay now
```

C# doesn't support automatic unboxing in the same meaning as Java, because it doesn't have a separate set of primitive types and object types. All types that have both primitive and object version in Java, are automatically implemented by the C# compiler as either primitive (value) types or object (reference) types.

In both languages, automatic boxing does not downcast automatically, i.e. the following code won't compile:

C#:

```
int i = 42;

object o = i;          // box
```

```
int j = o;              // unbox (error)
Console.WriteLine(j); // unreachable line, author might have expected
output "42"
```

Java:

```
int i = 42;

Object o = i;          // box

int j = o;             // unbox (error)

System.out.println(j); // unreachable line, author might have expected
output "42"
```

Type Helpers

Modern Object Pascal has yet another way to perform operations on simple types, close to boxing, called type helpers in FreePascal or record helpers in Delphi and FreePascal in Delphi mode.

The dialects mentioned are Object Pascal compile-to-native languages, and so miss some of the features that C# and Java can implement. Notably run-time type inference on strongly typed variables.

But the feature is related to boxing.

It allows the programmer to use constructs like:

```
{$ifdef fpc}{$mode delphi}{$endif}

uses sysutils;  // this unit contains wraps for the simple types

var

  x:integer=100;

  s:string;

begin

  s:= x.ToString;

  writeln(s);

end.
```

Data Structure

In computer science, a data structure is a data organization, management, and storage format that enables efficient access and modification. More precisely, a data structure is a collection of data values, the relationships among them, and the functions or operations that can be applied to the data.

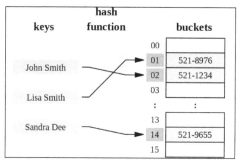

A data structure known as a hash table.

Usage

Data structures serve as the basis for abstract data types (ADT). The ADT defines the logical form of the data type. The data structure implements the physical form of the data type.

Different types of data structures are suited to different kinds of applications, and some are highly specialized to specific tasks. For example, relational databases commonly use B-tree indexes for data retrieval, while compiler implementations usually use hash tables to look up identifiers.

Data structures provide a means to manage large amounts of data efficiently for uses such as large databases and internet indexing services. Usually, efficient data structures are key to designing efficient algorithms. Some formal design methods and programming languages emphasize data structures, rather than algorithms, as the key organizing factor in software design. Data structures can be used to organize the storage and retrieval of information stored in both main memory and secondary memory.

Implementation

Data structures are generally based on the ability of a computer to fetch and store data at any place in its memory, specified by a pointer—a bit string, representing a memory address, that can be itself stored in memory and manipulated by the program. Thus, the array and record data structures are based on computing the addresses of data items with arithmetic operations, while the linked data structures are based on storing addresses of data items within the structure itself.

The implementation of a data structure usually requires writing a set of procedures that create and manipulate instances of that structure. The efficiency of a data structure cannot be analyzed separately from those operations. This observation motivates the theoretical concept of an abstract data type, a data structure that is defined indirectly by the operations that may be performed on it, and the mathematical properties of those operations (including their space and time cost).

Language Support

Most assembly languages and some low-level languages, such as BCPL (Basic Combined Programming Language), lack built-in support for data structures. On the other hand, many high-level programming languages and some higher-level assembly languages, such as MASM, have special syntax or other built-in support for certain data structures, such as records and arrays. For example, the C (a direct descendant of BCPL) and Pascal languages support structs and records, respectively, in addition to vectors (one-dimensional arrays) and multi-dimensional arrays.

Most programming languages feature some sort of library mechanism that allows data structure implementations to be reused by different programs. Modern languages usually come with standard libraries that implement the most common data structures. Examples are the C++ Standard Template Library, the Java Collections Framework, and the Microsoft .NET Framework.

Modern languages also generally support modular programming, the separation between the interface of a library module and its implementation. Some provide opaque data types that allow clients to hide implementation details. Object-oriented programming languages, such as C++, Java, and Smalltalk, typically use classes for this purpose.

Many known data structures have concurrent versions which allow multiple computing threads to access a single concrete instance of a data structure simultaneously.

Tree in Data Structure

In computer science, a tree is a widely used abstract data type (ADT) that simulates a hierarchical tree structure, with a root value and subtrees of children with a parent node, represented as a set of linked nodes.

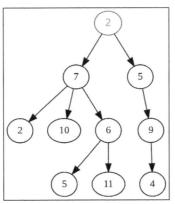

A generic, and so non-binary, unsorted, some labels duplicated, arbitrary diagram of a tree.
The node labeled 7 has three children, labeled 2, 10 and 6, and one
parent, labeled 2. The root node, at the top, has no parent.

A tree data structure can be defined recursively as a collection of nodes (starting at a root node), where each node is a data structure consisting of a value, together with a list of references to nodes (the "children"), with the constraints that no reference is duplicated, and none points to the root.

Alternatively, a tree can be defined abstractly as a whole (globally) as an ordered tree, with a value assigned to each node. Both these perspectives are useful: while a tree can be analyzed mathematically as a whole, when actually represented as a data structure it is usually represented and worked with separately by node (rather than as a set of nodes and an adjacency list of edges between nodes, as one may represent a digraph, for instance). For example, looking at a tree as a whole, one can talk about "the parent node" of a given node, but in general as a data structure a given node only contains the list of its children, but does not contain a reference to its parent (if any).

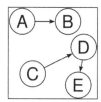

Not a tree: Two non-connected parts, A→B and C→D→E. There is more than one root.

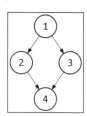

Not a tree: Undirected cycle 1-2-4-3. 4 has more than one parent (inbound edge).

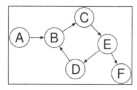

Not a tree: Cycle B→C→E→D→B. B has more than one parent (inbound edge).

Not a tree: Cycle A→A. A is the root but it also has a parent.

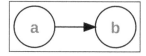

Each linear list is trivially a tree. A tree is a nonlinear data structure, compared to arrays, linked lists, stacks and queues which are linear data structures. A tree can be empty with no nodes or a tree is a structure consisting of one node called the root and zero or one or more subtrees.

Unordered Tree

Mathematically, an *unordered tree* (or "algebraic tree") can be defined as an algebraic structure (X,parent) where X is the non-empty carrier set of *nodes* and *parent* is a function on X which assigns each node x its "parent" node, *parent(x)*. The structure is subject to the condition that every non-empty subalgebra must have the same fixed point. That is, there must be a unique "root" node r, such that *parent(r)* = r and for every node x, some iterative application *parent(parent(...parent(x)...))* equals r.

There are several equivalent definitions. As the closest alternative, one can define unordered trees as *partial* algebras (X, *parent*) which are obtained from the total algebras by letting *parent(r)* be undefined. That is, the root r is the only node on which the *parent* function is not defined and for every node x, the root is reachable from x in the directed graph (X, *parent*). This definition is in fact coincident with that of an anti-arborescence.

The box on the right contains what can be regarded as a canonical definition of unordered trees. It just describes the partial algebra (X, *parent*) as a relational structure (X, <). Moreover, dedicated terminology can be provided for generalizations of unordered trees that correspond to distinguished subsets of the listed conditions: (3) – directed pseudoforest, (4) – directed acyclic graph , (3,4) – unordered forest, (1,2,3) – directed pseudotree.

Another equivalent definition of an unordered tree is that of a set-theoretic tree that is singly-rooted and whose height is at most ω (a finite-ish tree). That is, the algebraic structures (X, *parent*) are equivalent to partial orders that have a top element r and whose every principal upset (aka principal filter) is a finite chain. To be precise, we should speak about an inverse set-theoretic tree since the set-theoretic definition usually employs opposite ordering. The correspondence between (X, *parent*) and (X, ≤) is established via reflexive transitive closure / reduction, with the reduction resulting in the "partial" version without the root cycle.

The definition of trees in descriptive set theory (DST) utilizes the representation of partial orders (X, ≥) as prefix orders between finite sequences. In turns out that up to isomorphism, there is a one-to-one correspondence between the (inverse of) DST trees and the tree structures defined so far.

We can refer to the four equivalent characterizations as to *tree as an algebra, tree as a partial algebra, tree as a partial order*, and *tree as a prefix order*. There is also a fifth equivalent definition – that of a graph-theoretic rooted tree which is just a connected acyclic rooted graph.

The expression of trees as (partial) algebras $(X, parent)$ follows directly the implementation of tree structures using *parent pointers*. Typically, the partial version is used in which the root node has no parent defined. However, in some implementations or models even the $parent(r) = r$ circularity is established. Notable examples:

- The Linux VFS where "The root dentry has a d_parent that points to itself".

- The concept of an *instantiation tree* from object-oriented programming. In this case, the root node is the top metaclass – the only class that is a direct instance of itself.

The above definition admits *infinite* trees. This allows for the description of infinite structures supported by some implementations via lazy evaluation. A notable example is the infinite regress of eigenclasses from the Ruby object model. In this model, the tree established via superclass links between non-terminal objects is infinite and has an infinite branch (a single infinite branch of "helix" objects –).

Sibling Sets

In every unordered tree $(X, parent)$ there is a distinguished partition of the set X of nodes into *sibling sets*. Two non-root nodes x, y belong to the same sibling set if $parent(x) = parent(y)$. The root node r forms the singleton sibling set $\{r\}$. A tree is said to be *locally finite* or *finitely branching* if each of its sibling sets is finite.

Each pair of distinct siblings is incomparable in $\le$. This is why the word *unordered* is used in the definition. Such a terminology might become misleading when all sibling sets are singletons, i.e. when the set X of all nodes is totally ordered (and thus well-ordered) by $\le$. In such a case we might speak about a *singly-branching tree* instead.

Using Set Inclusion

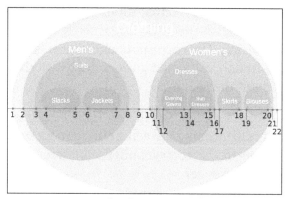

Tree as a laminar system of sets.

As with every partially ordered set, tree structures $(X, \le)$ can be represented by containment order – by set systems in which $\le$ is coincident with $\subseteq$, the induced inclusion order. Consider a structure (U, F) such that U is a non-empty set, and F is a set of subsets of U such that the following are satisfied (by Nested Set Collection definition):

- $\emptyset \notin F$. (That is, (U, F) is a hypergraph).

- $U \in F$.

- For every X, Y from F, $X \cap Y \in \{\emptyset, X, Y\}$. (That is, F is a *laminar* family).

- For every X from F, there are only finitely many Y from F such that $X \subseteq Y$.

Then the structure $(F, \subseteq)$ is an unordered tree whose root equals U. Conversely, if $(U, \leq)$ is an unordered tree, and F is the set $\{\downarrow x \mid x \in U\}$ of all principal ideals of $(U, \leq)$ then the set system (U, F) satisfies the above properties.

The set-system view of tree structures provides the default semantic model – in the majority of most popular cases, tree data structures represent containment hierarchy. This also offers a justification for order direction with the root at the top: The root node is a *greater* container than any other node. Notable examples:

- Directory structure of a file system. A directory contains its sub-directories.

- DOM tree. The document parts corresponent to DOM nodes are in subpart relation according to the tree order.

- Single inheritance in object-oriented programming. An instance of a class is also an instance of a superclass.

- Hierarchical taxonomy such as the Dewey Decimal Classification with sections of increasing specificity.

- BSP trees, quadtrees, octrees, R-trees and other tree data structures used for recursive space partitioning.

Well-founded Trees

An unordered tree $(X, \leq)$ is *well-founded* if the strict partial order $<$ is a well-founded relation. In particular, every finite tree is well-founded. Assuming the axiom of dependent choice a tree is well-founded if and only if it has no infinite branch.

Well-founded trees can be defined recursively – by forming trees from a disjoint union of smaller trees. For the precise definition, suppose that X is a set of nodes. Using the reflexivity of partial orders, we can identify any tree $(Y, \leq)$ on a subset of X with its partial order $(\leq)$ – a subset of $X \times X$. The set R of all relations R that form a well-founded tree (Y, R) on a subset Y of X is defined in stages R_i, so that $R = \cup \{R_i \mid i \text{ is ordinal}\}$. For each ordinal number i, let R belong to the i-th stage R_i if and only if R is equal to:

$$\cup F \cup ((\text{dom}(\cup F) \cup \{x\}) \times \{x\}),$$

where F is a subset of $\bigcup\{R_k \mid k < i\}$ such that elements of F are pairwise disjoint, and x is a node that does not belong to dom($\bigcup$F). (We use dom(S) to denote the domain of a relation S.) Observe that the lowest stage R_0 consists of single-node trees $\{(x,x)\}$ since only empty F is possible. In each stage, (possibly) new trees R are built by taking a forest $\bigcup$F with components F from lower stages and attaching a new root x atop of $\bigcup$F.

In contrast to the tree *height* which is at most ω, the *rank* of well-founded trees is unlimited.

Using Recursive Pairs

In computing, a common way to define well-founded trees is via recursive ordered pairs (F, x): A tree is a forest F together with a fresh node x. A *forest F* in turn is a possibly empty set of trees with pairwise disjoint sets of nodes. For the precise definition, proceed similarly as in the construction of *names* used in the set-theoretic technique of forcing. Let X be a set of nodes. In the superstructure over X, define sets T, F of trees and forests, respectively, and a map *nodes* : $T \to \wp(X)$ assigning each tree t its underlying set of nodes so that:

(trees over X)	$t \in T$	$\leftrightarrow$	t is a pair (F,x) from $\mathcal{F} \times X$ such that for all $s \in F, x \notin nodes(s)$,
(forests over X)	$F \in \mathcal{F}$	$\leftrightarrow$	F is a subset of T such that for every s, $t \in F$, $s \neq t$, $nodes(s) \cap nodes(t) = \varnothing$,
(nodes of trees)	$y \in nodes(t)$	$\leftrightarrow$	$t = (F,x) \in T$ and either $y = x$ or $y \in nodes(s)$ for some $s \in F$.

Circularities in the above conditions can be eliminated by stratifying each of T, F and *nodes* into stages Subsequently, define a subtree relation $\leq$ on T as the reflexive transitive closure of the immediate subtree relation $\prec$ defined between trees by:

$$s \prec t \quad \leftrightarrow \quad s \in \pi_1(t),$$

where $\pi_1(t)$ is the projection of t onto the first coordinate, i.e. it is the forest F such that $t = (F, x)$ for some $x \in X$. It can be observed that $(T, \leq)$ is a multitree: for every $t \in T$, the principal ideal $\downarrow t$ ordered by $\leq$ is a well-founded tree as a partial order. Moreover, for every tree $t \in T$, its nodes-order structure $(nodes(t), \leq_t)$ is given by $x \leq_t y$ if and only if there are forests $F, G \in F$ such that both (F, x) and (G, y) are subtrees of t and $(F, x) \leq (G, y)$.

Using Arrows

Another formalization as well as generalization of unordered trees can be obtained by reifying parent-child pairs of nodes. Each such ordered pair can be regarded as an abstract entity – an arrow. This results in a multidigraph (X, A, s, t) where X is the set of nodes, A is the set of *arrows*, and s and t are functions from A to X assigning each arrow its *source* and *target*, respectively. The structure is subject to the following conditions:

Condition 1: $(A, s \circ t^{-1})$ is an unordered tree, as a total algebra.

Condition 2: The t map is a bijection between arrows and nodes.

In Condition 1, the composition symbol $\circ$ is to be interpreted left-to-right. The condition says that inverse consecutivity of arrows is a total child-to-parent map. Let this parent map between arrows be denoted p, i.e. $p = s \circ t^{-1}$. Then we also have $s = p \circ t$, thus a multidigraph satisfying (1,2) can also be axiomatized as (X, A, p, t), with the parent map p instead of s as a definitory constituent. Observe that the root arrow is necessarily a loop, i.e. its source and target coincide.

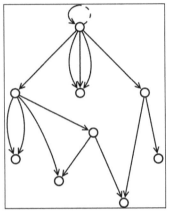

Arrow tree: the hard-link structure of VFS.

An important generalization of the above structure is established by allowing the target map t to be many-to-one. This means that Condition 2 is weakened to:

- The t map is surjective – each node is the target of some arrow.

Note that condition (1) asserts that only leaf arrows are allowed to have the same target. That is, the restriction of t to the range of p is still injective.

Multidigraphs satisfying (1,2') can be called arrow trees – their tree characteristics is imposed on arrows rather than nodes. These structures can be regarded as the most essential abstraction of the Linux VFS because they reflect the hard-link structure of filesystems. Nodes are called inodes, arrows are dentries (or hard links). The parent and target maps p and t are respectively represented by d_parent and d_inode fields in the dentry data structure. Each inode is assigned a fixed file type, of which the directory type plays a special role of designed parents: (a) only directory inodes can appear as hard-link source and (b) a directory inode cannot appear as the target of more than one hard-link.

Using dashed style for the first half of the root loop indicates that, similarly to the parent map, there is a *partial* version for the source map s in which the source of the root arrow is undefined. This variant is employed for further generalization.

Using Paths in a Digraph

Unordered trees naturally arise by "unfolding" of accessible pointed graphs. Let R = (X, R, r) be a *pointed relational structure*, i.e. such that X is the set of nodes, R is a relation between nodes (a subset of $X \times X$), and r is a distinguished "root" node. Assume further that R is *accessible*, which means that X equals the preimage of {r} under the reflexive transitive closure of R, and call such a structure an *accessible pointed graph* or *apg* for short.(∗) Then one can derive another apg R' = (X', R', r') – the *unfolding* of R – as follows:

- X' is the set of reversed *paths* to r, i.e. the set of non-empty finite sequences p of nodes (elements of X) such that (a) consecutive members of p are inversely R-related, and (b) the first member of p is the root r.

- R' is a relation between paths from X' such that paths p and q are R'-related if and only if p = q ∗ [x] for some node x (i.e. q is a maximal proper prefix of p, the "popped" p), and.

- r' is the one-element sequence [r].

Apparently, the structure (X', R') is an unordered tree in the "partial-algebra" version: R' is a partial map that relates each non-root element of X' to its parent by path popping. The root element is obviously r'. Moreover, the following properties are satisfied:

- R is isomorphic to its unfolding R'   if and only if   R is a tree (‡).
  (In particular, unfolding is idempotent, up to isomorphism).

- Unfolding preserves well-foundedness: If R is well-founded then so is R'.

- Unfolding preserves rank: If R is well-founded then the ranks of R and R' coincide.

Using Paths in a Multidigraph

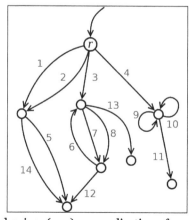

Accessible pointed quiver (apq): generalization of apg to multidigraphs.

As shown on the example of hard-link structure of file systems, many data structures in computing allow *multiple* links between nodes. Therefore, in order to properly exhibit the appearance of unordered trees among data structures it is necessary to generalize accessible pointed graphs to *multidigraph* setting. To simplify the terminology, we make use of the term *quiver* which is an established synonym for multidigraph.

Let an *accessible pointed quiver* or *apq* for short be defined as a structure $M = (X, A, s, t)$ where X is a set of *nodes*, A is a set of *arrows*, s is a *partial* function from A to X (the *source* map), and t is a total function from A to X (the *target* map). Thus, M is a partial multidigraph. The structure is subject to the following conditions:

- There is exactly one root arrow, a_r, whose source $s(a_r)$ is undefined.

- Every node $x \in X$ is reachable via a finite sequence of consecutive arrows starting with the root arrow a_r.

M is said to be a *tree* if the target map t is a bijection between arrows and nodes. The *unfolding* of M is formed by the sequences mentioned in (2) – which are the *accessibility paths* (cf. Path algebra). As an apq, the unfolding can be written as $M' = (X', A', s', t')$ where X' is the set of accessibility paths, A' coincides with X', s' coincides with path popping, and t' is the identity on X'. Like with apgs, unfolding is idempotent and always results in a tree. The *underlying apg* is obtained as the structure $(X, R, t(a_r))$ where $R = \{(t(a),s(a)) \mid a \in A \setminus \{a_r\}\}$.

The diagram above shows an example of an apq with 1+14 arrows. In JavaScript, Python or Ruby, the structure can be created by the following (exactly the same) code:

```
r = {};

r[1] = {}; r[2] = r[1]; r[3] = {}; r[4] = {};

r[1][5]      = {};     r[1][14]     = r[1][5];

r[3][7]      = {};     r[3][8]      = r[3][7]; r[3][13] = {};

r[4][9]    = r[4]; r[4][10]    = r[4];      r[4][11] = {};

r[3][7][6] = r[3]; r[3][7][12] = r[1][5];
```

Using Names

Unordered trees and their generalizations form the essence of naming systems. There are two prominent examples of naming systems: file systems and (nested) associative arrays. The multidigraph-based structures from previous subsections provided *anonymous* abstractions for both cases. To obtain naming capabilities, arrows are to be equipped with *names* as identifiers. A name must be locally unique – within each sibling set of arrows there can be at most one arrow labelled by a given name.

source	name	target
s(a)	σ(a)	t(a)

This can be formalized as a structure $E = (X, \Sigma, A, s, \sigma, t)$ where X is a set of *nodes*, Σ is a set of *names*, A is a set of *arrows*, s is a partial function from A to X, σ is a partial function from A to Σ, and t is a total function from A to X. For an arrow a, constituents of the triple $(s(a), \sigma(a), t(a))$ are respectively a's *source*, *name* and *target*. The structure is subject to the following conditions.

- The reduct (X, A, s, t) is an accessible pointed quiver (apq) as defined previously.

- The name function σ is undefined just for the source-less root arrow.

- The name function σ is injective in the restriction to every sibling set of arrows, i.e. for every non-root arrows a, b, if $s(a) = s(b)$ and $\sigma(a) = \sigma(b)$ then $a = b$.

This structure can be called a *nested dictionary* or *named apq*. In computing, such structures are ubiquitous. The table above shows that arrows can be considered un-reified as the set $A' = \{(s(a), \sigma(a), t(a)) \mid a \in A \setminus \{a_r\}\}$ of source-name-target triples. This leads to a relational structure (X, Σ, A') which can be viewed as a relational database table. Underlines in source and name indicate primary key. The structure can be rephrased as a deterministic labelled transition system: X is a set of states, Σ is a set of labels, A' is a set of labelled transitions. (Moreover, the root node $r = t(a_r)$ is an initial state, and the accessibility condition means that every state is reachable from the initial state).

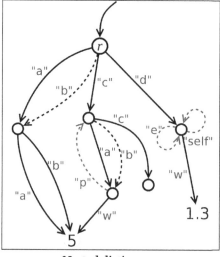

Nested dictionary.

The diagram on the right shows a nested dictionary E that has the same underlying multidigraph as the example The structure can be created by the code below. Like before, exactly the same code applies for JavaScript, Python and Ruby.

First, a substructure, E_0, is created by a single assignment of a literal {...} to r. This structure, depicted by full lines, is an arrow tree (therefore, it is a spanning tree). The literal in turn appears to be a JSON serialization of E_0.

Subsequently, the remaining arrows are created by assignments of already existing nodes. Arrows that cause cycles are displayed in blue.

```
r = {"a":{"a":5,"b":5},"c":{"a":{"w":5},"c":{}},"d":{"w":1.3}}


r["b"]            = r["a"]; r["c"]["b"] = r["c"]["a"]

r["c"]["a"]["p"] = r["c"]; r["d"]["e"] = r["d"]["self"] = r["d"]
```

In the Linux VFS, the name function σ is represented by the d_name field in the dentry data structure. The E_0 structure above demonstrates a correspondence between JSON-representable structures and hard-link structures of file systems. In both cases, there is a fixed set of built-in types of nodes of which one type is a container type, except that in JSON, there are in fact two such types – Object and Array. If the latter one is ignored (as well as the distinction between individual primitive data types) then the provided abstractions of file-systems and JSON data are the same – both are arrow trees equipped with naming σ and a distinction of container nodes.

Pathnames

The naming function σ of a nested dictionary E naturally extends from arrows to arrow paths. Each sequence $p = [a_1, ..., a_n]$ of consecutive arrows is implicitly assigned a *pathname* (cf. Pathname) – the sequence $\sigma(p) = [\sigma(a_1), ..., \sigma(a_n)]$ of arrow names. Local uniqueness carries over to arrow paths: different sibling paths have different pathnames. In particular, the root-originating arrow paths are in one-to-one correspondence with their pathnames. This correspondence provides a symbolic representation of the unfolding of E via pathnames – the nodes in E are globally identified via a tree of pathnames.

Ordered Tree

The structures introduced in the previous subsection form just the core "hierarchical" part of tree data structures that appear in computing. In most cases, there is also an additional "horizontal" ordering between siblings. In search trees the order is commonly established by the "key" or value associated with each sibling, but in many trees that is not the case. For example, XML documents, lists within JSON files, and many other structures have order that does not depend on the values in the nodes, but is itself data — sorting the paragraphs of a novel alphabetically would lose information.

The correspondent expansion of the previously described tree structures $(X, \leq)$ can be defined by endowing each sibling set with a linear order as follows. An alternative definition according to Kuboyama is presented in the next subsection.

An *ordered tree* is a structure $(X, \leq_V, \leq_S)$ where X is a non-empty set of nodes and $\leq_V$ and $\leq_S$ are relations on X called *vertical* (or also *hierarchical*) order and *sibling* order, respectively. The structure is subject to the following conditions:

- $(X, \leq_V)$ is a partial order that is an unordered tree.

- $(X, \leq_S)$ is a partial order.

- Distinct nodes are comparable in $<_S$ if and only if they are siblings: $(<_S) \cup (>_S)$ $= ((<_V) \circ (>_V)) \setminus \mathrm{id}_X$.

(The following condition can be omitted in the case of finite trees.)

- Every node has only finitely many preceding siblings, i.e. every principal ideal of $(X, \leq_S)$ is finite.

Conditions (2) and (3) say that $(X, \leq_S)$ is a component-wise linear order, each component being a sibling set. Condition (4) asserts that if a sibling set S is infinite then $(S, \leq_S)$ is isomorphic to $(\mathbb{N}, \leq)$, the usual ordering of natural numbers.

Given this, there are three (another) distinguished partial orders which are uniquely given by the following prescriptions:

$(<_H)$	=	$(\leq_V) \circ (<_S) \circ (\geq_V)$	(the horizontal order),
$(<_L)$	=	$(>_V) \cup (<_H)$	(the "discordant" linear order),
$(<_{L^-})$	=	$(<_V) \cup (<_H)$	(the "concordant" linear order).

This amounts to a "V-S-H-L$^{\pm}$" system of five partial orders $\leq_V, \leq_S, \leq_H, \leq_L, \leq_{L^-}$ on the same set X of nodes, in which, except for the pair $\{ \leq_S, \leq_H \}$, any two relations uniquely determine the other three.

Notes about notational conventions:

- The relation composition symbol $\circ$ used in this subsection is to be interpreted left-to-right (as $\circ_l$).

- Symbols $<$ and $\leq$ express the *strict* and *non-strict* versions of a partial order.

- Symbols $>$ and $\geq$ express the converse relations.

- The $\prec$ symbol is used for the covering relation of $\leq$ which is the *immediate* version of a partial order.

This yields six versions $\prec$, $<$, $\leq$, $\succ$, $>$, $\geq$ for a single partial order relation. Except for $\prec$ and $\succ$, each version uniquely determines the others. Passing from $\prec$ to $<$ requires that $<$ be transitively reducible. This is always satisfied for all of $<_V$, $<_S$ and $<_H$ but might not hold for $<_{L^+}$ or $<_{L^-}$ if X is infinite.

The partial orders $\leq_V$ and $\leq_H$ are complementary: $(<_V) \uplus (>_V) \uplus (<_H) \uplus (>_H) = X \times X \setminus \mathrm{id}_X$. As a consequence, the "concordant" linear order $<_{L^+}$ is a linear extension of $<_V$. Similarly, $<_{L^-}$ is a linear extension of $>_V$.

The covering relations $\prec_{L^-}$ and $\prec_{L^+}$ correspond to pre-order traversal and post-order traversal, respectively. If $x \prec_{L^-} y$ then, according to whether y has a previous sibling or not, the x node is either the "rightmost" non-strict descendant of the previous sibling of y or, in the latter case, x is the first child of y. Pairs (x,y) of the latter case form the relation $(\prec_{L^-}) \setminus (\prec_H)$ which is a partial map that assigns each non-leaf node its *first child* node. Similarly, $(\succ_{L^+}) \setminus (\succ_H)$ assigns each non-leaf node with finitely many children its *last* child node.

Definition using Horizontal Order

The Kuboyama's definition of "rooted ordered trees" makes use of the horizontal order $\leq_H$ as a definitory relation. Using the notation and terminology introduced so far, the definition can be expressed as follows.

An *ordered tree* is a structure $(X, \leq_V, \leq_H)$ such that conditions (1–5) are satisfied:

- $(X, \leq_V)$ is a partial order that is an unordered tree. (The *vertical* order).

- $(X, \leq_H)$ is a partial order. (The *horizontal* order).

- The partial orders $\leq_V$ and $\leq_H$ are complementary: $(<_V) \uplus (>_V) \uplus (<_H) \uplus (>_H) = X \times X \setminus \mathrm{id}_X$. (That is, pairs of nodes that are incomparable in $(<_V)$ are comparable in $(<_H)$ and vice versa).

- The partial orders $\leq_V$ and $\leq_H$ are "consistent": $(<_H) = (\leq_V) \circ (<_H) \circ (\geq_V)$. (That is, for every nodes x, y such that $x <_H y$, all descendants of x must precede all the descendants of y).

(Like before, the following condition can be omitted in the case of finite trees.)

- Every node has only finitely many preceding siblings. (That is, for every infinite sibling set S, $(S, \leq_H)$ has the order type of the natural numbers).

The sibling order $(\leq_S)$ is obtained by $(<_S) = (<_H) \cap ((<_V) \circ (>_V))$, i.e. two distinct nodes are in sibling order if and only if they are in horizontal order and are siblings.

Determinacy Table

The following table shows the determinacy of the "V-S-H-L$^{\pm}$" system. Relational expressions in the table's body are equal to one of $<_V$, $<_S$, $<_H$, $<_{L^-}$, or $<_{L^+}$ according to the column. It follows that except for the pair $\{ \leq_S, \leq_H \}$, an ordered tree $(X, \ldots)$ is uniquely determined by any two of the five relations.

	$<_V$	$<_S$	$<_H$	$<_{L^-}$	$<_{L^+}$
V,S			$(\leq_V) \circ (<_S) \circ (\geq_V)$		
V,H		$(<_H) \cap ((<_V)\circ(>_V))$		$(>_V) \cup (<_H)$	$(<_V) \cup (<_H)$
V,L$^-$		$(<_{L^-}) \cap ((<_V)\circ(>_V))$	$(<_{L^-}) \setminus (>_V)$		
V,L$^+$		$(<_{L^+}) \cap ((<_V)\circ(>_V))$	$(<_{L^+}) \setminus (<_V)$		
H,L$^-$	$(>_{L^-}) \setminus (<_H)$				
H,L$^+$	$(<_{L^+}) \setminus (<_H)$				
L$^-$,L$^+$	$(>_{L^-}) \cap (<_{L^+})$		$(<_{L^-}) \cap (<_{L^+})$		
S,L$^-$	$x <_V y \leftrightarrow y = \inf_{L^-}(Y)$ where Y is the image of {x} under $(\geq_S)\circ(>_{L^-})$				
S,L$^+$	$x <_V y \leftrightarrow y = \sup_{L^+}(Y)$ where Y is the image of {x} under $(\leq_S)\circ(<_{L^+})$				

In the last two rows, $\inf_{L^-}(Y)$ denotes the infimum of Y in $(X, \leq_{L^-})$, and $\sup_{L^+}(Y)$ denotes the supremum of Y in $(X, \leq_{L^+})$. In both rows, $(\leq_S)$ resp. $(\geq_S)$ can be equivalently replaced by the sibling equivalence $(\leq_S)\circ(\geq_S)$. In particular, the partition into sibling sets together with either of $\leq_{L^-}$ or $\leq_{L^+}$ is also sufficient to determine the ordered tree. The first prescription for $<_V$ can be read as: the parent of a non-root node x equals the infimum of the set of all immediate predecessors of siblings of x, where the words infimum and predecessors are meant w.r.t. $\leq_{L^-}$. Similarly with the second prescription, just use supremum, successors and $\leq_{L^+}$.

The relations $\leq_S$ and $\leq_H$ obviously cannot form a definitory pair. For the simplest example, consider an ordered tree with exactly two nodes – then one cannot tell which of them is the root.

XPath Axes

XPath Axis	Relation
ancestor	$<_V$
ancestor-or-self	$\leq_V$
child	$>_V$
descendant	$>_V$
descendant-or-self	$\geq_V$
following	$<_H$
following-sibling	$<_S$
parent	$<_V$

preceding	$>_H$
preceding-sibling	$>_S$
self	id_x

The table on the right shows a correspondence of introduced relations to XPath axes, which are used in structured document systems to access nodes that bear particular ordering relationships to a starting "context" node. For a context node x, its *axis* named by the specifier in the left column is the set of nodes that equals the image of $\{x\}$ under the correspondent relation. As of XPath 2.0, the nodes are "returned" in *document order*, which is the "discordant" linear order $\leq_{L^-}$. A "concordance" would be achieved, if the vertical order $\leq_V$ was defined oppositely, with the bottom-up direction outwards the root like in set theory in accordance to natural trees.

Traversal Maps

Below is the list of partial maps that are typically used for ordered tree traversal. Each map is a distinguished functional subrelation of $\leq_{L^-}$ or of its opposite.

- $\lessdot_V$ ... the *parent-node* partial map,

- $>_S$ ... the *previous-sibling* partial map,

- $\lessdot_S$ ... the *next-sibling* partial map,

- $(\lessdot_{L^-}) \setminus (\lessdot_H)$ ... the *first-child* partial map,

- $(>_{L^+}) \setminus (>_H)$ ... the *last-child* partial map,

- $>_{L^-}$ ... the *previous-node* partial map,

- $\lessdot_{L^-}$ ... the *next-node* partial map.

Generating Structure

The traversal maps constitute a partial unary algebra $(X, parent, previousSibling, ..., nextNode)$ that forms a basis for representing trees as linked data structures. At least conceptually, there are parent links, sibling adjacency links, and first / last child links. This also applies to unordered trees in general, which can be observed on the dentry data structure in the Linux VFS.

Similarly to the "V-S-H-L$^\pm$" system of partial orders, there are pairs of traversal maps that uniquely determine the whole ordered tree structure. Naturally, one such generating structure is $(X, \lessdot_V, \lessdot_S)$ which can be transcribed as $(X, parent, nextSibling)$ – the structure of parent and next-sibling links. Another important generating structure is $(X, firstChild, nextSibling)$ known as left-child right-sibling binary tree. This partial algebra establishes a one-to-one correspondence between binary trees and ordered trees.

Definition using Binary Trees

The correspondence to binary trees provides a concise definition of ordered trees as partial algebras. An *ordered tree* is a structure $(X, \text{lc}, \text{rs})$ where X is a non-empty set of nodes, and *lc*, *rs* are partial maps on X called *left-child* and *right-sibling*, respectively. The structure is subject to the following conditions:

- The partial maps *lc* and *rs* are disjoint, i.e. $(\text{lc}) \cap (\text{rs}) = \emptyset$.

- The inverse of $(\text{lc}) \cup (\text{rs})$ is a partial map p such that the partial algebra (X, p) is an unordered tree.

The partial order structure $(X, \leq_V, \leq_S)$ is obtained as follows:

$(<_S)$	=	(rs),
$(>_V)$	=	$(\text{lc}) \circ (\leq_S)$.

Encoding by Sequences

Ordered trees can be naturally encoded by finite sequences of natural numbers. Denote ω^* the set of all finite sequences of natural numbers. Then any non-empty subset W of ω^* that is closed under taking prefixes gives rise to an ordered tree: just take the prefix order for $\geq_V$ and the lexicographical order for $\leq_L$. Conversely, for an ordered tree $T = (X, \leq_V, \leq_L)$ assign each node x the sequence of sibling indices, i.e. the root is assigned the empty sequence and for every non-root node x, let $w(x) = w(parent(x)) * [i]$ where i is the number of preceding siblings of x and $*$ is the concatenation operator. Put $W = \{w(x) \mid x \in X\}$. Then W, equipped with the induced orders $\leq_V$ (the inverse of prefix order) and $\leq_L$ (the lexicographical order), is isomorphic to T.

Per-level Ordering

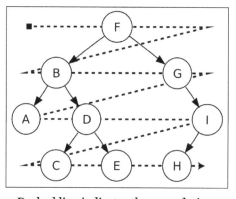

Dashed line indicates the $<_{B^-}$ ordering.

As a possible expansion of the "V-S-H-L$^{\pm}$" system, another distinguished relations between nodes can be defined, based on the tree's level structure. First, let us denote by $\sim_E$ the equivalence relation defined by $x \sim_E y$ if and only if x and y have the same number of ancestors. This yields a partition of the set of nodes into *levels* $L_0, L_1, \ldots$ (, L_n) – a coarsement of the partition into sibling sets. Then define relations $<_E$, $<_{B^-}$ and $<_{B^+}$ by :

$$(<_E) = (<_H) \cap (\sim_E) \qquad \text{((per) level order)},$$

$$(<_{B^-}) = (<_E) \cup ((\sim_E)^\circ (>_V)) \qquad \text{(breadth-first order, BFS ordering)},$$

$$(<_{B^+}) = (<_E) \cup ((<_V)^\circ (\sim_E)) \qquad \text{(breadth-first post-order)}.$$

It can be observed that $<_E$ is a strict partial order and $<_{B^-}$ and $<_{B^+}$ are strict total orders. Moreover, there is a similarity between the "V-S-L$^{\pm}$" and "V-E-B$^{\pm}$" systems: $<_E$ is component-wise linear and orthogonal to $<_V$, $<_{B^-}$ is linear extension of $<_E$ and of $>_V$, and $<_{B^+}$ is a linear extension of $<_E$ and of $<_V$.

Compiler

A compiler is a computer program that translates computer code written in one programming language (the source language) into another language (the target language). The name *compiler* is primarily used for programs that translate source code from a high-level programming language to a lower level language (e.g., assembly language, object code, or machine code) to create an executable program.

However, there are many different types of compilers. If the compiled program can run on a computer whose CPU or operating system is different from the one on which the compiler runs, the compiler is a cross-compiler. A bootstrap compiler is written in the language that it intends to compile. A program that translates from a low-level language to a higher level one is a decompiler. A program that translates between high-level languages is usually called a source-to-source compiler or transcompiler. A language rewriter is usually a program that translates the form of expressions without a change of language. The term compiler-compiler refers to tools used to create parsers that perform syntax analysis.

A compiler is likely to perform many or all of the following operations: Preprocessing, lexical analysis, parsing, semantic analysis (syntax-directed translation), conversion of input programs to an intermediate representation, code optimization and code generation. Compilers implement these operations in phases that promote efficient design and correct transformations of source input to target output. Program faults caused by incorrect compiler behavior can be very difficult to track down and work around; therefore, compiler implementers invest significant effort to ensure compiler correctness.

Compilers are not the only language processor used to transform source programs. An interpreter is computer software that transforms and then executes the indicated operations. The translation process influences the design of computer languages which leads to a preference of compilation or interpretation. In practice, an interpreter can be implemented for compiled languages and compilers can be implemented for interpreted languages.

Compiler Construction

A compiler implements a formal transformation from a high-level source program to a low-level target program. Compiler design can define an end to end solution or tackle a defined subset that interfaces with other compilation tools e.g. preprocessors, assemblers, linkers. Design requirements include rigorously defined interfaces both internally between compiler components and externally between supporting toolsets.

In the early days, the approach taken to compiler design was directly affected by the complexity of the computer language to be processed, the experience of the persons designing it, and the resources available. Resource limitations led to the need to pass through the source code more than once.

A compiler for a relatively simple language written by one person might be a single, monolithic piece of software. However, as the source language grows in complexity the design may be split into a number of interdependent phases. Separate phases provide design improvements that focus development on the functions in the compilation process.

One-pass versus Multi-pass Compilers

Classifying compilers by number of passes has its background in the hardware resource limitations of computers. Compiling involves performing lots of work and early computers did not have enough memory to contain one program that did all of this work. So compilers were split up into smaller programs which each made a pass over the source (or some representation of it) performing some of the required analysis and translations.

The ability to compile in a single pass has classically been seen as a benefit because it simplifies the job of writing a compiler and one-pass compilers generally perform compilations faster than multi-pass compilers. Thus, partly driven by the resource limitations of early systems, many early languages were specifically designed so that they could be compiled in a single pass (e.g., Pascal).

In some cases the design of a language feature may require a compiler to perform more than one pass over the source. For instance, consider a declaration appearing on line 20 of the source which affects the translation of a statement appearing on line 10. In this case, the first pass needs to gather information about declarations appearing after statements that they affect, with the actual translation happening during a subsequent pass.

The disadvantage of compiling in a single pass is that it is not possible to perform many of the sophisticated optimizations needed to generate high quality code. It can be difficult to count exactly how many passes an optimizing compiler makes. For instance, different phases of optimization may analyse one expression many times but only analyse another expression once.

Splitting a compiler up into small programs is a technique used by researchers interested in producing provably correct compilers. Proving the correctness of a set of small programs often requires less effort than proving the correctness of a larger, single, equivalent program.

Three-stage Compiler Structure

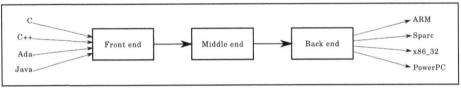

Compiler design.

Regardless of the exact number of phases in the compiler design, the phases can be assigned to one of three stages. The stages include a front end, a middle end, and a back end.

- The front end verifies syntax and semantics according to a specific source language. For statically typed languages it performs type checking by collecting type information. If the input program is syntactically incorrect or has a type error, it generates error and/or warning messages, usually identifying the location in the source code where the problem was detected; in some cases the actual error may be (much) earlier in the program. Aspects of the front end include lexical analysis, syntax analysis, and semantic analysis. The front end transforms the input program into an intermediate representation (IR) for further processing by the middle end. This IR is usually a lower-level representation of the program with respect to the source code.

- The *middle end* performs optimizations on the IR that are independent of the CPU architecture being targeted. This source code/machine code independence is intended to enable generic optimizations to be shared between versions of the compiler supporting different languages and target processors. Examples of middle end optimizations are removal of useless (dead code elimination) or unreachable code (reachability analysis), discovery and propagation of constant values (constant propagation), relocation of computation to a less frequently executed place (e.g., out of a loop), or specialization of computation based on the context. Eventually producing the "optimized" IR that is used by the back end.

- The *back end* takes the optimized IR from the middle end. It may perform more analysis, transformations and optimizations that are specific for the target CPU architecture. The back end generates the target-dependent assembly code, performing register allocation in the process. The back end performs instruction scheduling, which re-orders instructions to keep parallel execution units busy by filling delay slots. Although most optimization problems are NP-hard, heuristic techniques for solving them are well-developed and currently implemented in production-quality compilers. Typically the output of a back end is machine code specialized for a particular processor and operating system.

This front/middle/back-end approach makes it possible to combine front ends for different languages with back ends for different CPUs while sharing the optimizations of the middle end. Practical examples of this approach are the GNU Compiler Collection, LLVM, and the Amsterdam Compiler Kit, which have multiple front-ends, shared optimizations and multiple back-ends.

Front End

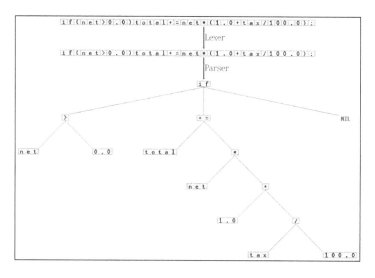

Lexer and parser example for C. Starting from the sequence of characters "`if(net>0.0) total+=net*(1.0+tax/100.0);`", the scanner composes a sequence of tokens, and categorizes each of them, for example as identifier, reserved word, number literal, or operator. The latter sequence is transformed by the parser into a syntax tree, which is then treated by the remaining compiler phases. The scanner and parser handles the regular and properly context-free parts of the grammar for C, respectively.

The front end analyzes the source code to build an internal representation of the program, called the intermediate representation (IR). It also manages the symbol table, a data structure mapping each symbol in the source code to associated information such as location, type and scope.

While the frontend can be a single monolithic function or program, as in a scannerless parser, it is more commonly implemented and analyzed as several phases, which may execute sequentially or concurrently. This method is favored due to its modularity and separation of concerns. Most commonly today, the frontend is broken into three phases: lexical analysis (also known as lexing), syntax analysis (also known as scanning or parsing), and semantic analysis. Lexing and parsing comprise the syntactic analysis (word syntax and phrase syntax, respectively), and in simple cases these modules (the lexer and parser) can be automatically generated from a grammar for the language, though in more complex cases these require manual modification. The lexical grammar and phrase grammar are usually context-free grammars, which simplifies analysis significantly, with context-sensitivity handled at the semantic analysis phase. The semantic analysis phase is generally more complex and written by hand, but can be partially or fully automated using attribute grammars. These phases themselves can be further broken down: lexing as scanning and evaluating, and parsing as building a concrete syntax tree (CST, parse tree) and then transforming it into an abstract syntax tree (AST, syntax tree). In some cases additional phases are used, notably *line reconstruction* and *preprocessing,* but these are rare.

The main phases of the front end include the following:

- *Line reconstruction* converts the input character sequence to a canonical form ready for the parser. Languages which strop their keywords or allow arbitrary spaces within identifiers require this phase. The top-down, recursive-descent, table-driven parsers used in the 1960s typically read the source one character at a time and did not require a separate tokenizing phase. Atlas Autocode and Imp (and some implementations of ALGOL and Coral 66) are examples of stropped languages whose compilers would have a *Line Reconstruction* phase.

- *Preprocessing* supports macro substitution and conditional compilation. Typically the preprocessing phase occurs before syntactic or semantic analysis; e.g. in the case of C, the preprocessor manipulates lexical tokens rather than syntactic forms. However, some languages such as Scheme support macro substitutions based on syntactic forms.

- *Lexical analysis* (also known as *lexing* or *tokenization*) breaks the source code text into a sequence of small pieces called *lexical tokens.* This phase can be divided into two stages: the *scanning,* which segments the input text into syntactic units called *lexemes* and assign them a category; and the *evaluating,* which converts lexemes into a processed value. A token is a pair consisting of a *token name* and an optional *token value.* Common token categories may include identifiers, keywords, separators, operators, literals and comments, although the set of token categories varies in different programming languages. The lexeme syntax is typically a regular language, so a finite state automaton constructed from a regular expression can be used to recognize it. The software doing lexical analysis is called a lexical analyzer. This may not be a separate step—it can be combined with the parsing step in scannerless parsing, in which case parsing is done at the character level, not the token level.

- *Syntax analysis* (also known as *parsing*) involves parsing the token sequence to identify the syntactic structure of the program. This phase typically builds a parse tree, which replaces the linear sequence of tokens with a tree structure built according to the rules of a formal grammar which define the language's syntax. The parse tree is often analyzed, augmented, and transformed by later phases in the compiler.

- *Semantic analysis* adds semantic information to the parse tree and builds the symbol table. This phase performs semantic checks such as type checking (checking for type errors), or object binding (associating variable and function references with their definitions), or definite assignment (requiring all local variables to be initialized before use), rejecting incorrect programs or issuing warnings. Semantic analysis usually requires a complete parse tree, meaning that this phase logically follows the parsing phase, and logically precedes the code generation phase, though it is often possible to fold multiple phases into one pass over the code in a compiler implementation.

Middle End

The middle end, also known as *optimizer,* performs optimizations on the intermediate representation in order to improve the performance and the quality of the produced machine code. The middle end contains those optimizations that are independent of the CPU architecture being targeted.

The main phases of the middle end include the following:

- Analysis: This is the gathering of program information from the intermediate representation derived from the input; data-flow analysis is used to build use-define chains, together with dependence analysis, alias analysis, pointer analysis, escape analysis, etc. Accurate analysis is the basis for any compiler optimization. The control flow graph of every compiled function and the call graph of the program are usually also built during the analysis phase.

- Optimization: The intermediate language representation is transformed into functionally equivalent but faster (or smaller) forms. Popular optimizations are inline expansion, dead code elimination, constant propagation, loop transformation and even automatic parallelization.

Compiler analysis is the prerequisite for any compiler optimization, and they tightly work together. For example, dependence analysis is crucial for loop transformation.

The scope of compiler analysis and optimizations vary greatly; their scope may range from operating within a basic block, to whole procedures, or even the whole program. There is a trade-off between the granularity of the optimizations and the cost of compilation. For example, peephole optimizations are fast to perform during compilation but only affect a small local fragment of the code, and can be performed independently of the context in which the code fragment appears. In contrast, interprocedural optimization requires more compilation time and memory space, but enable optimizations which are only possible by considering the behavior of multiple functions simultaneously.

Interprocedural analysis and optimizations are common in modern commercial compilers from HP, IBM, SGI, Intel, Microsoft, and Sun Microsystems. The free software GCC was criticized for a long time for lacking powerful interprocedural optimizations, but it is changing in this respect. Another open source compiler with full analysis and optimization infrastructure is Open64, which is used by many organizations for research and commercial purposes.

Due to the extra time and space needed for compiler analysis and optimizations, some compilers skip them by default. Users have to use compilation options to explicitly tell the compiler which optimizations should be enabled.

Back End

The back end is responsible for the CPU architecture specific optimizations and for code generation. The main phases of the back end include the following:

- *Machine dependent optimizations*: Optimizations that depend on the details of the CPU architecture that the compiler targets. A prominent example is peephole optimizations, which rewrites short sequences of assembler instructions into more efficient instructions.

- *Code generation*: The transformed intermediate language is translated into the output language, usually the native machine language of the system. This involves resource and storage decisions, such as deciding which variables to fit into registers and memory and the selection and scheduling of appropriate machine instructions along with their associated addressing modes. Debug data may also need to be generated to facilitate debugging.

Compiler Correctness

Compiler correctness is the branch of software engineering that deals with trying to show that a compiler behaves according to its language specification. Techniques include developing the compiler using formal methods and using rigorous testing (often called compiler validation) on an existing compiler.

Compiled versus Interpreted Languages

Higher-level programming languages usually appear with a type of translation in mind: either designed as compiled language or interpreted language. However, in practice there is rarely anything about a language that *requires* it to be exclusively compiled or exclusively interpreted, although it is possible to design languages that rely on re-interpretation at run time. The categorization usually reflects the most popular or widespread implementations of a language — for instance, BASIC is sometimes called an interpreted language, and C a compiled one, despite the existence of BASIC compilers and C interpreters.

Interpretation does not replace compilation completely. It only hides it from the user and makes it gradual. Even though an interpreter can itself be interpreted, a directly executed program is needed somewhere at the bottom of the stack.

Further, compilers can contain interpreters for optimization reasons. For example, where an expression can be executed during compilation and the results inserted into the output program, then it prevents it having to be recalculated each time the program runs, which can greatly speed up the final program. Modern trends toward just-in-time compilation and bytecode interpretation at times blur the traditional categorizations of compilers and interpreters even further.

Some language specifications spell out that implementations *must* include a compilation facility; for example, Common Lisp. However, there is nothing inherent in the definition of Common Lisp that stops it from being interpreted. Other languages have features that are very easy to implement in an interpreter, but make writing a compiler much harder; for example, APL, SNOBOL4, and many scripting languages allow programs to construct arbitrary source code at runtime with regular string operations, and then execute that code by passing it to a special evaluation function. To implement these features in a compiled language, programs must usually be shipped with a run-time library that includes a version of the compiler itself.

Types

One classification of compilers is by the platform on which their generated code executes. This is known as the *target platform*.

A *native* or *hosted* compiler is one whose output is intended to directly run on the same type of computer and operating system that the compiler itself runs on. The output of a cross compiler is designed to run on a different platform. Cross compilers are often used when developing software for embedded systems that are not intended to support a software development environment.

The output of a compiler that produces code for a virtual machine (VM) may or may not be executed on the same platform as the compiler that produced it. For this reason such compilers are not usually classified as native or cross compilers.

The lower level language that is the target of a compiler may itself be a high-level programming language. C, viewed by some as a sort of portable assembly language, is frequently the target language of such compilers. For example, Cfront, the original compiler for C++, used C as its target language. The C code generated by such a compiler is usually not intended to be readable and maintained by humans, so indent style and creating pretty C intermediate code are ignored. Some of the features of C that make it a good target language include the #line directive, which can be generated by the compiler to support debugging of the original source, and the wide platform support available with C compilers.

While a common compiler type outputs machine code, there are many other types:

- Source-to-source compilers are a type of compiler that takes a high-level language as its input and outputs a high-level language. For example, an automatic parallelizing compiler will frequently take in a high-level language program as an input and then transform the code and annotate it with parallel code annotations (e.g. OpenMP) or language constructs (e.g. Fortran's DOALL statements).

- Bytecode compilers that compile to assembly language of a theoretical machine, like some Prolog implementations.

  ○ This Prolog machine is also known as the Warren Abstract Machine (or WAM).

  ○ Bytecode compilers for Java, Python are also examples of this category.

- Just-in-time compilers (JIT compiler) defer compilation until runtime. JIT compilers exist for many modern languages including Python, JavaScript, Smalltalk, Java, Microsoft .NET's Common Intermediate Language (CIL) and others. A JIT compiler generally runs inside an interpreter. When the interpreter detects that a code path is "hot", meaning it is executed frequently, the JIT compiler will be invoked and compile the "hot" code for increased performance.

  ○ For some languages, such as Java, applications are first compiled using a bytecode compiler and delivered in a machine-independent intermediate representation. A bytecode interpreter executes the bytecode, but the JIT compiler will translate the bytecode to machine code when increased performance is necessary.

- Hardware compilers (also known as syntheses tools) are compilers whose output is a description of the hardware configuration instead of a sequence of instructions.

- ◦ The output of these compilers target computer hardware at a very low level, for example a field-programmable gate array (FPGA) or structured application-specific integrated circuit (ASIC). Such compilers are said to be hardware compilers, because the source code they compile effectively controls the final configuration of the hardware and how it operates. The output of the compilation is only an interconnection of transistors or lookup tables.

- ◦ An example of hardware compiler is XST, the Xilinx Synthesis Tool used for configuring FPGAs. Similar tools are available from Altera, Synplicity, Synopsys and other hardware vendors.

- An *assembler* is a program that compiles human readable assembly language to machine code, the actual instructions executed by hardware. The inverse program that translates machine code to assembly language is called a disassembler.

- A program that translates from a low-level language to a higher level one is a decompiler.

- A program that translates between high-level languages is usually called a language translator, source-to-source compiler, language converter, or language rewriter. The last term is usually applied to translations that do not involve a change of language.

- A program that translates into an object code format that is not supported on the compilation machine is called a cross compiler and is commonly used to prepare code for embedded applications.

- A program that rewrites object code back into the same type of object code while applying optimisations and transformations is a binary recompiler.

Phases of a Compiler

Compiler operates in various phases each phase transforms the source program from one representation to another. Every phase takes inputs from its previous stage and feeds its output to the next phase of the compiler.

There are 6 phases in a compiler. Each of this phase help in converting the high-level langue the machine code. The phases of a compiler are:

- Lexical analysis.

- Syntax analysis.

- Semantic analysis.

- Intermediate code generator.

- Code optimizer.

- Code generator.

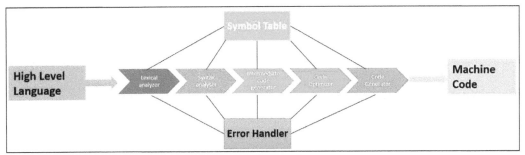

Phases of Compiler.

All these phases convert the source code by dividing into tokens, creating parse trees, and optimizing the source code by different phases.

Phase 1: Lexical Analysis

Lexical Analysis is the first phase when compiler scans the source code. This process can be left to right, character by character, and group these characters into tokens.

Here, the character stream from the source program is grouped in meaningful sequences by identifying the tokens. It makes the entry of the corresponding tickets into the symbol table and passes that token to next phase.

The primary functions of this phase are:

- Identify the lexical units in a source code.

- Classify lexical units into classes like constants, reserved words, and enter them in different tables. It will Ignore comments in the source program.

- Identify token which is not a part of the language.

Example:

x = y + 10

Tokens:

X	identifier
=	Assignment operator
Y	identifier
+	Addition operator
10	Number

Phase 2: Syntax Analysis

Consider parse tree for the following example:

`(a+b)*c`

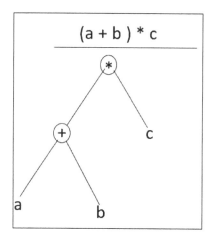

In Parse Tree:

- Interior node: Record with an operator filed and two files for children.

- Leaf: records with 2/more fields; one for token and other information about the token.

- Ensure that the components of the program fit together meaningfully.

- Gathers type information and checks for type compatibility.

- Checks operands are permitted by the source language.

Phase 3: Semantic Analysis

Semantic analysis checks the semantic consistency of the code. It uses the syntax tree of the previous phase along with the symbol table to verify that the given source code is semantically consistent. It also checks whether the code is conveying an appropriate meaning.

Semantic Analyzer will check for Type mismatches, incompatible operands, a function called with improper arguments, an undeclared variable, etc.

Functions of Semantic analyses phase are:

- Helps you to store type information gathered and save it in symbol table or syntax tree.

- Allows you to perform type checking.

- In the case of type mismatch, where there are no exact type correction rules which satisfy the desired operation a semantic error is shown.

- Collects type information and checks for type compatibility.

- Checks if the source language permits the operands or not.

Example:

```
float x = 20.2;

float y = x*30;
```

In the above code, the semantic analyzer will typecast the integer 30 to float 30.0 before multiplication.

Phase 4: Intermediate Code Generation

Once the semantic analysis phase is over the compiler, generates intermediate code for the target machine. It represents a program for some abstract machine.

Intermediate code is between the high-level and machine level language. This intermediate code needs to be generated in such a manner that makes it easy to translate it into the target machine code.

Functions on Intermediate Code generation:

- It should be generated from the semantic representation of the source program

- Holds the values computed during the process of translation

- Helps you to translate the intermediate code into target language

- Allows you to maintain precedence ordering of the source language

- It holds the correct number of operands of the instruction

For example:

```
total = count + rate * 5
```

Intermediate code with the help of address code method is:

```
t1 := int_to_float(5)

t2 := rate * t1

t3 := count + t2

total := t3
```

Phase 5: Code Optimization

The next phase of is code optimization or Intermediate code. This phase removes unnecessary code line and arranges the sequence of statements to speed up the execution of the program without wasting resources. The main goal of this phase is to improve on the intermediate code to generate a code that runs faster and occupies less space.

The primary functions of this phase are:

- It helps you to establish a trade-off between execution and compilation speed.

- Improves the running time of the target program.

- Generates streamlined code still in intermediate representation.

- Removing unreachable code and getting rid of unused variables.

- Removing statements which are not altered from the loop.

Example:

Consider the following code:

```
a = intofloat(10)
b = c * a
d = e + b
f = d
```

Can become:

```
b =c * 10.0
f = e+b
```

Phase 6: Code Generation

Code generation is the last and final phase of a compiler. It gets inputs from code optimization phases and produces the page code or object code as a result. The objective of this phase is to allocate storage and generate relocatable machine code.

It also allocates memory locations for the variable. The instructions in the intermediate code are converted into machine instructions. This phase coverts the optimize or intermediate code into the target language.

The target language is the machine code. Therefore, all the memory locations and registers are also selected and allotted during this phase. The code generated by this phase is executed to take inputs and generate expected outputs.

Example:

$$a = b + 60.0$$

Would be possibly translated to registers:

```
MOVF a, R1

MULF #60.0, R2

ADDF R1, R2
```

References

- Fog, Agner (2010-02-16). "Calling conventions for different C++ compilers and operating systems: Chapter 3, Data Representation" (PDF). Retrieved 2010-08-30

- Seymour, Lipschutz (2014). Data structures (Revised first ed.). New Delhi, India: McGraw Hill Education. ISBN 9781259029967. OCLC 927793728

- Bovet, Daniel; Cesati, Marco (2005). Understanding the Linux Kernel. O'Reilly. ISBN 9780596554910

- The-Structure-of-a-Compiler: brainkart.com, Retrieved 9 August, 2020

- Cooper, Keith Daniel; Torczon, Linda (2012). Engineering a compiler (2nd ed.). Amsterdam: Elsevier/Morgan Kaufmann. p. 8. ISBN 9780120884780. OCLC 714113472

4
Arrays, Strings and Variables

Arrays consist of a set of like variables stored at contiguous memory locations. Strings refer to series of characters either as a literal constant or some kind of variable. Variable is the storage address assigned to a storage area that stores value. This chapter has been carefully written to provide an easy understanding of arrays, strings and variables.

Array

An array is collection of items stored at contiguous memory locations. The idea is to store multiple items of same type together. This makes it easier to calculate the position of each element by simply adding an offset to a base value, i.e., the memory location of the first element of the array (generally denoted by the name of the array).

For simplicity, we can think of an array a fleet of stairs where on each step is placed a value (let's say one of your friends). Here, you can identify the location of any of your friends by simply knowing the count of the step they are on.

Remember: "Location of next index depends on the data type we use".

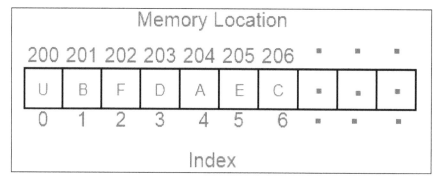

The image can be looked as a top-level view of a staircase where you are at the base of staircase. Each element can be uniquely identified by their index in the array.

Types of indexing in array:

- 0 (zero-based indexing): The first element of the array is indexed by subscript of 0.

- 1 (one-based indexing): The first element of the array is indexed by subscript of 1.

- n (n-based indexing): The base index of an array can be freely chosen. Usually programming languages allowing n-based indexing also allow negative index values and other scalar data types like enumerations, or characters may be used as an array index.

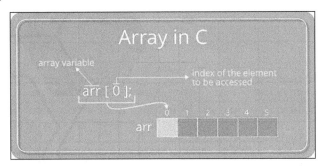

Advantages of using arrays:

- Arrays allow random access of elements. This makes accessing elements by position faster.

- Arrays have better cache locality that can make a pretty big difference in performance.

Examples:

```
// A character array in C/C++/Java
char arr1[] = {'g', 'e', 'e', 'k', 's'};


// An Integer array in C/C++/Java
int arr2[] = {10, 20, 30, 40, 50};


// Item at i'th index in array is typically accessed
// as "arr[i]".  For example arr1[0] gives us 'g'
```

```
// and arr2[3] gives us 40.
```

Usually, an array of characters is called a 'string', whereas an array of ints or floats is called simply an array.

Arrays in Java

Arrays in Java work differently than they do in C/C++. Following are some important point about Java arrays:

- In Java all arrays are dynamically allocated.

- Since arrays are objects in Java, we can find their length using member length. This is different from C/C++ where we find length using sizeof.

- A Java array variable can also be declared like other variables with [] after the data type.

- The variables in the array are ordered and each have an index beginning from 0.

- Java array can be also be used as a static field, a local variable or a method parameter.

- The size of an array must be specified by an int value and not long or short.

- The direct superclass of an array type is Object.

- Every array type implements the interfaces Cloneable and java.io.Serializable.

Array can contain primitive's data types as well as objects of a class depending on the definition of array. In case of primitive's data types, the actual values are stored in contiguous memory locations. In case of objects of a class, the actual objects are stored in heap segment.

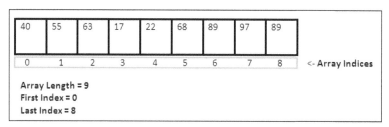

Creating, Initializing, and Accessing an Array

One-Dimensional Arrays: The general form of a one-dimensional array declaration is:

```
type var-name[];
```

```
OR

type[] var-name;
```

An array declaration has two components: the type and the name. type declares the element type of the array. The element type determines the data type of each element that comprises the array. Like array of int type, we can also create an array of other primitive data types like char, float, double..etc or user defined data type(objects of a class). Thus, the element type for the array determines what type of data the array will hold.

Example:

```
// both are valid declarations

int intArray[];

or int[] intArray;


byte byteArray[];

short shortsArray[];

boolean booleanArray[];

long longArray[];

float floatArray[];

double doubleArray[];

char charArray[];


// an array of references to objects of

// the class MyClass (a class created by

// user)

MyClass myClassArray[];


Object[]  ao,        // array of Object

Collection[] ca;   // array of Collection

                    // of unknown type
```

Although the above first declaration establishes the fact that intArray is an array variable, no array actually exists. It simply tells to the compiler that this (intArray) variable will hold an array of the integer type. To link intArray with an actual, physical array of integers, you must allocate one using new and assign it to intArray.

Instantiating an Array in Java

When an array is declared, only a reference of array is created. To actually create or give memory to array, you create an array like this: The general form of new as it applies to one-dimensional arrays appears as follows:

```
var-name = new type [size];
```

Here, type specifies the type of data being allocated, size specifies the number of elements in the array, and var-name is the name of array variable that is linked to the array. That is, to use new to allocate an array, you must specify the type and number of elements to allocate.

Example:

```
int intArray[];    //declaring array

intArray = new int[20];  // allocating memory to array
```

or

```
int[] intArray = new int[20]; // combining both statements in one
```

- The elements in the array allocated by new will automatically be initialized to zero (for numeric types), false (for boolean), or null (for reference types).Refer Default array values in Java.

- Obtaining an array is a two-step process. First, you must declare a variable of the desired array type. Second, you must allocate the memory that will hold the array, using new, and assign it to the array variable. Thus, in Java all arrays are dynamically allocated.

Array Literal

In a situation, where the size of the array and variables of array are already known, array literals can be used.

```
int[] intArray = new int[]{ 1,2,3,4,5,6,7,8,9,10 };

 // Declaring array literal
```

- The length of this array determines the length of the created array.

- There is no need to write the new int[] part in the latest versions of Java.

Accessing Java Array Elements using for Loop

Each element in the array is accessed via its index. The index begins with 0 and ends at (total array size)-1. All the elements of array can be accessed using Java for Loop.

```
// accessing the elements of the specified array
for (int i = 0; i < arr.length; i++)

    System.out.println("Element at index " + i +

                            " : "+ arr[i]);
```

Implementation

```
// Java program to illustrate creating an array
// of integers, puts some values in the array,
// and prints each value to standard output.


class GFG
{
        public static void main (String[] args)

        {
        // declares an Array of integers.
        int[] arr;


        // allocating memory for 5 integers.
        arr = new int[5];


        // initialize the first elements of the array
        arr[0] = 10;


        // initialize the second elements of the array
        arr[1] = 20;
```

```
//so on...
arr[2] = 30;
arr[3] = 40;
arr[4] = 50;


// accessing the elements of the specified array
for (int i = 0; i < arr.length; i++)
        System.out.println("Element at index " + i +
                                " : "+ arr[i]);


    }
}
```

Output:

```
Element at index 0 : 10
Element at index 1 : 20
Element at index 2 : 30
Element at index 3 : 40
Element at index 4 : 50
```

You can also access java arrays using foreach loops.

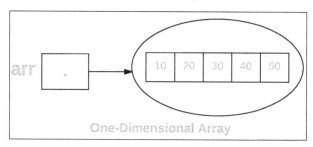

One-Dimensional Array

Arrays of Objects

An array of objects is created just like an array of primitive type data items in the following way.

```
Student[] arr = new Student[7]; //student is a user-defined class
```

The studentArray contains seven memory spaces each of size of student class in which the address of seven Student objects can be stored. The Student objects have to be instantiated using the constructor of the Student class and their references should be assigned to the array elements in the following way.

```
Student[] arr = new Student[5];

// Java program to illustrate creating an array of

// objects


class Student

{

        public int roll_no;

        public String name;

        Student(int roll_no, String name)

        {

                this.roll_no = roll_no;

                this.name = name;

        }

}


// Elements of array are objects of a class Student.

public class GFG

{

        public static void main (String[] args)

        {

                // declares an Array of integers.

                Student[] arr;


                // allocating memory for 5 objects of type Student.

                arr = new Student[5];
```

```
        // initialize the first elements of the array

        arr[0] = new Student(1,"aman");


        // initialize the second elements of the array

        arr[1] = new Student(2,"vaibhav");


        // so on...
        arr[2] = new Student(3,"shikar");

        arr[3] = new Student(4,"dharmesh");

        arr[4] = new Student(5,"mohit");


        // accessing the elements of the specified array

        for (int i = 0; i < arr.length; i++)

            System.out.println("Element at " + i + " : " +

                                arr[i].roll_no +" "+ arr[i].name);

    }

}
```

Output:

```
Element at 0 : 1 aman

Element at 1 : 2 vaibhav

Element at 2 : 3 shikar

Element at 3 : 4 dharmesh

Element at 4 : 5 mohit
```

What Happens if we try to Access Element Outside the Array Size?

JVM throws ArrayIndexOutOfBoundsException to indicate that array has been accessed with an illegal index. The index is either negative or greater than or equal to size of array.

```
class GFG

{
```

```
        public static void main (String[] args)

        {

                int[] arr = new int[2];

                arr[0] = 10;

                arr[1] = 20;


                for (int i = 0; i <= arr.length; i++)

                        System.out.println(arr[i]);

        }

}
```

Runtime error:

```
Exception in thread "main" java.lang.ArrayIndexOutOfBoundsException: 2

    at GFG.main(File.java:12)
```

Output:

```
10

20
```

Multidimensional Arrays

Multidimensional arrays are arrays of arrays with each element of the array holding the reference of other array. These are also known as Jagged Arrays. A multidimensional array is created by appending one set of square brackets ([]) per dimension. Examples:

```
int[][] intArray = new int[10][20]; //a 2D array or matrix

int[][][] intArray = new int[10][20][10]; //a 3D array
```

class multiDimensional

```
{

        public static void main(String args[])

        {

                // declaring and initializing 2D array

                int arr[][] = { {2,7,9},{3,6,1},{7,4,2} };
```

```
        // printing 2D array

        for (int i=0; i< 3 ; i++)

        {

                for (int j=0; j < 3 ; j++)

                        System.out.print(arr[i][j] + " ");


                System.out.println();

        }

    }

}
```

Output:

2 7 9

3 6 1

7 4 2

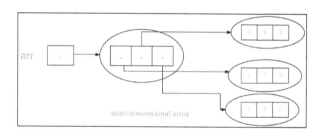

Multi-dimensional array

Passing Arrays to Methods

Like variables, we can also pass arrays to methods. For example, below program pass array to method sum for calculating sum of array's values.

```
// Java program to demonstrate

// passing of array to method


class Test

{

    // Driver method

    public static void main(String args[])
```

```
    {

        int arr[] = {3, 1, 2, 5, 4};


        // passing array to method m1

        sum(arr);


    }


    public static void sum(int[] arr)

    {

        // getting sum of array values

        int sum = 0;


        for (int i = 0; i < arr.length; i++)

            sum+=arr[i];


        System.out.println("sum of array values : " + sum);

    }

}
```

Output:

```
sum of array values : 15
```

Returning Arrays from Methods

As usual, a method can also return an array. For example, below program returns an array from method m1.

```
// Java program to demonstrate

// return of array from method

class Test

{
```

```
    // Driver method
    public static void main(String args[])
    {
        int arr[] = m1();

        for (int i = 0; i < arr.length; i++)
            System.out.print(arr[i]+" ");

    }

    public static int[] m1()
    {
        // returning array
        return new int[]{1,2,3};
    }
}
```

Output:

```
1 2 3
```

Class Objects for Arrays

Every array has an associated Class object, shared with all other arrays with the same component type.

```
// Java program to demonstrate
// Class Objects for Arrays

class Test
{
    public static void main(String args[])
    {
```

```
        int intArray[] = new int[3];

        byte byteArray[] = new byte[3];

        short shortsArray[] = new short[3];


        // array of Strings
        String[] strArray = new String[3];


        System.out.println(intArray.getClass());

        System.out.println(intArray.getClass().getSuperclass());

        System.out.println(byteArray.getClass());

        System.out.println(shortsArray.getClass());

        System.out.println(strArray.getClass());

    }

}
```

Output:

```
class [I

class java.lang.Object

class [B

class [S

class [Ljava.lang.String;
```

Explanation:

- The string "[I" is the run-time type signature for the class object "array with component type int".

- The only direct superclass of any array type is java.lang.Object.

- The string "[B" is the run-time type signature for the class object "array with component type byte".

- The string "[S" is the run-time type signature for the class object "array with component type short".

- The string "[L" is the run-time type signature for the class object "array with component type of a Class". The Class name is then followed.

Array Members

Now as you know that arrays are object of a class and direct superclass of arrays is class Object. The members of an array type are all of the following:

- The public final field length, which contains the number of components of the array. Length may be positive or zero.

- All the members inherited from class Object; the only method of Object that is not inherited is its clone method.

- The public method clone(), which overrides clone method in class Object and throws no checked exceptions.

Cloning of Arrays

When you clone a single dimensional array, such as Object[], a "deep copy" is performed with the new array containing copies of the original array's elements as opposed to references.

```java
// Java program to demonstrate
// cloning of one-dimensional arrays


class Test
{
    public static void main(String args[])
    {
        int intArray[] = {1,2,3};


        int cloneArray[] = intArray.clone();


        // will print false as deep copy is created
        // for one-dimensional array
        System.out.println(intArray == cloneArray);


        for (int i = 0; i < cloneArray.length; i++) {
            System.out.print(cloneArray[i]+" ");
```

```
            }

        }

}
```

Output:

```
false

1 2 3
```

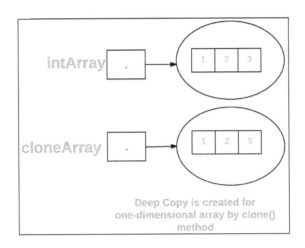

A clone of a multidimensional array (like Object[][]) is a "shallow copy" however, which is to say that it creates only a single new array with each element array a reference to an original element array but subarrays are shared.

```java
// Java program to demonstrate
// cloning of multi-dimensional arrays


class Test

{

        public static void main(String args[])

        {

                int intArray[][] = {{1,2,3},{4,5}};


                int cloneArray[][] = intArray.clone();


                // will print false
```

```
System.out.println(intArray == cloneArray);


// will print true as shallow copy is created
// i.e. sub-arrays are shared
System.out.println(intArray[0] == cloneArray[0]);
System.out.println(intArray[1] == cloneArray[1]);


    }
}
```

Output:

```
false

true

true
```

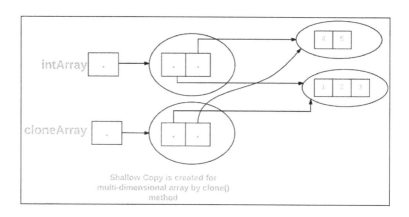

Shallow Copy is created for
multi-dimensional array by clone()
method

C++ Arrays

C++ provides a data structure, the array, which stores a fixed-size sequential collection of elements of the same type. An array is used to store a collection of data, but it is often more useful to think of an array as a collection of variables of the same type.

Instead of declaring individual variables, such as number0, number1, ..., and number99, you declare one array variable such as numbers and use numbers[0], numbers[1], and ..., numbers[99] to represent individual variables. A specific element in an array is accessed by an index.

All arrays consist of contiguous memory locations. The lowest address corresponds to the first element and the highest address to the last element.

Declaring Arrays

To declare an array in C++, the programmer specifies the type of the elements and the number of elements required by an array as follows:

```
type arrayName [ arraySize ];
```

This is called a single-dimension array. The arraySize must be an integer constant greater than zero and type can be any valid C++ data type. For example, to declare a 10-element array called balance of type double, use this statement:

```
double balance[10];
```

Initializing Arrays

You can initialize C++ array elements either one by one or using a single statement as follows:

```
double balance[5] = {1000.0, 2.0, 3.4, 17.0, 50.0};
```

The number of values between braces { } cannot be larger than the number of elements that we declare for the array between square brackets [ ]. Following is an example to assign a single element of the array.

If you omit the size of the array, an array just big enough to hold the initialization is created. Therefore, if you write:

```
double balance[] = {1000.0, 2.0, 3.4, 17.0, 50.0};
```

You will create exactly the same array as you did in the previous example.

```
balance[4] = 50.0;
```

The above statement assigns element number 5th in the array a value of 50.0. Array with 4th index will be 5th, i.e., last element because all arrays have 0 as the index of their first element which is also called base index. Following is the pictorial representation of the same array.

	0	1	2	3	4
balance	1000.0	2.0	3.4	7.0	50.0

Accessing Array Elements

An element is accessed by indexing the array name. This is done by placing the index of the element within square brackets after the name of the array. For example;

```
double salary = balance[9];
```

The previous statement will take 10th element from the array and assign the value to salary variable.

This program makes use of setw() function to format the output. When the above code is compiled and executed, it produces the following result:

```
Element          Value

       0           100

       1           101

       2           102

       3           103

       4           104

       5           105

       6           106

       7           107

       8           108

       9           109
```

Arrays in C++

Arrays are important to C++ and should need lots of more detail. There are following few important concepts, which should be clear to a C++ programmer:

- Multi-dimensional arrays: C++ supports multidimensional arrays. The simplest form of the multidimensional array is the two-dimensional array.

- Pointer to an array: You can generate a pointer to the first element of an array by simply specifying the array name, without any index.

- Passing arrays to functions: You can pass to the function a pointer to an array by specifying the array's name without an index.

- Return array from functions: C++ allows a function to return an array.

Advantages of Array

Advantages of Array are as follows:

Saves Memory

Memory can be allocated dynamically in an array. This advantage of array helps to save the memory of the system. It also helps when the pre-defined array has insufficient memory. At runtime memory can be allocated manually during run time. Also when memory allocation is not dynamic it stored the data in contiguous memory locations. The amount of storage required depends on the data type or size.

Cache Friendly

In an array, values are near each other in memory. They can be accessed easily from CPU to cache. This brings to a conclusion that iteration over an array is much faster than any other iteration. It parses the array an array of reference may be an advantage here.

Predictable Timings with Array

In both the hash table and array the access time is provided. However, the hash table is a bit complicated and it usually involves multiple steps where each step may involve cache misses and memory reload. When arrays are taken into consideration the system is well aware of the precise address of the array and wherein memory is it allocated and stored. Hence accessing arrays is not only fast but also it is predictable.

Easier Debugging

When taken into consideration a linked list, it is usually time-consuming to check if an index is valid or not. Similarly, it is difficult to check it in a hash table as well. But when it comes to an array it has its specified indexes and hence optimal to use. It can be directly traversed with the index position.

More Compact in Memory Usage

An array requires memory space only for the values, the start address and its length. On the contrary, a linked list needs a pointer for every value which is inserted. It acquires memory for every address and also when extra data is inserted it also needs memory for the same. Hash table also needs memory depending on how it is implemented. This implementation decides how memory is allocated and usually, it requires extra allocation.

Advantages over Variables

An array is considered to be a homogenous collection of data. Here the word collection means that it helps in storing multiple values which are under the same variable. For any purpose, if the user wishes to store multiple values of similar type, an array is the best option which can be used. As a result for any purpose if a user wishes to store multiple values of a similar type then arrays can be used and utilized efficiently.

Advantages over Data Structures

An array is also a collection of data which stores data of the same type and in a sequential manner. As this data is stored in a sequential manner it is efficient to track it by using just its index values. This is not easy when taken into consideration the non-sequential data structures. In these cases every time you need to traverse to a particular desired position and then access its value.

Helps in Reusability of Code

One of the major advantages of an array is that they can be declared once and reused multiple times. It represents multiple values by making use of a single variable. This helps in improvement of reusability of code and also improves the readability of the code. If in this situation no array is used then we will need to store multiple values in multiple variables.

Zero-length Arrays

Zero-length arrays is also an advantage which is considered to be flexible and are used to implement variable length arrays. When a structure is taken into consideration then the user often ends up wasting memory and the constants are too large. When zero-length arrays are used then the allocated structures do not consume any memory. They act as pointers. They can be said as zero-length arrays are pointers whose contents are in line at itself.

Multi-dimensional Arrays

These can be defined as an array of arrays. Data which is present in tabular format like 1D, 2D, etc. can be defined. The total number of elements can be stored in the multi-dimensional array and can be calculated by multiplying the size of all dimensions.

Applications

Arrays are used to implement mathematical vectors and matrices, as well as other kinds of rectangular tables. Many databases, small and large, consist of (or include) one-dimensional arrays whose elements are records.

Arrays are used to implement other data structures, such as lists, heaps, hash tables, deques, queues, stacks, strings, and VLists. Array-based implementations of other data structures are frequently simple and space-efficient (implicit data structures), requiring little space overhead, but may have poor space complexity, particularly when modified, compared to tree-based data structures (compare a sorted array to a search tree).

One or more large arrays are sometimes used to emulate in-program dynamic memory allocation, particularly memory pool allocation. Historically, this has sometimes been the only way to allocate "dynamic memory" portably.

Arrays can be used to determine partial or complete control flow in programs, as a compact alternative to (otherwise repetitive) multiple IF statements. They are known in this context as control tables and are used in conjunction with a purpose built interpreter whose control flow is altered according to values contained in the array. The array may contain subroutine pointers (or relative subroutine numbers that can be acted upon by SWITCH statements) that direct the path of the execution.

Element Identifier and Addressing Formulas

When data objects are stored in an array, individual objects are selected by an index that is usually a non-negative scalar integer. Indexes are also called subscripts. An index *maps* the array value to a stored object.

There are three ways in which the elements of an array can be indexed:

- 0 (zero-based indexing):
  - The first element of the array is indexed by subscript of 0.
- 1 (one-based indexing):
  - The first element of the array is indexed by subscript of 1.
- n (n-based indexing):
  - The base index of an array can be freely chosen. Usually programming languages allowing *n-based indexing* also allow negative index values and other scalar data types like enumerations, or characters may be used as an array index.

Using zero based indexing is the design choice of many influential programming languages, including C, Java and Lisp. This leads to simpler implementation where the subscript refers to an offset from the starting position of an array, so the first element has an offset of zero.

Arrays can have multiple dimensions, thus it is not uncommon to access an array using multiple indices. For example, a two-dimensional array A with three rows and four columns might provide access to the element at the 2nd row and 4th column by the expression A[1][3] in the case of a zero-based indexing system. Thus two indices are used for a two-dimensional array, three for a three-dimensional array, and *n* for an *n*-dimensional array.

The number of indices needed to specify an element is called the dimension, dimensionality, or rank of the array. In standard arrays, each index is restricted to a certain range of consecutive integers (or consecutive values of some enumerated type), and the address of an element is computed by a "linear" formula on the indices.

One-dimensional Arrays

A one-dimensional array (or single dimension array) is a type of linear array. Accessing its elements involves a single subscript which can either represent a row or column index.

As an example consider the C declaration `int anArrayName[10];` which declares a one-dimensional array of ten integers. Here, the array can store ten elements of type `int` . This array has indices starting from zero through nine. For example, the expressions an`ArrayName[0]` and `anArrayName[9]` are the first and last elements respectively.

For a vector with linear addressing, the element with index i is located at the address $B + c \times i$, where B is a fixed *base address* and c a fixed constant, sometimes called the *address increment* or *stride*. If the valid element indices begin at 0, the constant B is simply the address of the first element of the array. For this reason, the C programming language specifies that array indices always begin at 0; and many programmers will call that element "zeroth" rather than "first".

However, one can choose the index of the first element by an appropriate choice of the base address B. For example, if the array has five elements, indexed 1 through 5, and the base address B is replaced by $B + 30c$, then the indices of those same elements will be 31 to 35. If the numbering does not start at 0, the constant B may not be the address of any element.

Multidimensional Arrays

For a multidimensional array, the element with indices i,j would have address $B + c \cdot i + d \cdot j$, where the coefficients c and d are the *row* and *column address increments*, respectively.

More generally, in a k-dimensional array, the address of an element with indices $i_1, i_2, ..., i_k$ is:

$$B + c_1 \cdot i_1 + c_2 \cdot i_2 + ... + c_k \cdot i_k.$$

For example: int a[2][3];

This means that array a has 2 rows and 3 columns, and the array is of integer type. Here we can store 6 elements they will be stored linearly but starting from first row linear then continuing with second row. The above array will be stored as $a_{11}, a_{12}, a_{13}, a_{21}, a_{22}, a_{23}$.

This formula requires only k multiplications and k additions, for any array that can fit in memory. Moreover, if any coefficient is a fixed power of 2, the multiplication can be replaced by bit shifting. The coefficients c_k must be chosen so that every valid index tuple maps to the address of a distinct element.

If the minimum legal value for every index is 0, then B is the address of the element whose indices are all zero. As in the one-dimensional case, the element indices may be changed by changing the base address B. Thus, if a two-dimensional array has rows and columns indexed from 1 to 10 and 1 to 20, respectively, then replacing B by $B + c_1 - 3c_2$ will cause them to be renumbered from 0 through 9 and 4 through 23, respectively. Taking advantage of this feature, some languages (like FORTRAN 77) specify that array indices begin at 1, as in mathematical tradition while other languages (like Fortran 90, Pascal and Algol) let the user choose the minimum value for each index.

Dope Vectors

The addressing formula is completely defined by the dimension d, the base address B, and the increments $c_1, c_2, ..., c_k$. It is often useful to pack these parameters into a record called the array's *descriptor* or *stride vector* or *dope vector*. The size of each element, and the minimum and maximum values allowed for each index may also be included in the dope vector. The dope vector is a complete handle for the array, and is a convenient way to pass arrays as arguments to procedures. Many useful array slicing operations (such as selecting a sub-array, swapping indices, or reversing the direction of the indices) can be performed very efficiently by manipulating the dope vector.

Compact Layouts

Often the coefficients are chosen so that the elements occupy a contiguous area of memory. However, that is not necessary. Even if arrays are always created with contiguous elements, some array slicing operations may create non-contiguous sub-arrays from them.

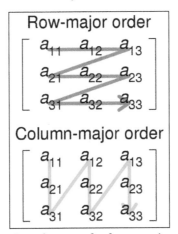

Illustration of row- and column-major order.

There are two systematic compact layouts for a two-dimensional array. For example, consider the matrix:

$$A = \begin{bmatrix} 1 & 2 & 3 \\ 4 & 5 & 6 \\ 7 & 8 & 9 \end{bmatrix}.$$

In the row-major order layout (adopted by C for statically declared arrays), the elements in each row are stored in consecutive positions and all of the elements of a row have a lower address than any of the elements of a consecutive row:

1	2	3	4	5	6	7	8	9

In column-major order (traditionally used by Fortran), the elements in each column are consecutive in memory and all of the elements of a column have a lower address than any of the elements of a consecutive column:

1	4	7	2	5	8	3	6	9

For arrays with three or more indices, "row major order" puts in consecutive positions any two elements whose index tuples differ only by one in the *last* index. "Column major order" is analogous with respect to the *first* index.

In systems which use processor cache or virtual memory, scanning an array is much faster if successive elements are stored in consecutive positions in memory, rather than sparsely scattered. Many algorithms that use multidimensional arrays will scan them in a predictable order. A programmer (or a sophisticated compiler) may use this information to choose between row- or column-major layout for each array. For example, when computing the product $A \cdot B$ of two matrices, it would be best to have A stored in row-major order, and B in column-major order.

Resizing

Static arrays have a size that is fixed when they are created and consequently do not allow elements to be inserted or removed. However, by allocating a new array and copying the contents of the old array to it, it is possible to effectively implement a *dynamic* version of an array;. If this operation is done infrequently, insertions at the end of the array require only amortized constant time.

Some array data structures do not reallocate storage, but do store a count of the number of elements of the array in use, called the count or size. This effectively makes the array a dynamic array with a fixed maximum size or capacity; Pascal strings are examples of this.

Non-linear Formulas

More complicated (non-linear) formulas are occasionally used. For a compact two-dimensional triangular array, for instance, the addressing formula is a polynomial of degree 2.

Efficiency

Both *store* and *select* take (deterministic worst case) constant time. Arrays take linear

$(O(n))$ space in the number of elements n that they hold. In an array with element size k and on a machine with a cache line size of B bytes, iterating through an array of n elements requires the minimum of ceiling(nk/B) cache misses, because its elements occupy contiguous memory locations. This is roughly a factor of B/k better than the number of cache misses needed to access n elements at random memory locations. As a consequence, sequential iteration over an array is noticeably faster in practice than iteration over many other data structures, a property called locality of reference (this does *not* mean however, that using a perfect hash or trivial hash within the same (local) array, will not be even faster - and achievable in constant time). Libraries provide low-level optimized facilities for copying ranges of memory (such as memcpy) which can be used to move contiguous blocks of array elements significantly faster than can be achieved through individual element access. The speedup of such optimized routines varies by array element size, architecture, and implementation.

Memory-wise, arrays are compact data structures with no per-element overhead. There may be a per-array overhead (e.g., to store index bounds) but this is language-dependent. It can also happen that elements stored in an array require *less* memory than the same elements stored in individual variables, because several array elements can be stored in a single word; such arrays are often called *packed* arrays. An extreme (but commonly used) case is the bit array, where every bit represents a single element.

A single octet can thus hold up to 256 different combinations of up to 8 different conditions, in the most compact form. Array accesses with statically predictable access patterns are a major source of data parallelism.

Comparison with other Data Structures

	Linked list	Array	Dynamic array	Balanced tree	Random access list	Hashed array tree
Indexing	$\Theta(n)$	$\Theta(1)$	$\Theta(1)$	$\Theta(\log n)$	$\Theta(\log n)$	$\Theta(1)$
Insert/delete at beginning	$\Theta(1)$	N/A	$\Theta(n)$	$\Theta(\log n)$	$\Theta(1)$	$\Theta(n)$
Insert/delete at end	$\Theta(1)$ when last element is known; $\Theta(n)$ when last element is unknown	N/A	$\Theta(1)$ amortized	$\Theta(\log n)$	$\Theta(\log n)$ updating	$\Theta(1)$ amortized
Insert/delete in middle	search time + $\Theta(1)$	N/A	$\Theta(n)$	$\Theta(\log n)$	$\Theta(\log n)$ updating	$\Theta(n)$
Wasted space (average)	$\Theta(n)$	0	$\Theta(n)$	$\Theta(n)$	$\Theta(n)$	$\Theta(\sqrt{n})$

Dynamic arrays or growable arrays are similar to arrays but add the ability to insert and delete elements; adding and deleting at the end is particularly efficient. However, they reserve linear ($\Theta(n)$) additional storage, whereas arrays do not reserve additional storage.

Associative arrays provide a mechanism for array-like functionality without huge storage overheads when the index values are sparse. For example, an array that contains values only at indexes 1 and 2 billion may benefit from using such a structure. Specialized associative arrays with integer keys include Patricia tries, Judy arrays, and van Emde Boas trees.

Balanced trees require O(log n) time for indexed access, but also permit inserting or deleting elements in O(log n) time, whereas growable arrays require linear ($\Theta(n)$) time to insert or delete elements at an arbitrary position. Linked lists allow constant time removal and insertion in the middle but take linear time for indexed access. Their memory use is typically worse than arrays, but is still linear.

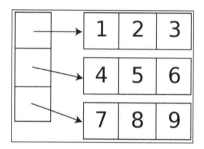

An Iliffe vector is an alternative to a multidimensional array structure. It uses a one-dimensional array of references to arrays of one dimension less. For two dimensions, in particular, this alternative structure would be a vector of pointers to vectors, one for each row(pointer on c or c++). Thus an element in row i and column j of an array A would be accessed by double indexing ($A[i][j]$ in typical notation). This alternative structure allows jagged arrays, where each row may have a different size — or, in general, where the valid range of each index depends on the values of all preceding indices. It also saves one multiplication (by the column address increment) replacing it by a bit shift (to index the vector of row pointers) and one extra memory access (fetching the row address), which may be worthwhile in some architectures.

Dimension

The dimension of an array is the number of indices needed to select an element. Thus, if the array is seen as a function on a set of possible index combinations, it is the dimension of the space of which its domain is a discrete subset. Thus a one-dimensional array is a list of data, a two-dimensional array a rectangle of data, a three-dimensional array a block of data, etc.

This should not be confused with the dimension of the set of all matrices with a given domain, that is, the number of elements in the array. For example, an array with 5 rows and

4 columns is two-dimensional, but such matrices form a 20-dimensional space. Similarly, a three-dimensional vector can be represented by a one-dimensional array of size three.

Bit Array

A bit array (also known as bit map, bit set, bit string, or bit vector) is an array data structure that compactly stores bits. It can be used to implement a simple set data structure. A bit array is effective at exploiting bit-level parallelism in hardware to perform operations quickly. A typical bit array stores kw bits, where w is the number of bits in the unit of storage, such as a byte or word, and k is some nonnegative integer. If w does not divide the number of bits to be stored, some space is wasted due to internal fragmentation.

A bit array is a mapping from some domain (almost always a range of integers) to values in the set $\{0, 1\}$. The values can be interpreted as dark/light, absent/present, locked/unlocked, valid/invalid, et cetera. The point is that there are only two possible values, so they can be stored in one bit. As with other arrays, the access to a single bit can be managed by applying an index to the array. Assuming its size (or length) to be n bits, the array can be used to specify a subset of the domain (e.g. $\{0, 1, 2, ..., n-1\}$), where a 1-bit indicates the presence and a 0-bit the absence of a number in the set. This set data structure uses about n/w words of space, where w is the number of bits in each machine word. Whether the least significant bit (of the word) or the most significant bit indicates the smallest-index number is largely irrelevant, but the former tends to be preferred (on little-endian machines).

Basic Operations

Although most machines are not able to address individual bits in memory, nor have instructions to manipulate single bits, each bit in a word can be singled out and manipulated using bitwise operations. In particular:

- OR can be used to set a bit to one: 11101010 OR 00000100 = 11101110.

- AND can be used to set a bit to zero: 11101010 AND 11111101 = 11101000.

- AND together with zero-testing can be used to determine if a bit is set:

    ◦ 11101010 AND 00000001 = 00000000 = 0.

    ◦ 11101010 AND 00000010 = 00000010 ≠ 0.

- XOR can be used to invert or toggle a bit:

    ◦ 11101010 XOR 00000100 = 11101110.

- ◦   11101110 XOR 00000100 = 11101010.

- NOT can be used to invert all bits.

    - ◦   NOT 10110010 = 01001101.

To obtain the bit mask needed for these operations, we can use a bit shift operator to shift the number 1 to the left by the appropriate number of places, as well as bitwise negation if necessary.

Given two bit arrays of the same size representing sets, we can compute their union, intersection, and set-theoretic difference using n/w simple bit operations each ($2n/w$ for difference), as well as the complement of either:

```
for i from 0 to n/w-1

    complement_a[i] := not a[i]

    union[i]        := a[i] or b[i]

    intersection[i] := a[i] and b[i]

    difference[i]   := a[i] and (not b[i])
```

If we wish to iterate through the bits of a bit array, we can do this efficiently using a doubly nested loop that loops through each word, one at a time. Only n/w memory accesses are required:

```
for i from 0 to n/w-1

    index := 0    // if needed

    word := a[i]

    for b from 0 to w-1

        value := word and 1 ≠ 0

        word := word shift right 1

        // do something with value

        index := index + 1    // if needed
```

Both of these code samples exhibit ideal locality of reference, which will subsequently receive large performance boost from a data cache. If a cache line is k words, only about n/wk cache misses will occur.

More Complex Operations

As with character strings it is straightforward to define *length*, *substring*, lexicographical *compare*, *concatenation*, *reverse* operations. The implementation of some of these operations is sensitive to endianness.

Population/Hamming Weight

If we wish to find the number of 1 bits in a bit array, sometimes called the population count or Hamming weight, there are efficient branch-free algorithms that can compute the number of bits in a word using a series of simple bit operations. We simply run such an algorithm on each word and keep a running total. Counting zeros is similar.

Inversion

Vertical flipping of a one-bit-per-pixel image, or some FFT algorithms, requires flipping the bits of individual words (so b31 b30 ... b0 becomes b0 ... b30 b31). When this operation is not available on the processor, it's still possible to proceed by successive passes, in this example on 32 bits:

```
exchange two 16bit halfwords

exchange bytes by pairs (0xddccbbaa -> 0xccddaabb)

...

swap bits by pairs

swap bits (b31 b30 ... b1 b0 -> b30 b31 ... b0 b1)

```

The last operation can be written ((x&0x55555555)<<1) | (x&0x-aaaaaaaa)>>1)).

Find First One

The find first set or *find first one* operation identifies the index or position of the 1-bit with the smallest index in an array, and has widespread hardware support (for arrays not larger than a word) and efficient algorithms for its computation. When a priority queue is stored in a bit array, find first one can be used to identify the highest priority element in the queue. To expand a word-size *find first one* to longer arrays, one can find the first nonzero word and then run *find first one* on that word. The related operations *find first zero, count leading zeros, count leading ones, count trailing zeros, count trailing ones,* and *log base 2* can also be extended to a bit array in a straightforward manner.

Compression

A bit array is the most dense storage for "random" bits, that is, where each bit is equally likely to be 0 or 1, and each one is independent. But most data is not random, so it may be possible to store it more compactly. For example, the data of a typical fax image is not random and can be compressed. Run-length encoding is commonly used to compress these long streams. However, most compressed data formats are not so easy to access randomly; also by compressing bit arrays too aggressively we run the risk of losing the benefits due to bit-level parallelism (vectorization). Thus, instead of compressing bit arrays as streams of bits, we might compress them as streams of bytes or words.

Advantages and Disadvantages

Bit arrays, despite their simplicity, have a number of marked advantages over other data structures for the same problems:

- They are extremely compact; no other data structures can store n independent pieces of data in n/w words.

- They allow small arrays of bits to be stored and manipulated in the register set for long periods of time with no memory accesses.

- Because of their ability to exploit bit-level parallelism, limit memory access, and maximally use the data cache, they often outperform many other data structures on practical data sets, even those that are more asymptotically efficient.

However, bit arrays aren't the solution to everything. In particular:

- Without compression, they are wasteful set data structures for sparse sets (those with few elements compared to their range) in both time and space. For such applications, compressed bit arrays, Judy arrays, tries, or even Bloom filters should be considered instead.

- Accessing individual elements can be expensive and difficult to express in some languages. If random access is more common than sequential and the array is relatively small, a byte array may be preferable on a machine with byte addressing. A word array, however, is probably not justified due to the huge space overhead and additional cache misses it causes, unless the machine only has word addressing.

Applications

Because of their compactness, bit arrays have a number of applications in areas where space or efficiency is at a premium. Most commonly, they are used to represent a simple group of boolean flags or an ordered sequence of boolean values. Bit arrays are used for priority queues, where the bit at index k is set if and only if k is in the queue; this data structure is used, for example, by the Linux kernel, and benefits strongly from a find-first-zero operation in hardware.

Bit arrays can be used for the allocation of memory pages, inodes, disk sectors, etc. In such cases, the term *bitmap* may be used. However, this term is frequently used to refer to raster images, which may use multiple bits per pixel.

Another application of bit arrays is the Bloom filter, a probabilistic set data structure that can store large sets in a small space in exchange for a small probability of error. It is also possible to build probabilistic hash tables based on bit arrays that accept either false positives or false negatives.

Bit arrays and the operations on them are also important for constructing succinct data structures, which use close to the minimum possible space. In this context, operations like finding the nth 1 bit or counting the number of 1 bits up to a certain position become important.

Bit arrays are also a useful abstraction for examining streams of compressed data, which often contain elements that occupy portions of bytes or are not byte-aligned. For example, the compressed Huffman coding representation of a single 8-bit character can be anywhere from 1 to 255 bits long.

In information retrieval, bit arrays are a good representation for the posting lists of very frequent terms. If we compute the gaps between adjacent values in a list of strictly increasing integers and encode them using unary coding, the result is a bit array with a 1 bit in the nth position if and only if n is in the list. The implied probability of a gap of n is $1/2^n$. This is also the special case of Golomb coding where the parameter M is 1; this parameter is only normally selected when $-\log(2-p)/\log(1-p) \leq 1$, or roughly the term occurs in at least 38% of documents.

Language Support

The APL programming language fully supports bit arrays of arbitrary shape and size as a Boolean datatype distinct from integers. All major implementations (Dyalog APL, APL2, APL Next, NARS2000, Gnu APL, etc.) pack the bits densely into whatever size the machine word is. Bits may be accessed individually via the usual indexing notation (A[3]) as well as through all of the usual primitive functions and operators where they are often operated on using a special case algorithm such as summing the bits via a table lookup of bytes.

The C programming language's *bit fields*, pseudo-objects found in structs with size equal to some number of bits, are in fact small bit arrays; they are limited in that they cannot span words. Although they give a convenient syntax, the bits are still accessed using bitwise operators on most machines, and they can only be defined statically (like C's static arrays, their sizes are fixed at compile-time). It is also a common idiom for C programmers to use words as small bit arrays and access bits of them using bit operators. A widely available header file included in the X11 system, xtrapbits.h, is "a portable way for systems to define bit field manipulation of arrays of bits." A more explanatory description of aforementioned approach can be found in the comp.lang.c faq.

In C++, although individual `bools` typically occupy the same space as a byte or an integer, the STL type `vector<bool>` is a partial template specialization in which bits are packed as a space efficiency optimization. Since bytes (and not bits) are the smallest addressable unit in C++, the [] operator does *not* return a reference to an element, but instead returns a proxy reference. This might seem a minor point, but it means that `vector<bool>` is *not* a standard STL container, which is why the use of `vector<bool>` is generally discouraged. Another unique STL class, `bitset`, creates a vector of bits fixed at a particular size at compile-time, and in its interface and syntax more resembles the idiomatic use of words as bit sets by C programmers. It also has some additional power, such as the ability to efficiently count the number of bits that are set. The Boost C++ Libraries provide a `dynamic_bitset` class whose size is specified at run-time.

The D programming language provides bit arrays in its standard library, Phobos, in `std.bitmanip`. As in C++, the [] operator does not return a reference, since individual bits are not directly addressable on most hardware, but instead returns a `bool`.

In Java, the class `BitSet` creates a bit array that is then manipulated with functions named after bitwise operators familiar to C programmers. Unlike the `bitset` in C++, the Java `BitSet` does not have a "size" state (it has an effectively infinite size, initialized with 0 bits); a bit can be set or tested at any index. In addition, there is a class `EnumSet`, which represents a Set of values of an enumerated type internally as a bit vector, as a safer alternative to bit fields.

The .NET Framework supplies a `BitArray` collection class. It stores boolean values, supports random access and bitwise operators, can be iterated over, and its `Length` property can be changed to grow or truncate it. Although Standard ML has no support for bit arrays, Standard ML of New Jersey has an extension, the `BitArray` structure, in its SML/NJ Library. It is not fixed in size and supports set operations and bit operations, including, unusually, shift operations.

Haskell likewise currently lacks standard support for bitwise operations, but both GHC and Hugs provide a `Data.Bits` module with assorted bitwise functions and operators, including shift and rotate operations and an "unboxed" array over boolean values may be used to model a Bit array, although this lacks support from the former module.

In Perl, strings can be used as expandable bit arrays. They can be manipulated using the usual bitwise operators (~ | & ^), and individual bits can be tested and set using the *vec* function.

In Ruby, you can access (but not set) a bit of an integer (`Fixnum` or `Bignum`) using the bracket operator ([]), as if it were an array of bits. Apple's Core Foundation library contains CFBitVector and CFMutableBitVector structures. PL/I supports arrays of *bit strings* of arbitrary length, which may be either fixed-length or varying. The array elements may be *aligned*— each element begins on a byte or word boundary— or *unaligned*— elements immediately follow each other with no padding.

PL/pgSQL and PostgreSQL's SQL support *bit strings* as native type. There are two SQL bit types: `bit(n)` and `bit varying(n)`, where n is a positive integer.

Hardware description languages such as VHDL, Verilog, and SystemVerilog natively support bit vectors as these are used to model storage elements like flip-flops, hardware busses and hardware signals in general. In hardware verification languages such as OpenVera, *e* and SystemVerilog, bit vectors are used to sample values from the hardware models, and to represent data that is transferred to hardware during simulations.

Dynamic Array

Several values are inserted at the end of a dynamic array using geometric expansion. Grey cells indicate space reserved for expansion. Most insertions are fast (constant time), while some are slow due to the need for reallocation ($\Theta(n)$ time, labelled with turtles). The *logical size* and *capacity* of the final array are shown.

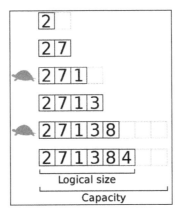

In computer science, a dynamic array, growable array, resizable array, dynamic table, mutable array, or array list is a random access, variable-size list data structure that allows elements to be added or removed. It is supplied with standard libraries in many modern mainstream programming languages. Dynamic arrays overcome a limit of static arrays, which have a fixed capacity that needs to be specified at allocation.

A dynamic array is not the same thing as a dynamically allocated array, which is an array whose size is fixed when the array is allocated, although a dynamic array may use such a fixed-size array as a back end.

Bounded-size Dynamic Arrays and Capacity

A simple dynamic array can be constructed by allocating an array of fixed-size, typically larger than the number of elements immediately required. The elements of the dynamic array are stored contiguously at the start of the underlying array, and the remaining positions towards the end of the underlying array are reserved, or unused. Elements can be added at the end of a dynamic array in constant time by using the reserved space, until this space is completely consumed. When all space is consumed, and an additional element is to be added, then the underlying fixed-sized array needs to be increased in size. Typically resizing is expensive because it involves allocating a new underlying array and copying each element from the original array. Elements can be removed from the end of a dynamic array in constant time, as no resizing is required. The number of elements used by the dynamic array contents is its *logical size* or *size*, while the size of the underlying array is called the dynamic array's *capacity* or *physical size*, which is the maximum possible size without relocating data.

A fixed-size array will suffice in applications where the maximum logical size is fixed (e.g. by specification), or can be calculated before the array is allocated. A dynamic array might be preferred if:

- The maximum logical size is unknown, or difficult to calculate, before the array is allocated.

- It is considered that a maximum logical size given by a specification is likely to change.

- The amortized cost of resizing a dynamic array does not significantly affect performance or responsiveness.

Geometric Expansion and Amortized Cost

To avoid incurring the cost of resizing many times, dynamic arrays resize by a large amount, such as doubling in size, and use the reserved space for future expansion. The operation of adding an element to the end might work as follows:

```
function insertEnd(dynarray a, element e)

    if (a.size == a.capacity)

        // resize a to twice its current capacity:

        a.capacity ← a.capacity * 2

        // (copy the contents to the new memory location here)

    a[a.size] ← e

    a.size ← a.size + 1
```

As n elements are inserted, the capacities form a geometric progression. Expanding the array by any constant proportion a ensures that inserting n elements takes $O(n)$ time overall, meaning that each insertion takes amortized constant time. Many dynamic arrays also deallocate some of the underlying storage if its size drops below a certain threshold, such as 30% of the capacity. This threshold must be strictly smaller than $1/a$ in order to provide hysteresis (provide a stable band to avoid repeatedly growing and shrinking) and support mixed sequences of insertions and removals with amortized constant cost. Dynamic arrays are a common example when teaching amortized analysis.

Growth Factor

The growth factor for the dynamic array depends on several factors including a space-time trade-off and algorithms used in the memory allocator itself. For growth factor a, the average time per insertion operation is about $a/(a-1)$, while the number of wasted cells is bounded above by $(a-1)n$. If memory allocator uses a first-fit allocation algorithm, then growth factor values such as $a=2$ can cause dynamic array expansion to run out of memory even though a significant amount of memory may still be available.

Below are growth factors used by several popular implementations:

Implementation	Growth factor (a)
Java ArrayList	1.5 (3/2)
Python PyListObject	~1.125 (n + n >> 3)
Microsoft Visual C++ 2013	1.5 (3/2)
G++ 5.2.0	2
Clang 3.6	2
Facebook folly/FBVector	1.5 (3/2)

Performance

Comparison of list data structures						
	Linked list	Array	Dynamic array	Balanced tree	Random access list	Hashed array tree
Indexing	$\Theta(n)$	$\Theta(1)$	$\Theta(1)$	$\Theta(\log n)$	$\Theta(\log n)$	$\Theta(1)$
Insert/delete at beginning	$\Theta(1)$	N/A	$\Theta(n)$	$\Theta(\log n)$	$\Theta(1)$	$\Theta(n)$
Insert/delete at end	$\Theta(1)$ when last element is known; $\Theta(n)$ when last element is unknown	N/A	$\Theta(1)$ amortized	$\Theta(\log n)$	$\Theta(\log n)$ updating	$\Theta(1)$ amortized
Insert/delete in middle	search time + $\Theta(1)$	N/A	$\Theta(n)$	$\Theta(\log n)$	$\Theta(\log n)$ updating	$\Theta(n)$
Wasted space (average)	$\Theta(n)$	0	$\Theta(n)$	$\Theta(n)$	$\Theta(n)$	$\Theta(\sqrt{n})$

The dynamic array has performance similar to an array, with the addition of new operations to add and remove elements:

- Getting or setting the value at a particular index (constant time).

- Iterating over the elements in order (linear time, good cache performance).

- Inserting or deleting an element in the middle of the array (linear time).

- Inserting or deleting an element at the end of the array (constant amortized time).

Dynamic arrays benefit from many of the advantages of arrays, including good locality of reference and data cache utilization, compactness (low memory use), and random access. They usually have only a small fixed additional overhead for storing information about the size and capacity. This makes dynamic arrays an attractive tool for building cache-friendly data structures. However, in languages like Python or Java that enforce reference semantics, the dynamic array generally will not store the actual data, but rather it will store references to the data that resides in other areas of memory. In this case, accessing items in the array sequentially will actually involve accessing multiple non-contiguous areas of memory, so the many advantages of the cache-friendliness of this data structure are lost.

Compared to linked lists, dynamic arrays have faster indexing (constant time versus linear time) and typically faster iteration due to improved locality of reference; however, dynamic arrays require linear time to insert or delete at an arbitrary location, since all following elements must be moved, while linked lists can do this in constant time. This disadvantage is mitigated by the gap buffer and *tiered vector* variants. Also, in a highly fragmented memory region, it may be expensive or impossible to find contiguous space for a large dynamic array, whereas linked lists do not require the whole data structure to be stored contiguously.

A balanced tree can store a list while providing all operations of both dynamic arrays and linked lists reasonably efficiently, but both insertion at the end and iteration over the list are slower than for a dynamic array, in theory and in practice, due to non-contiguous storage and tree traversal/manipulation overhead.

String

In computer programming, a string is traditionally a sequence of characters, either as a literal constant or as some kind of variable. The latter may allow its elements to be mutated and the length changed, or it may be fixed (after creation). A string is generally considered as a data type and is often implemented as an array data structure of bytes (or words) that stores a sequence of elements, typically characters, using some character encoding. *String* may also denote more general arrays or other sequence (or list) data types and structures.

Depending on the programming language and precise data type used, a variable declared to be a string may either cause storage in memory to be statically allocated for a predetermined maximum length or employ dynamic allocation to allow it to hold a variable number of elements.

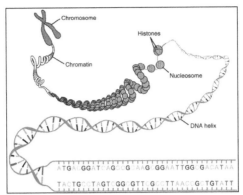

Strings are applied e.g. in Bioinformatics to describe DNA strands composed of nitrogenous bases.

When a string appears literally in source code, it is known as a string literal or an anonymous string. In formal languages, which are used in mathematical logic and theoretical computer science, a string is a finite sequence of symbols that are chosen from a set called an alphabet.

String Datatypes

A string datatype is a datatype modeled on the idea of a formal string. Strings are such an important and useful datatype that they are implemented in nearly every programming language. In some languages they are available as primitive types and in others as composite types. The syntax of most high-level programming languages allows for a string, usually quoted in some way, to represent an instance of a string datatype; such a meta-string is called a *literal* or *string literal*.

String Length

Although formal strings can have an arbitrary finite length, the length of strings in real languages is often constrained to an artificial maximum. In general, there are two types of string datatypes: *fixed-length strings*, which have a fixed maximum length to be determined at compile time and which use the same amount of memory whether this maximum is needed or not, and *variable-length strings*, whose length is not arbitrarily fixed and which can use varying amounts of memory depending on the actual requirements at run time. Most strings in modern programming languages are variable-length strings. Of course, even variable-length strings are limited in length – by the size of available computer memory. The string length can be stored as a separate integer (which may put another artificial limit on the length) or implicitly through a termination character, usually a character value with all bits zero such as in C programming language.

Character Encoding

String datatypes have historically allocated one byte per character, and, although the exact character set varied by region, character encodings were similar enough that programmers could often get away with ignoring this, since characters a program treated specially (such as period and space and comma) were in the same place in all the encodings a program would encounter. These character sets were typically based on ASCII or EBCDIC. If text in one encoding was displayed on a system using a different encoding, text was often mangled, though often somewhat readable and some computer users learned to read the mangled text.

The normal solutions involved keeping single-byte representations for ASCII and using two-byte representations for CJK ideographs. Use of these with existing code led to problems with matching and cutting of strings, the severity of which depended on how the character encoding was designed. Some encodings such as the EUC family guarantee that a byte value in the ASCII range will represent only that ASCII character, making the encoding safe for systems that use those characters as field separators. Other encodings such as ISO-2022 and Shift-JIS do not make such guarantees, making matching on byte codes unsafe. These encodings also were not "self-synchronizing", so that locating character boundaries required backing up to the start of a string, and pasting two strings together could result in corruption of the second string.

Unicode has simplified the picture somewhat. Most programming languages now have a datatype for Unicode strings. Unicode's preferred byte stream format UTF-8 is designed not to have the problems described above for older multibyte encodings. UTF-8, UTF-16 and UTF-32 require the programmer to know that the fixed-size code units are different than the "characters", the main difficulty currently is incorrectly designed APIs that attempt to hide this difference (UTF-32 does make *code points* fixed-sized, but these are not "characters" due to composing codes).

Implementations

Some languages, such as C++ and Ruby, normally allow the contents of a string to be changed after it has been created; these are termed *mutable* strings. In other languages, such as Java and Python, the value is fixed and a new string must be created if any alteration is to be made; these are termed *immutable* strings (some of these languages also provide another type that is mutable, such as Java and .NET `StringBuilder`, the thread-safe Java `StringBuffer`, and the Cocoa `NSMutableString`).

Strings are typically implemented as arrays of bytes, characters, or code units, in order to allow fast access to individual units or substrings—including characters when they have a fixed length. A few languages such as Haskell implement them as linked lists instead. Some languages, such as Prolog and Erlang, avoid implementing a dedicated string datatype at all, instead adopting the convention of representing strings as lists of character codes.

Representations

Representations of strings depend heavily on the choice of character repertoire and the method of character encoding. Older string implementations were designed to work with repertoire and encoding defined by ASCII, or more recent extensions like the ISO 8859 series. Modern implementations often use the extensive repertoire defined by Unicode along with a variety of complex encodings such as UTF-8 and UTF-16.

The term *byte string* usually indicates a general-purpose string of bytes, rather than strings of only (readable) characters, strings of bits, or such. Byte strings often imply that bytes can take any value and any data can be stored as-is, meaning that there should be no value interpreted as a termination value.

Most string implementations are very similar to variable-length arrays with the entries storing the character codes of corresponding characters. The principal difference is that, with certain encodings, a single logical character may take up more than one entry in the array. This happens for example with UTF-8, where single codes (UCS code points) can take anywhere from one to four bytes, and single characters can take an arbitrary number of codes. In these cases, the logical length of the string (number of characters) differs from the physical length of the array (number of bytes in use). UTF-32 avoids the first part of the problem.

Null-terminated

The length of a string can be stored implicitly by using a special terminating character; often this is the null character (NUL), which has all bits zero, a convention used and perpetuated by the popular C programming language. Hence, this representation is commonly referred to as a C string. This representation of an n-character string takes n + 1 space (1 for the terminator), and is thus an implicit data structure.

In terminated strings, the terminating code is not an allowable character in any string. Strings with *length* field do not have this limitation and can also store arbitrary binary data.An example of a *null-terminated string* stored in a 10-byte buffer, along with its ASCII (or more modern UTF-8) representation as 8-bit hexadecimal numbers is:

F	R	A	N	K	NUL	k	e	f	w
46_{16}	52_{16}	41_{16}	$4E_{16}$	$4B_{16}$	00_{16}	$6B_{16}$	65_{16}	66_{16}	77_{16}

The length of the string in the above example, "FRANK", is 5 characters, but it occupies 6 bytes. Characters after the terminator do not form part of the representation; they may be either part of other data or just garbage. (Strings of this form are sometimes called *ASCIZ strings*, after the original assembly language directive used to declare them).

Byte- and Bit-terminated

Using a special byte other than null for terminating strings has historically appeared in both hardware and software, though sometimes with a value that was also a printing character. $ was used by many assembler systems, : used by CDC systems (this character had a value of zero), and the ZX80 used "since this was the string delimiter in its BASIC language.

Somewhat similar, "data processing" machines like the IBM 1401 used a special word mark bit to delimit strings at the left, where the operation would start at the right. This bit had to be clear in all other parts of the string. This meant that, while the IBM 1401 had a seven-bit word, almost no-one ever thought to use this as a feature, and override the assignment of the seventh bit to (for example) handle ASCII codes.

Early microcomputer software relied upon the fact that ASCII codes do not use the high-order bit, and set it to indicate the end of a string. It must be reset to 0 prior to output.

Length-prefixed

The length of a string can also be stored explicitly, for example by prefixing the string with the length as a byte value. This convention is used in many Pascal dialects; as a consequence, some people call such a string a Pascal string or P-string. Storing the string length as byte limits the maximum string length to 255. To avoid such limitations, improved implementations of P-strings use 16-, 32-, or 64-bit words to store the string length. When the *length* field covers the address space, strings are limited only by the available memory.

If the length is bounded, then it can be encoded in constant space, typically a machine word, thus leading to an implicit data structure, taking $n + k$ space, where k is the number of characters in a word (8 for 8-bit ASCII on a 64-bit machine, 1 for 32-bit UTF-32/UCS-4 on a 32-bit machine, etc.). If the length is not bounded, encoding a length n takes $\log(n)$ space, so length-prefixed strings are a succinct data structure, encoding a string of length n in $\log(n) + n$ space.

In the latter case, the length-prefix field itself doesn't have fixed length, therefore the actual string data needs to be moved when the string grows such that the length field needs to be increased.

Here is a Pascal string stored in a 10-byte buffer, along with its ASCII / UTF-8 representation:

length	F	R	A	N	K	k	e	f	w
05_{16}	46_{16}	52_{16}	41_{16}	$4E_{16}$	$4B_{16}$	$6B_{16}$	65_{16}	66_{16}	77_{16}

Strings as Records

Many languages, including object-oriented ones, implement strings as records with an internal structure like:

```
class string {

  size_t length;

  char *text;

};
```

However, since the implementation is usually hidden, the string must be accessed and modified through member functions. `text` is a pointer to a dynamically allocated memory area, which might be expanded as needed.

Other Representations

Both character termination and length codes limit strings: For example, C character arrays that contain null (NUL) characters cannot be handled directly by C string library functions: Strings using a length code are limited to the maximum value of the length code. Both of these limitations can be overcome by clever programming.

It is possible to create data structures and functions that manipulate them that do not have the problems associated with character termination and can in principle overcome length code bounds. It is also possible to optimize the string represented using techniques from run length encoding (replacing repeated characters by the character value and a length) and Hamming encoding.

While these representations are common, others are possible. Using ropes makes certain string operations, such as insertions, deletions, and concatenations more efficient. The core data structure in a text editor is the one that manages the string (sequence of characters) that represents the current state of the file being edited. While that state could be stored in a single long consecutive array of characters, a typical text editor instead uses an alternative representation as its sequence data structure—a gap buffer, a linked list of lines, a piece table, or a rope—which makes certain string operations, such as insertions, deletions, and undoing previous edits, more efficient.

Security Concerns

The differing memory layout and storage requirements of strings can affect the security of the program accessing the string data. String representations requiring a terminating character are commonly susceptible to buffer overflow problems if the terminating character is not present, caused by a coding error or an attacker deliberately altering the data. String representations adopting a separate length field are also susceptible if the length can be manipulated. In such cases, program code accessing the string data requires bounds checking to ensure that it does not inadvertently access or change data outside of the string memory limits.

String data is frequently obtained from user input to a program. As such, it is the responsibility of the program to validate the string to ensure that it represents the expected format. Performing limited or no validation of user input can cause a program to be vulnerable to code injection attacks.

Non-text Strings

While character strings are very common uses of strings, a string in computer science may refer generically to any sequence of homogeneously typed data. A bit string or byte string, for example, may be used to represent non-textual binary data retrieved from a communications medium. This data may or may not be represented by a string-specific datatype, depending on the needs of the application, the desire of the programmer, and the capabilities of the programming language being used. If the programming language's string implementation is not 8-bit clean, data corruption may ensue.

C programmers draw a sharp distinction between a "string", aka a "string of characters", which by definition is always null terminated, vs. a "byte string" or "pseudo string" which may be stored in the same array but is often not null terminated. Using C string handling functions on such a "byte string" often seems to work, but later leads to security problems.

String Processing Algorithms

There are many algorithms for processing strings, each with various trade-offs. Competing algorithms can be analyzed with respect to run time, storage requirements, and so forth.

Some categories of algorithms include:

- String searching algorithms for finding a given substring or pattern.
- String manipulation algorithms.
- Sorting algorithms.
- Regular expression algorithms.
- Parsing a string.
- Sequence mining.

Advanced string algorithms often employ complex mechanisms and data structures, among them suffix trees and finite state machines. The name *stringology* was coined in 1984 by computer scientist Zvi Galil for the issue of algorithms and data structures used for string processing.

Character String-oriented Languages and Utilities

Character strings are such a useful datatype that several languages have been designed in order to make string processing applications easy to write. Examples include the following languages:

- Awk.

- Icon.

- MUMPS.

- Perl.

- Rexx.

- Ruby.

- Sed.

- SNOBOL.

- Tcl.

- TTM.

Many Unix utilities perform simple string manipulations and can be used to easily program some powerful string processing algorithms. Files and finite streams may be viewed as strings. Some APIs like Multimedia Control Interface, embedded SQL or printf use strings to hold commands that will be interpreted.

Recent scripting programming languages, including Perl, Python, Ruby, and Tcl employ regular expressions to facilitate text operations. Perl is particularly noted for its regular expression use, and many other languages and applications implement Perl compatible regular expressions. Some languages such as Perl and Ruby support string interpolation, which permits arbitrary expressions to be evaluated and included in string literals.

Character String Functions

String functions are used to create strings or change the contents of a mutable string. They also are used to query information about a string. The set of functions and their names varies depending on the computer programming language.

The most basic example of a string function is the string length function – the function that returns the length of a string (not counting any terminator characters or any of the string's internal structural information) and does not modify the string. This function is often named `length` or `len`. For example, `length("hello world")` would return 11.

Another common function is concatenation, where a new string is created by appending two strings, often this is the + addition operator.

Some microprocessor's instruction set architectures contain direct support for string operations, such as block copy (e.g. In intel x86m `REPNZ MOVSB`).

Formal Theory

Let Σ be a finite set of symbols (alternatively called characters), called the alphabet. No assumption is made about the nature of the symbols. A string (or word) over Σ is any finite sequence of symbols from Σ. For example, if $\Sigma = \{0, 1\}$, then *01011* is a string over Σ.

The *length* of a string s is the number of symbols in s (the length of the sequence) and can be any non-negative integer; it is often denoted as $|s|$. The *empty string* is the unique string over Σ of length 0, and is denoted ε or λ. The set of all strings over Σ of length n is denoted Σ^n. For example, if $\Sigma = \{0, 1\}$, then $\Sigma^2 = \{00, 01, 10, 11\}$. Note that $\Sigma^0 = \{\varepsilon\}$ for any alphabet Σ.

The set of all strings over Σ of any length is the Kleene closure of Σ and is denoted Σ^*. In terms of Σ^n,

$$\Sigma^* = \bigcup_{n \in \mathbb{N} \cup \{0\}} \Sigma^n .$$

For example, if $\Sigma = \{0, 1\}$, then $\Sigma^* = \{\varepsilon, 0, 1, 00, 01, 10, 11, 000, 001, 010, 011, ...\}$. Although the set Σ^* itself is countably infinite, each element of Σ^* is a string of finite length. A set of strings over Σ (i.e. any subset of Σ^*) is called a *formal language* over Σ. For example, if $\Sigma = \{0, 1\}$, the set of strings with an even number of zeros, $\{\varepsilon, 1, 00, 11, 001, 010, 100, 111, 0000, 0011, 0101, 0110, 1001, 1010, 1100, 1111, ...\}$, is a formal language over Σ.

Concatenation and Substrings

Concatenation is an important binary operation on Σ^*. For any two strings s and t in Σ^*, their concatenation is defined as the sequence of symbols in s followed by the sequence of characters in t, and is denoted st. For example, if $\Sigma = \{a, b, ..., z\}$, $s = $ `bear,` and $t = $ `hug`, then $st = $ `bearhug` and $ts = $ `hugbear`.

String concatenation is an associative, but non-commutative operation. The empty string ε serves as the identity element; for any string s, $\varepsilon s = s\varepsilon = s$. Therefore, the set Σ^* and the concatenation operation form a monoid, the free monoid generated by Σ. In addition, the length function defines a monoid homomorphism from Σ^* to the non-negative integers (that is, a function $L : \Sigma^* \mapsto \mathbb{N} \cup \{0\},$, such that $L(st) = L(s) + L(t) \quad \forall s, t \in \Sigma^*.$).

A string s is said to be a *substring* or *factor* of t if there exist (possibly empty) strings u and v such that $t = usv$. The relation "is a substring of" defines a partial order on Σ^*, the least element of which is the empty string.

Prefixes and Suffixes

A string s is said to be a prefix of t if there exists a string u such that $t = su$. If u is non-empty, s is said to be a *proper* prefix of t. Symmetrically, a string s is said to be a suffix of t if there exists a string u such that $t = us$. If u is nonempty, s is said to be a *proper* suffix of t. Suffixes and prefixes are substrings of t. Both the relations "is a prefix of" and "is a suffix of" are prefix orders.

Reversal

The reverse of a string is a string with the same symbols but in reverse order. For example, if s = abc (where a, b, and c are symbols of the alphabet), then the reverse of s is cba. A string that is the reverse of itself (e.g., s = madam) is called a palindrome, which also includes the empty string and all strings of length 1.

Rotations

A string $s = uv$ is said to be a rotation of t if $t = vu$. For example, if Σ = {0, 1} the string 0011001 is a rotation of 0100110, where u = 00110 and v = 01. As another example, the string abc has three different rotations, viz. abc itself (with u=abc, v=ε), bca (with u=bc, v=a), and cab (with u=c, v=ab).

Lexicographical Ordering

It is often useful to define an ordering on a set of strings. If the alphabet Σ has a total order (cf. alphabetical order) one can define a total order on Σ^* called lexicographical order. For example, if Σ = {0, 1} and 0 < 1, then the lexicographical order on Σ^* includes the relationships ε < 0 < 00 < 000 < ... < 0001 < 001 < 01 < 010 < 011 < 0110 < 01111 < 1 < 10 < 100 < 101 < 111 < 1111 < 11111 ... The lexicographical order is total if the alphabetical order is, but isn't well-founded for any nontrivial alphabet, even if the alphabetical order is.

String Operations

A number of additional operations on strings commonly occur in the formal theory.

Topology

Strings admit the following interpretation as nodes on a graph, where k is the number of symbols in Σ:

- Fixed-length strings of length n can be viewed as the integer locations in an n-dimensional hypercube with sides of length $k-1$.

- Variable-length strings (of finite length) can be viewed as nodes on a perfect k-ary tree.

- Infinite strings (otherwise not considered here) can be viewed as infinite paths on a k-node complete graph.

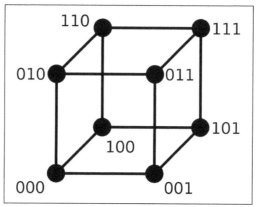

(Hyper)cube of binary strings of length 3.

The natural topology on the set of fixed-length strings or variable-length strings is the discrete topology, but the natural topology on the set of infinite strings is the limit topology, viewing the set of infinite strings as the inverse limit of the sets of finite strings. This is the construction used for the p-adic numbers and some constructions of the Cantor set, and yields the same topology. Isomorphisms between string representations of topologies can be found by normalizing according to the lexicographically minimal string rotation.

Substring

A substring is a contiguous sequence of characters within a string. For instance, "*the best of*" is a substring of "*It was the best of times*". This is not to be confused with subsequence, which is a generalization of substring. For example, "*Itwastimes*" is a subsequence of "*It was the best of times*", but not a substring.

"string" is a substring of "substring".

Prefix and suffix are special cases of substring. A prefix of a string S is a substring of S that occurs at the *beginning* of S. A suffix of a string S is a substring that occurs at the *end* of S. The list of all substrings of the string "*apple*" would be "*apple*", "*appl*", "*pple*", "*app*", "*ppl*", "*ple*", "*ap*", "*pp*", "*pl*", "*le*", "*a*", "*p*", "*l*", "*e*", "". A string u is a substring (or factor) of a string t if there exists two strings p and s such that $t = pus$. In particular, the empty string is a substring of every string.

Example: The string $u =$ ana is equal to substrings (and subsequences) of $t =$ banana at two different offsets:

```
banana
 | | | | |
 ana| |
  | | |
  ana
```

The first occurrence is obtained with $p = b$ and $s =$ na, while the second occurrence is obtained with $p =$ ban and s being the empty string.

A substring of a string is a prefix of a suffix of the string, and equivalently a suffix of a prefix. If u is a substring of t, it is also a subsequence, which is a more general concept. The occurrences of a given pattern in a given string can be found with a string searching algorithm. Finding the longest string which is equal to a substring of two or more strings is known as the longest common substring problem.

Prefix

A string p is a prefix of a string t if there exists a string s such that $t = ps$. A *proper prefix* of a string is not equal to the string itself; some sources in addition restrict a proper prefix to be non-empty. A prefix can be seen as a special case of a substring.

Example: The string ban is equal to a prefix (and substring and subsequence) of the string banana:

```
banana
| | |
ban
```

The square subset symbol is sometimes used to indicate a prefix, so that $p \sqsubseteq t$ denotes that p is a prefix of t. This defines a binary relation on strings, called the prefix relation, which is a particular kind of prefix order.

Suffix

A string s is a suffix of a string t if there exists a string p such that $t = ps$. A *proper suffix* of a string is not equal to the string itself. A more restricted interpretation is that it is also not empty. A suffix can be seen as a special case of a substring.

Example: The string `nana` is equal to a suffix (and substring and subsequence) of the string banana:

```
banana
   | | | |
   nana
```

A suffix tree for a string is a trie data structure that represents all of its suffixes. Suffix trees have large numbers of applications in string algorithms. The suffix array is a simplified version of this data structure that lists the start positions of the suffixes in alphabetically sorted order; it has many of the same applications.

Border

A border is suffix and prefix of the same string, e.g. "bab" is a border of "babab" (and also of "babooneatingakebab").

Superstring

A superstring of a finite set P of strings is a single string that contains every string in P as a substring. For example, bcclabccefab is a superstring of P = {abcc, efab, bccla}, and efabccla is a shorter one. Generally, one is interested in finding superstrings whose length is as small as possible; a concatenation of all strings of P in any order gives a trivial superstring of P. A string that contains every possible permutation of a specified character set is called a superpermutation.

Variable

In computer programming, a variable or scalar is a storage address (identified by a memory address) paired with an associated symbolic name, which contains some known or unknown quantity of information referred to as a *value*. The variable name is the usual way to reference the stored value, in addition to referring to the variable itself, depending on the context. This separation of name and content allows the name to be used independently of the exact information it represents. The identifier in computer source code can be bound to a value during run time, and the value of the variable may thus change during the course of program execution.

Variables in programming may not directly correspond to the concept of variables in mathematics. The latter is abstract, having no reference to a physical object such as storage address. The value of a computing variable is not necessarily part of an equation or formula as in mathematics. Variables in computer programming are frequently given long names to make them relatively descriptive of their use, whereas variables in mathematics often have terse, one- or two-character names for brevity in transcription and manipulation.

A variable's storage address may be referenced by several different identifiers, a situation known as aliasing. Assigning a value to the variable using one of the identifiers will change the value that can be accessed through the other identifiers.

Compilers have to replace variables' symbolic names with the actual addresses of the data. While a variable's name, type, and address often remain fixed, the data stored in the address may be changed during program execution.

Actions on a Variable

In imperative programming languages, values can generally be accessed or changed at any time. In pure functional and logic languages, variables are bound to expressions and keep a single value during their entire lifetime due to the requirements of referential transparency. In imperative languages, the same behavior is exhibited by (named) constants (symbolic constants), which are typically contrasted with (normal) variables.

Depending on the type system of a programming language, variables may only be able to store a specified data type (e.g. integer or string). Alternatively, a datatype may be associated only with the current value, allowing a single variable to store anything supported by the programming language.

Variables and scope:

- Automatic variables: Each local variable in a function comes into existence only when the function is called, and disappears when the function is exited. Such variables are known as automatic variables.

- External variables: These are variables that are external to a function on and can be accessed by name by any function. These variables remain in existence permanently; rather that appearing and disappearing as functions are called and exited, retain their values even after the functions that set them have returned.

Identifiers Referencing a Variable

An identifier referencing a variable can be used to access the variable in order to read out the value, or alter the value, or edit other attributes of the variable, such as access permission, locks, semaphores, etc.

For instance, a variable might be referenced by the identifier "total_count" and the variable can contain the number 1956. If the same variable is referenced by the identifier "r" as well, and if using this identifier "r", the value of the variable is altered to

2009, then reading the value using the identifier "`total_count`" will yield a result of 2009 and not 1956.

If a variable is only referenced by a single identifier that can simply be called *the name of the variable*. Otherwise, we can speak of *one of the names of the variable*. For instance, in the previous example, the "`total_count`" is a name of the variable in question, and "`r`" is another name of the same variable.

Typing

In statically typed languages such as Java or ML, a variable also has a *type*, meaning that only certain kinds of values can be stored in it. For example, a variable of type "integer" is prohibited from storing text values.

In dynamically typed languages such as Python, it is values, not variables, which carry type. In Common Lisp, both situations exist simultaneously: A variable is given a type (if undeclared, it is assumed to be T, the universal supertype) which exists at compile time. Values also have types, which can be checked and queried at runtime.

Typing of variables also allows polymorphisms to be resolved at compile time. However, this is different from the polymorphism used in object-oriented function calls (referred to as *virtual functions* in C++) which resolves the call based on the value type as opposed to the supertypes the variable is allowed to have.

Variables often store simple data, like integers and literal strings, but some programming languages allow a variable to store values of other datatypes as well. Such languages may also enable functions to be parametric polymorphic. These functions operate like variables to represent data of multiple types. For example, a function named `length` may determine the length of a list. Such a `length` function may be parametric polymorphic by including a type variable in its type signature, since the number of elements in the list is independent of the elements' types.

Parameters

The *formal parameters* (or *formal arguments*) of functions are also referred to as variables. For instance, in this Python code segment,

```
>>> def addtwo(x):
...        return x + 2
...
>>> addtwo(5)
7
```

the variable named x is a *parameter* because it is given a value when the function is called. The integer 5 is the *argument* which gives x its value. In most languages, function parameters have local scope. This specific variable named x can only be referred to within the addtwo function (though of course other functions can also have variables called x).

Memory Allocation

The specifics of variable allocation and the representation of their values vary widely, both among programming languages and among implementations of a given language. Many language implementations allocate space for *local variables*, whose extent lasts for a single function call on the *call stack*, and whose memory is automatically reclaimed when the function returns. More generally, in *name binding*, the name of a variable is bound to the address of some particular block (contiguous sequence) of bytes in memory, and operations on the variable manipulate that block. Referencing is more common for variables whose values have large or unknown sizes when the code is compiled. Such variables reference the location of the value instead of storing the value itself, which is allocated from a pool of memory called the *heap*.

Bound variables have values. A value, however, is an abstraction, an idea; in implementation, a value is represented by some *data object*, which is stored somewhere in computer memory. The program, or the runtime environment, must set aside memory for each data object and, since memory is finite, ensure that this memory is yielded for reuse when the object is no longer needed to represent some variable's value.

Objects allocated from the heap must be reclaimed—especially when the objects are no longer needed. In a garbage-collected language (such as C#, Java, Python, Golang and Lisp), the runtime environment automatically reclaims objects when extant variables can no longer refer to them. In non-garbage-collected languages, such as C, the program (and the programmer) must explicitly allocate memory, and then later free it, to reclaim its memory. Failure to do so leads to memory leaks, in which the heap is depleted as the program runs, risks eventual failure from exhausting available memory.

When a variable refers to a data structure created dynamically, some of its components may be only indirectly accessed through the variable. In such circumstances, garbage collectors (or analogous program features in languages that lack garbage collectors) must deal with a case where only a portion of the memory reachable from the variable needs to be reclaimed.

Naming Conventions

Unlike their mathematical counterparts, programming variables and constants commonly take multiple-character names, e.g. COST or total. Single-character names are most commonly used only for auxiliary variables; for instance, i, j, k for array index variables.

Some naming conventions are enforced at the language level as part of the language syntax which involves the format of valid identifiers. In almost all languages, variable names cannot start with a digit (0–9) and cannot contain whitespace characters. Whether or not punctuation marks are permitted in variable names varies from language to language; many languages only permit the underscore ("_") in variable names and forbid all other punctuation. In some programming languages, sigils (symbols or punctuation) are affixed to variable identifiers to indicate the variable's datatype or scope.

Case-sensitivity of variable names also varies between languages and some languages require the use of a certain case in naming certain entities; Most modern languages are case-sensitive; some older languages are not. Some languages reserve certain forms of variable names for their own internal use; in many languages, names beginning with two underscores ("__") often fall under this category.

However, beyond the basic restrictions imposed by a language, the naming of variables is largely a matter of style. At the machine code level, variable names are not used, so the exact names chosen do not matter to the computer. Thus names of variables identify them, for the rest they are just a tool for programmers to make programs easier to write and understand. Using poorly chosen variable names can make code more difficult to review than non-descriptive names, so names which are clear are often encouraged.

Programmers often create and adhere to code style guidelines which offer guidance on naming variables or impose a precise naming scheme. Shorter names are faster to type but are less descriptive; longer names often make programs easier to read and the purpose of variables easier to understand. However, extreme verbosity in variable names can also lead to less comprehensible code.

Variable Types (Based on Lifetime)

In terms of the classifications of variables, we can classify variables based on the lifetime of them. The different types of variables are static, stack-dynamic, explicit heap-dynamic, and implicit heap-dynamic. A static variable is also known as global variable, it is bound to a memory cell before execution begins and remains to the same memory cell until termination. A typical example is the static variables in C and C++. A Stack-dynamic variable is known as local variable, which is bound when the declaration statement is executed, and it is deallocated when the procedure returns. The main examples are local variables in C subprograms and Java methods. Explicit Heap-Dynamic variables are nameless (abstract) memory cells that are allocated and deallocated by explicit run-time instructions specified by the programmer. The main examples are dynamic objects in C++ (via new and delete) and all objects in Java. Implicit Heap-Dynamic variables are bound to heap storage only when they are assigned values. Allocation and release occur when values are reassigned to variables. As a result, Implicit heap-dynamic variables have the highest degree of flexibility. The main examples are some variables in JavaScript, PHP and all variables in APL.

Local Variable

In computer science, a local variable is a variable that is given *local scope*. Local variable references in the function or block in which it is declared override the same variable name in the larger scope. In programming languages with only two levels of visibility, local variables are contrasted with global variables. On the other hand, many ALGOL-derived languages allow any number of nested levels of visibility, with private variables, functions, constants and types hidden within them, either by nested blocks or nested functions. Local variables are fundamental to procedural programming, and more generally modular programming: variables of local scope are used to avoid issues with side-effects that can occur with global variables.

Local variables may have a lexical or dynamic scope, though lexical (static) scoping is far more common. In lexical scoping (or lexical scope; also called static scoping or static scope), if a variable name's scope is a certain block, then its scope is the program text of the block definition: Within that block's text, the variable name exists, and is bound to the variable's value, but outside that block's text, the variable name does not exist. By contrast, in dynamic scoping (or dynamic scope), if a variable name's scope is a certain block, then its scope is that block and all functions transitively called by that block (except when overridden again by another declaration); after the block ends, the variable name does not exist. Some languages, like Perl and Common Lisp, allow the programmer to choose static or dynamic scoping when defining or redefining a variable. Examples of languages that use dynamic scoping include Logo, Emacs lisp, and the shell languages bash, dash, and the MirBSD Korn shell (mksh)'s "local" declaration. Most other languages provide lexically scoped local variables.

In most languages, local variables are automatic variables stored on the call stack directly. This means that when a recursive function calls itself, local variables in each instance of the function are given distinct addresses. Hence variables of this scope can be declared, written to, and read, without any risk of side-effects to functions outside of the block in which they are declared.

Programming languages that employ *call by value* semantics provide a called subroutine with its own local copy of the arguments passed to it. In most languages, these local parameters are treated the same as other local variables within the subroutine. In contrast, *call by reference* and *call by name* semantics allow the parameters to act as aliases of the values passed as arguments, allowing the subroutine to modify variables outside its own scope.

Static Local Variables

A special type of local variable, called a *static local*, is available in many mainstream languages (including C/C++, Visual Basic, and VB.NET) which allows a value to be retained from one call of the function to another – it is a static variable with local scope.

In this case, recursive calls to the function also have access to the (single, statically allocated) variable. In all of the above languages, static variables are declared as such with a special *storage class* keyword (e.g., `static`).

Static locals in global functions have the same lifetime as static global variables, because their value remains in memory for the life of the program, but have function scope (not global scope), as with automatic local variables. This is distinct from other usages of the `static` keyword, which has several different meanings in various languages.

Local Variables in Perl

Perl supports both dynamic and lexically-scoped local variables. The keyword `local` is used to define local dynamically-scoped variables, while `my` is used for local lexically-scoped variables. Since dynamic scoping is less common today, the Perl documentation warns that "`local` isn't what most people think of as "local". Instead, the `local` keyword gives a temporary, dynamically-scoped value to a global (package) variable, which lasts until the end of the enclosing block. However, the variable is visible to any function called from within the block. To create lexically-scoped local variables, use the `my` operator instead.

To understand how it works consider the following code:

```
$a = 1;
sub f() {
    local $a;
    $a = 2;
    g();
}
sub g() {
    print "$a\n";
}
g();
f();
g();
```

this will output:

```
1
2
1
```

This happens since the global variable $a is modified to a new *temporary* (local) meaning inside f(), but the global value is restored upon leaving the scope of f(). Using my in this case instead of local would have printed 1 three times since in that case the $a variable would be limited to the static scope of the function f() and not seen by g(). Randal L. Schwartz and Tom Phoenix argue that the operator local should have had a different name like save.

Local Variables in Ruby

Ruby as a language was inspired also by Perl, but in this case, the notation was made simpler: a global variable name must be preceded by a $ sign, like $variable_name, while a local variable has simply no $ sign in front of its name, like variable_name (while in perl all scalar values have a $ in front). Ruby only provides built-in support for statically-scoped local variables like Perl's my, not dynamically-scoped local variables like Perl's local. There is at least one library for Ruby that provides dynamically-scoped variables.

Global Variable

In computer programming, a global variable is a variable with global scope, meaning that it is visible (hence accessible) throughout the program, unless shadowed. The set of all global variables is known as the *global environment* or *global state*. In compiled languages, global variables are generally static variables, whose extent (lifetime) is the entire runtime of the program, though in interpreted languages (including command-line interpreters), global variables are generally dynamically allocated when declared, since they are not known ahead of time.

In some languages, all variables are global, or global by default, while in most modern languages variables have limited scope, generally lexical scope, though global variables are often available by declaring a variable at the top level of the program. In other languages, however, global variables do not exist; these are generally modular programming languages that enforce a module structure, or class-based object-oriented programming languages that enforce a class structure.

Use

Interaction mechanisms with global variables are called global environment mechanisms. The global environment paradigm is contrasted with the local environment paradigm, where all variables are local with no shared memory (and therefore all interactions can be reconducted to message passing).

Global variables are used extensively to pass information between sections of code that do not share a caller/callee relation like concurrent threads and signal handlers. Languages (including C) where each file defines an implicit namespace eliminate most of the problems seen with languages with a global namespace though some problems may persist without proper encapsulation. Without proper locking (such as with a mutex), code using global variables will not be thread-safe except for read only values in protected memory.

Environment Variables

Environment variables are a facility provided by some operating systems. Within the OS's shell (ksh in Unix, bash in Linux, COMMAND.COM in DOS and CMD.EXE in Windows) they are a kind of variable: For instance, in unix and related systems an ordinary variable becomes an environment variable when the `export` keyword is used. Program code other than shells has to access them by API calls, such as `getenv()` and `setenv()`.

They are local to the process in which they were set. That means if we open two terminal windows (Two different processes running shell) and change value of environment variable in one window, that change will not be seen by other window.

When a child process is created, it inherits all the environment variables and their values from the parent process. Usually, when a program calls another program, it first creates a child process by forking, then the child adjusts the environment as needed and lastly the child replaces itself with the program to be called. Child processes therefore cannot use environment variables to communicate with their peers, avoiding the action at a distance problem.

Global-only and Global-by-default

A number of non-structured languages, such as (early versions of) BASIC, COBOL and Fortran I only provide global variables. Fortran II introduced subroutines with local variables, and the COMMON keyword for accessing global variables. Usage of COMMON in FORTRAN continued in FORTRAN 77, and influenced later languages such as PL/SQL. Named COMMON groups for globals behave somewhat like structured namespaces. Variables are also global by default in FORTH, Lua, Perl, and most shells.

By Language

C and C++

The C language does not have a `global` keyword. However, variables declared outside a function have "file scope," meaning they are visible within the file. Variables declared with file scope are visible between their declaration and the end of the compilation unit (`.c` file) (unless shadowed by a like-named object in a nearer scope, such as a local variable); and they implicitly have external linkage and are thus visible to not only the `.c` file or compilation unit containing their declarations but also to every other compilation unit that is linked to form the complete program. External linkage, however, is not sufficient for such a variable's use in other files: For a compilation unit to correctly access such a global variable, it will need to know its type. This is accomplished by declaring the variable in each file using the extern keyword. (It will be *declared* in each file but may be *defined* in only one.) Such extern declarations are often placed in a shared header file, since it is common practice for all .c files in a project to include at least one .h file: the standard header file errno.h is an example, making the errno variable accessible to all modules in a project. Where this global access mechanism is judged problematic, it can be disabled using the static keyword which restricts a variable to file scope, and will cause attempts to import it with extern to raise a compilation (or linking) error.

An example of a "global" variable in C:

```c
#include <stdio.h>


// This is the file-scope variable (with internal linkage), visible only in
// this compilation unit.
static int shared = 3;


// This one has external linkage (not limited to this compilation unit).
extern int over_shared;


// Also internal linkage.
int over_shared_too = 2;


static void ChangeShared() {
    // Reference to the file-scope variable in a function.
    shared = 5;
}


static void LocalShadow() {
    // Local variable that will hide the global of the same name.
    int shared;
```

```
  // This will affect only the local variable and will have no effect on
the

  // file-scope variable of the same name.

  shared = 1000;

}


static void ParamShadow(int shared) {

  // This will affect only the parameter and will have no effect on the
file-

  // scope variable of the same name.

  shared = -shared;

}


int main() {

  // Reference to the file-scope variable.


  printf("%d\n", shared);


  ChangeShared();


  printf("%d\n", shared);


  LocalShadow();


  printf("%d\n", shared);


  ParamShadow(1);


  printf("%d\n", shared);
```

```
    return 0;

}
```

As the variable is an external one, there is no need to pass it as a parameter to use it in a function besides main. It belongs to every function in the module.

The output will be:

3

5

5

5

Java

Some languages, like Java, don't have global variables. In Java, all variables that are not local variables are fields of a class. Hence all variables are in the scope of either a class or a method. In Java, static fields (also known as class variables) exist independently of any instances of the class and one copy is shared among all instances; hence public static fields are used for many of the same purposes as global variables in other languages because of their similar "sharing" behavior:

```
public class Global {

    public static int a;

}
```

PHP

PHP has a `global` keyword and a number of unusual ways of using global variables. Variables declared outside functions have file scope (which is for most purposes the widest scope). However, they are not accessible inside functions unless imported with the `global` keyword (i.e., the keyword *accesses* global variables, it does not *declare* them).

However, some predefined variables, known as *superglobals* are always accessible. They are all arrays. A general purpose one is the `$GLOBALS` superglobal, which contains all the variables defined out of function scope. Changes to its elements change the original variables, and additions create new variables. The superglobals `$_POST` and `$_GET` are widely used in web programming.

Other Languages

- In Python and MATLAB a global variable can be declared anywhere with the global keyword.

• Ruby's global variables are distinguished by a '$' sigil. A number of predefined globals exist, for instance $$ is the current process ID.

Instance Variable

In object-oriented programming with classes, an instance variable is a variable defined in a class (i.e. a member variable), for which each instantiated object of the class has a separate copy, or instance. An instance variable is similar to a class variable. An instance variable is a variable which is declared in a class but outside the constructor and the method/function. Instance variables are created when an object is instantiated, and are accessible to all the methods, the constructor and block in the class. Access modifiers can be given to the instance variable.

An instance variable is not a class variable although there are similarities. It is a type of class attribute (or class property, field, or data member). The same dichotomy between *instance* and *class* members applies to methods ("member functions") as well; a class may have both instance methods and class methods. Each instance variable lives in memory for the life of the object it is owned by.

Variables are properties an object knows about itself. All instances of an object have their own copies of instance variables, even if the value is the same from one object to another. One object instance can change values of its instance variables without affecting all other instances. Instance variables can be used by all methods of a class unless the method is declared as static.

Example:

```
struct Request {


    static int count1; // variable name is not of importance

    int number;


    Request() {
       number = count1; // modifies the instance variable "this->number"

        ++count1; // modifies the class variable "Request::count1"

    }


};


int Request::count1 = 0;
```

In this C++ example, the instance variable `Request::number` is a copy of the class variable `Request::count1` where each instance constructed is assigned a sequential value of `count1` before it is incremented. Since `number` is an instance variable, each `Request` object contains its own distinct value; in contrast, there is only one object `Request::count1` available to all instances with the same value.

Steps in Variable

Here are the following three simple steps:

- Create variables with appropriate names.
- Store your values in those two variables.
- Retrieve and use the stored values from the variables.

Creating Variables

Creating variables is also called declaring variables in C programming. Different programming languages have different ways of creating variables inside a program. For example, C programming has the following simple way of creating variables:

```
#include <stdio.h>


int main() {

    int a;

    int b;

}
```

The above program creates two variables to reserve two memory locations with names a and b. We created these variables using int keyword to specify variable data type which means we want to store integer values in these two variables. Similarly, you can create variables to store long, float, char or any other data type. For example:

```
/* variable to store long value */

long a;


/* variable to store float value */

float b;
```

You can create variables of similar type by putting them in a single line but separated by comma as follows:

```
#include <stdio.h>


int main() {

    int a, b;

}
```

Listed below are the key points about variables that you need to keep in mind:

- A variable name can hold a single type of value. For example, if variable a has been defined int type, then it can store only integer.

- C programming language requires a variable creation, i.e., declaration before its usage in your program. You cannot use a variable name in your program without creating it, though programming language like Python allows you to use a variable name without creating it.

- You can use a variable name only once inside your program. For example, if a variable a has been defined to store an integer value, then you cannot define a again to store any other type of value.

- There are programming languages like Python, PHP, Perl, etc., which do not want you to specify data type at the time of creating variables. So you can store integer, float, or long without specifying their data type.

- You can give any name to a variable like age, sex, salary, year1990 or anything else you like to give, but most of the programming languages allow to use only limited characters in their variables names. For now, we will suggest to use only a....z, A....Z, 0....9 in your variable names and start their names using alphabets only instead of digits.

- Almost none of the programming languages allow to start their variable names with a digit, so 1990year will not be a valid variable name whereas year1990 or ye1990ar are valid variable names.

Store Values in Variables

Now, let's store some values in those variables:

```
#include <stdio.h>


int main() {
```

```
    int a;

    int b;


    a = 10;

    b = 20;

}
```

The above program has two additional statements where we are storing 10 in variable a and 20 is being stored in variable b. Almost all the programming languages have similar way of storing values in variable where we keep variable name in the left hand side of an equal sign = and whatever value we want to store in the variable, we keep that value in the right hand side.

Now, we have completed two steps, first we created two variables and then we stored required values in those variables. Now variable a has value 10 and variable b has value 20. In other words we can say, when above program is executed, the memory location named a will hold 10 and memory location b will hold 20.

Access Stored Values in Variables

If we do not use the stored values in the variables, then there is no point in creating variables and storing values in them. We know that the above program has two variables a and b and they store the values 10 and 20, respectively. So let's try to print the values stored in these two variables. Following is a C program, which prints the values stored in its variables:

```c
#include <stdio.h>


int main() {
    int a;
    int b;


    a = 10;
    b = 20;


    printf( "Value of a = %d\n", a );
    printf( "Value of b = %d\n", b );

}
```

When the above program is executed, it produces the following result:

```
Value of a = 10
Value of b = 20
```

We are making use of %d, which will be replaced with the values of the given variable in printf() statements. We can print both the values using a single printf() statement as follows:

```c
#include <stdio.h>


int main() {
    int a;
    int b;


    a = 10;
    b = 20;


    printf( "Value of a = %d and value of b = %d\n", a, b );
}
```

When the above program is executed, it produces the following result:

```
Value of a = 10 and value of b = 20
```

If you want to use float variable in C programming, then you will have to use %f instead of %d, and if you want to print a character value, then you will have to use %c. Similarly, different data types can be printed using different % and characters.

Variables in Java

Following is the equivalent program written in Java programming language. This program will create two variables a and b and very similar to C programming, it will assign 10 and 20 in these variables and finally print the values of the two variables in two ways:

```java
public class DemoJava {
    public static void main(String []args) {
        int a;
        int b;
```

```
    a = 10;
    b = 20;

    System.out.println("Value of a = " + a);
    System.out.println("Value of b = " + b);
    System.out.println("Value of a = " + a + " and value of b = " + b);

    }

}
```

When the above program is executed, it produces the following result:

```
Value of a = 10
Value of b = 20
Value of a = 10 and value of b = 20
```

Variables in Python

Following is the equivalent program written in Python. This program will create two variables a and b and at the same time, assign 10 and 20 in those variables. Python does not want you to specify the data type at the time of variable creation and there is no need to create variables in advance.

```
a = 10
b = 20

print "Value of a = ", a
print "Value of b = ", b
print "Value of a = ", a, " and value of b = ", b
```

When the above program is executed, it produces the following result:

```
Value of a =  10
Value of b =  20
Value of a =  10  and value of b =  20
```

You can use the following syntax in C and Java programming to declare variables and assign values at the same time:

```
#include <stdio.h>
```

```
int main() {
    int a = 10;
    int b = 20;


    printf( "Value of a = %d and value of b = %d\n", a, b );
}
```

When the above program is executed, it produces the following result:

```
Value of a = 10 and value of b = 20
```

References

- David R. Richardson (2002), The Book on Data Structures. iUniverse, 112 pages. ISBN 0-595-24039-9, ISBN 978-0-595-24039-5

- Introduction-to-arrays: geeksforgeeks.org, Retrieved 13 May, 2020

- "C++ STL vector: definition, growth factor, member functions". Archived from the original on 2015-08-06. Retrieved 2015-08-05

- Conrad Irwin. "LSpace: Dynamic scope for Ruby". December 2012 http://cirw.in/blog/lspace Retrieved 2013-10-16

- Computer-programming-variables, computer-programming: tutorialspoint.com, Retrieved 3 July, 2020

- Cpp-arrays, cplusplus: tutorialspoint.com, Retrieved 17 March, 2020

- "The Java Tutorials, Understanding Class Members". docs.oracle.com. Oracle. Archived from the original on 11 October 2014. Retrieved 23 October 2014

5
Programming Tools

Different types of tools are used in computer programming namely compilers, linkers, assemblers, disassemblers, load testers, performance analysts, GUI development tool, debuggers, PyScripter, etc. This chapter closely examines these programming tools to provide an extensive understanding of the subject.

A software or a programming tool is a set of computer programs that are used by the developers to create, maintain, debug, or support other applications and programs.

Software development tools are simply tools (generally software themselves) that programmers practice to create other software. For Example – language libraries, code editors, debuggers, etc. Any software deploy tool that enables a programmer to build stable software matching the needs or goals of a customer is placed into this category.

Agile development tools can be of different types like linkers, compilers, code editors, GUI designers, assemblers, debuggers, performance analysis tools, and many others. There are some factors that need to consider while selecting the corresponding development tool, based on the type of design.

Few of such factors are displayed below:

- Company criteria.

- Usefulness of tool.

- Integration of one tool with another.

- Choosing an appropriate environment.

- Learning curve.

Software development tools play a very important role in the IT field, although they are less substantial than the tools used by other professionals.Software development tools can be things like interpreters that work directly with code, but they can also be tools that help to make the lives of developers simpler and easier. For instance, while a user panel assigned to answering the questions of programmers and sharing knowledge might not have a direct influence on the development of a particular piece of software, but it does provide relevant solutions for developers who necessitate answers to vital questions.

So, you can find a very wide variety of other options in the category of software development tools. Anything that might help to boost the efficiency and accuracy can be conceivably be added to this category, including communication tools like Slack, libraries like Stack Overflow, and repositories like GitHub.

In other words, the selection of software engineering tools to be used in its development process can completely shape or break a project. Once the targeted ecosystem and programming languages are chosen, and the requirements and end goals are also well-enough understood, the next task is starting the work of a software development project is to choose the tools that will be utilized throughout the process. It's also important to be knowledgeable of the types of tools that are available for employment, their benefits, and the implications for using them.

You can find software development tools in many different places, and in numerous different configurations. For instance, APIs comprises of tools that enable software developers to achieve a specific goal, such as programming language libraries. SDKs include a very wide range of programming tools that allow programmers to create software for specific platforms and systems. Integrated development environments provide entire toolbars for programmers, allowing them to create programs in a single environment, test them in the same environment and even deploy them at the opportune time.

Many changes in IT happen as an indirect result of the development or induction of some other technological innovation. Some changes in the development of IT systems come and go faster as compared to fashion in clothing. IT trends are less like a straight timeline of incremental advances, and more like a churning cycle of twirling ideas that gain fame and then fall out of service as people strive to see what works and what doesn't, what's more effective, and vice versa.

Originally, software development tools hold only of those tools that are used during the actual design and testing phases of software development. However, today, there are software management tools that can be used throughout the software development life cycle. The original software development toolbox might have contained a basic text editor, as well as a linking loader, a compiler, and a tool for debugging software. Today, things are much more complicated, with tools that can be used during quality assurance, all phases of testing, and even during the design and deployment phases. Some examples of project management solution that helps developers organize and stay productive during projects are Microsoft Project, Wrike, etc.

Software development tools continue to evolve and change, as the needs of programmers grow. In the near future, we may be using more of our development efforts in developing systems that can emerge and acquire by themselves (machine learning), but someone still has to process those systems. Human power is still like to be needed to operate the tools.

SAS

SAS is a statistical software suite developed by SAS Institute for data management, advanced analytics, multivariate analysis, business intelligence, criminal investigation, and predictive analytics.

SAS is a software suite that can mine, alter, manage and retrieve data from a variety of sources and perform statistical analysis on it. SAS provides a graphical point-and-click user interface for non-technical users and more advanced options through the SAS language.

SAS programs have DATA steps, which retrieve and manipulate data, and PROC steps, which analyze the data. Each step consists of a series of statements.

The DATA step has executable statements that result in the software taking an action, and declarative statements that provide instructions to read a data set or alter the data's appearance. The DATA step has two phases: compilation and execution. In the compilation phase, declarative statements are processed and syntax errors are identified. Afterwards, the execution phase processes each executable statement sequentially. Data sets are organized into tables with rows called "observations" and columns called "variables". Additionally, each piece of data has a descriptor and a value.

The PROC step consists of PROC statements that call upon named procedures. Procedures perform analysis and reporting on data sets to produce statistics, analyses, and graphics. There are more than 300 named procedures and each one contains a substantial body of programming and statistical work.PROC statements can also display results, sort data or perform other operations. SAS macros are pieces of code or variables that are coded once and referenced to perform repetitive tasks.

SAS data can be published in HTML, PDF, Excel, RTF and other formats using the Output Delivery System, which was first introduced in 2007. The SAS Enterprise Guide is SAS's point-and-click interface. It generates code to manipulate data or perform analysis automatically and does not require SAS programming experience to use.

The SAS software suite has more than 200 components Some of the SAS components include:

- Base SAS : Basic procedures and data management.

- SAS/STAT : Statistical analysis.

- SAS/GRAPH : Graphics and presentation.

- SAS/OR : Operations research.

- SAS/ETS : Econometrics and Time Series Analysis.

- SAS/IML : Interactive matrix language.

- SAS/AF : Applications facility.

- SAS/QC : Quality control.

- SAS/INSIGHT : Data mining.

- SAS/PH : Clinical trial analysis.

- Enterprise Miner : Data mining.

- Enterprise Guide : GUI based code editor & project manager.

- SAS EBI : Suite of Business Intelligence Applications.

- SAS Grid Manager : Manager of SAS grid computing environment.

PyScripter

PyScripter is a free and open-source software Python integrated development environment (IDE) for Windows. It is built in Object Pascal and Python.

It originally started as a lightweight IDE designed to serve the purpose of providing a strong scripting solution for Delphi applications. Over time, it has evolved into a full-featured stand- alone Python IDE. It is built in Delphi using P4D and is extensible using Python scripts. Being built in a compiled language make it rather lightweight compared to some of the other IDEs. Currently, it is only available for Microsoft Windows operating systems.

Features

Syntax Highlighting Editor

PyScripter software interface.

- Unicode based.

- Full support for encoded Python source files.

- Brace highlighting.

- Python source code utilities: (un)tabify, (un)comment, (un)indent, etc.

- Code completion and call tips.

- Code and debugger hints.

- Syntax checking during typing.

- Context-sensitive help on Python keywords.

- Parameterized code templates.

- Accept files dropped from Explorer.

- File change notification.

- Converting line breaks in Windows, Unix, Macintosh.

- Print preview and print syntax highlighted Python code.

- Syntax highlighting of HTML, XML and CSS files.

- Split-view file editing.

- Firefox-like search and replace.

- Side-by-side file editing.

Integrated Python Interpreter

- Code completion.
- Call tips.
- Command history.
- Execute scripts without first saving.

Integrated Python Debugger

- Remote Python debugger.
- Call stack.
- Variables window.
- Watches window.
- Conditional breakpoints.
- Debugger hints.
- Post-mortem analysis.
- Can run or debug files without first saving.

Editor Views

- Disassembly.
- HTML documentation (pydoc).

File Explorer

- Easy configuration and browsing of the Python path.
- Integrated version control using Tortoise CVS or Tortoise SVN.

Project Manager

- Import extant directories.
- Multiple run configurations.

Integrated Unit Testing

- Automatic test generation.
- Unit testing GUI.

External Tools (External Run and Capture Output)

- Integration with Python tools such as PyLint, TabNanny, Profile, etc.

- Powerful parameter functionality for customized external tool integration.

Other

- Code explorer.

- Access to Python manuals via help menu.

- To do list.

- Find and replace in files.

- Integrated regular expression testing.

- Choice of Python version to run via command-line parameters.

- Run Python script externally, highly configurable.

- Find definition, references.

- Find definition by clicking and browsing history.

- Modern GUI with docked forms and configurable look and feel (themes).

- Persistent configurable IDE options.

Disassembler

A disassembler is a computer program that translates machine language into assembly language—the inverse operation to that of an assembler. A disassembler differs from a decompiler, which targets a high-level language rather than an assembly language. Disassembly, the output of a disassembler, is often formatted for human-readability rather than suitability for input to an assembler, making it principally a reverse-engineering tool.

Assembly language source code generally permits the use of constants and programmer comments. These are usually removed from the assembled machine code by the assembler. If so, a disassembler operating on the machine code would produce disassembly lacking these constants and comments; the disassembled output becomes more difficult for a human to interpret than the original annotated source code. Some disassemblers provide a built-in code commenting feature where the generated output gets enriched with comments regarding called API functions or parameters of called functions. Some disassemblers make use of the symbolic debugging information present in object files such as ELF. For example, IDA allows the human user to make up mnemonic symbols for values or regions of code in an interactive session: human insight applied to the disassembly process often parallels human creativity in the code writing process.

On CISC platforms with variable-width instructions, more than one disassembly may be valid. Disassemblers do not handle code that varies during execution.

Problems of Disassembly

Writing a disassembler which produces code which, when assembled, produces exactly the original binary is possible; however, there are often differences. This poses demands on the expressivity of the assembler. For example, an x86 assembler takes an arbitrary choice between two binary codes for something as simple as MOV AX, BX. If the original code uses the other choice, the original code simply cannot be reproduced at any given point in time. However, even when a fully correct disassembly is produced, problems remain if the program requires modification. For example, the same machine language jump instruction can be generated by assembly code to jump to a specified location (for example, to execute specific code), or to jump a specified number of bytes (for example, to skip over an unwanted branch). A disassembler cannot know what is intended, and may use either syntax to generate a disassembly which reproduces the original binary. However, if a programmer wants to add instructions between the jump instruction and its destination, it is necessary to understand the program's operation to determine whether the jump should be absolute or relative, i.e., whether its destination should remain at a fixed location, or be moved so as to skip both the original and added instructions.

Examples of Disassemblers

A disassembler may be stand-alone or interactive. A stand-alone disassembler, when executed, generates an assembly language file which can be examined; an interactive one shows the effect of any change the user makes immediately. For example, the disassembler may initially not know that a section of the program is actually code, and treat it as data; if the user specifies that it is code, the resulting disassembled code is shown immediately, allowing the user to examine it and take further action during the same run.

Any interactive debugger will include some way of viewing the disassembly of the program being debugged. Often, the same disassembly tool will be packaged as a stand-alone disassembler distributed along with the debugger. For example, objdump, part of GNU Binutils, is related to the interactive debugger gdb.

- Binary Ninja.

- DEBUG.

- Interactive Disassembler (IDA).

- Ghidra.

- Hiew.

- Hopper Disassembler.

- Netwide Disassembler (Ndisasm), companion to the Netwide Assembler (NASM).

- OLIVER (CICS interactive test/debug) includes disassemblers for Assembler, COBOL, and PL/1.

- OllyDbg is a 32-bit assembler level analysing debugger.

- Radare2.

- SIMON (batch interactive test/debug) includes disassemblers for Assembler, COBOL, and PL/1.

- Sourcer, a commenting 16-bit/32-bit disassembler for DOS, OS/2 and Windows by V Communications in the 1990s.

Disassemblers and Emulators

A dynamic disassembler can be incorporated into the output of an emulator or hypervisor to 'trace out', line-by-line, the real time execution of any executed machine instructions. In this case, as well as lines containing the disassembled machine code, the registers and/or data changes (or any other changes of "state", such as condition codes) that each individual instruction causes can be shown alongside or beneath the disassembled instruction. This provides extremely powerful debugging information for ultimate problem resolution, although the size of the resultant output can sometimes be quite large, especially if active for an entire program's execution. OLIVER provided these features from the early 1970s as part of its CICS debugging product offering and is now to be found incorporated into the XPEDITER product from Compuware.

Length Disassembler

A length disassembler, also known as length disassembler engine (LDE), is a tool that, given a sequence of bytes (instructions), outputs the number of bytes taken by the parsed instruction. Notable open source projects for the x86 architecture include ldisasm, Tiny x86 Length Disassembler and Extended Length Disassembler Engine for x86-64.

Debugger

A debugger or debugging tool is a computer program used to test and debug other programs (the "target" program). The main use of a debugger is to run the target program under controlled conditions that permit the programmer to track its operations in progress and monitor changes in computer resources (most often memory areas used by the target program or the computer's operating system) that may indicate malfunctioning code. Typical debugging facilities include the ability to run or halt the target program at specific points, display the contents of memory, CPU registers or storage devices (such as disk drives), and modify memory or register contents in order to enter selected test data that might be a cause of faulty program execution.

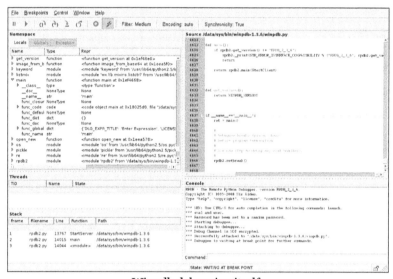

Winpdb debugging itself.

The code to be examined might alternatively be running on an *instruction set simulator* (ISS), a technique that allows great power in its ability to halt when specific conditions are encountered, but which will typically be somewhat slower than executing the code directly on the appropriate (or the same) processor. Some debuggers offer two modes of operation, full or partial simulation, to limit this impact.

A "trap" occurs when the program cannot normally continue because of a programming bug or invalid data. For example, the program might have tried to use an instruction not available on the current version of the CPU or attempted to access unavailable or protected memory. When the program "traps" or reaches a preset condition, the debugger typically shows the location in the original code if it is a source-level debugger or symbolic debugger, commonly now seen in integrated development environments. If it is a low-level debugger or a machine-language debugger it shows the line in the disassembly (unless it also has online access to the original source code and can display the appropriate section of code from the assembly or compilation).

Features

Typically, debuggers offer a query processor, a symbol resolver, an expression inter-preter, and a debug support interface at its top level. Debuggers also offer more sophis-ticated functions such as running a program step by step (single-stepping or program animation), stopping (breaking) (pausing the program to examine the current state) at some event or specified instruction by means of a breakpoint, and tracking the values of variables. Some debuggers have the ability to modify program state while it is running. It may also be possible to continue execution at a different location in the program to bypass a crash or logical error.

The same functionality which makes a debugger useful for correcting bugs allows it to be used as a software cracking tool to evade copy protection, digital rights man-agement, and other software protection features. It often also makes it useful as a general verification tool, fault coverage, and performance analyzer, especially if instruction path lengths are shown. Early microcomputers with disk-based storage often benefitted from the ability to diagnose and recover corrupted directory or reg-istry data records, to "undelete" files marked as deleted, or to crack file password protection.

Most mainstream debugging engines, such as gdb and dbx, provide console-based com-mand line interfaces. Debugger front-ends are popular extensions to debugger engines that provide IDE integration, program animation, and visualization features.

Record and Replay Debugging

"Record and replay debugging", also known as "software flight recording" or "program execution recording" captures application state changes and stores them to disk as each instruction in a program executes. The recording can then be replayed over and over, and interactively debugged to diagnose and resolve defects. Record and replay debug-ging is very useful for remote debugging and for resolving intermittent, non-determin-istic, and other hard-to-reproduce defects.

Reverse Debugging

Some debuggers include a feature called "reverse debugging", also known as "historical debugging" or "backwards debugging". These debuggers make it possible to step a pro-gram's execution backwards in time. Various debuggers include this feature. Microsoft Visual Studio offers IntelliTrace reverse debugging for C#, Visual Basic .NET, and some other languages, but not C++. Reverse debuggers also exist for C, C++, Java, Python, Perl, and other languages. Some are open source; some are proprietary commercial software. Some reverse debuggers slow down the target by orders of magnitude, but the best reverse debuggers cause a slowdown of 2× or less. Reverse debugging is very useful for certain types of problems, but is still not commonly used yet.

Language Dependency

Some debuggers operate on a single specific language while others can handle multiple languages transparently. For example, if the main target program is written in COBOL but calls assembly language subroutines and PL/1 subroutines, the debugger may have to dynamically switch modes to accommodate the changes in language as they occur.

Memory Protection

Some debuggers also incorporate memory protection to avoid storage violations such as buffer overflow. This may be extremely important in transaction processing environments where memory is dynamically allocated from memory 'pools' on a task by task basis.

Hardware Support for Debugging

Most modern microprocessors have at least one of these features in their CPU design to make debugging easier:

- Hardware support for single-stepping a program, such as the trap flag.

- An instruction set that meets the Popek and Goldberg virtualization requirements makes it easier to write debugger software that runs on the same CPU as the software being debugged; such a CPU can execute the inner loops of the program under test at full speed, and still remain under debugger control.

- In-system programming allows an external hardware debugger to reprogram a system under test (for example, adding or removing instruction breakpoints). Many systems with such ISP support also have other hardware debug support.

- Hardware support for code and data breakpoints, such as address comparators and data value comparators or, with considerably more work involved, page fault hardware.

- JTAG access to hardware debug interfaces such as those on ARM architecture processors or using the Nexus command set. Processors used in embedded systems typically have extensive JTAG debug support.

- Micro controllers with as few as six pins need to use low pin-count substitutes for JTAG, such as BDM, Spy-Bi-Wire, or debugWIRE on the Atmel AVR. DebugWIRE, for example, uses bidirectional signaling on the RESET pin.

Debugger Front-ends

Some of the most capable and popular debuggers implement only a simple command line interface (CLI)—often to maximize portability and minimize resource consumption.

Developers typically consider debugging via a graphical user interface (GUI) easier and more productive. This is the reason for visual front-ends, that allow users to monitor and control subservient CLI-only debuggers via graphical user interface. Some GUI debugger front-ends are designed to be compatible with a variety of CLI-only debuggers, while others are targeted at one specific debugger.

Automatic Programming

In computer science, the term automatic programming identifies a type of computer programming in which some mechanism generates a computer program to allow human programmers to write the code at a higher abstraction level. There has been little agreement on the precise definition of automatic programming, mostly because its meaning has changed over time. Program synthesis is one type of automatic programming where a procedure is created from scratch, based on mathematical requirements.

Generative Programming

Generative programming and the related term meta-programming are concepts whereby programs can be written "to manufacture software components in an automated way" just as automation has improved "production of traditional commodities such as garments, automobiles, chemicals, and electronics." The goal is to improve programmer productivity. It is often related to code-reuse topics such as component-based software engineering.

Source-code Generation

Source-code generation is the process of generating source code based on a description of the problem or an ontological model such as a template and is accomplished with a programming tool such as a template processor or an integrated development environment (IDE). These tools allow the generation of source code through any of various means.

Programs that could generate COBOL code include:

- the DYL250/DYL260/DYL270/DYL280 series.

- Business Controls Corporation's SB-5.

- Peat Marwick Mitchell's PMM2170 application-program-generator package.

These application generators supported COBOL inserts and overrides. A macro processor, such as the C preprocessor, which replaces patterns in source code according to relatively simple rules, is a simple form of source-code generator. Source-to-source code generation tools also exist.

Low-code Applications

A low-code development platform (LCDP) is software that provides an environment programmers use to create application software through graphical user interfaces and configuration instead of traditional computer programming.

Documentation Generator

A documentation generator is a programming tool that generates software documentation intended for programmers (API documentation) or end users (end-user guide), or both, from a set of source code files, and in some cases, binary files. Some generators, such as Doxygen or Javadoc, use special comments to drive the generation.

Types of Generation

Document generation can be divided in several types:

- Batch generation (generic technique).
- Text block correspondence (documents created based on pre-defined text blocks).
- Forms (forms for websites).
- Documentation synthesis:
  - Documentation can be inferred from code.
  - Documentation can be inferred from execution traces.
  - Documentation can be inferred from mailing lists.

Some integrated development environments provide interactive access to documentation, code metadata, etc.

Integrated Development Environment

An IDE, or Integrated Development Environment, enables programmers to consolidate the different aspects of writing a computer program.

An IDE normally consists of a source code editor, build automation tools, and a debugger. Most modern IDEs have intelligent code completion. Some IDEs contain a compiler, interpreter, or both. The boundary between an integrated development environment and other parts of the broader software development environment is not well-defined. Sometimes a version control system, or various tools to simplify the construction of a graphical user interface (GUI), are integrated. Many modern IDEs also have a class browser, an object browser, and a class hierarchy diagram, for use in object-oriented software development.

High-level language programs are usually written (coded) as ASCII text into a source code file. A unique file extension (Examples: .asm .c .cpp .java .js .py) is used to identify it as a source code file. As you might guess for our examples – Assembly, "C", "C++", Java, JavaScript, and Python, however, they are just ASCII text files (other text files usually use the extension of .txt). The source code produced by the programmer must be converted to an executable machine code file specifically for the computer's CPU (usually an Intel or Intel-compatible CPU within today's world of computers). There are several steps in getting a program from its source code stage to running the program on your computer. Historically, we had to use several software programs (a text editor, a compiler, a linker, and operating system commands) to make the conversion and run the program. However, today all those software programs with their associated tasks have been integrated into one program. However, this one program is really many software items that create an environment used by programmers to develop software. Thus the name: Integrated Development Environment or IDE.

Programs written in a high-level language are either directly executed by some kind of interpreter or converted into machine code by a compiler (and assembler and linker) for the CPU to execute. JavaScript, Perl, Python, and Ruby are examples of interpreted programming languages. C, C++, C#, Java, and Swift are examples of compiled programming languages. The following figure shows the progression of activity in an IDE as a programmer enters the source code and then directs the IDE to compile and run the program.

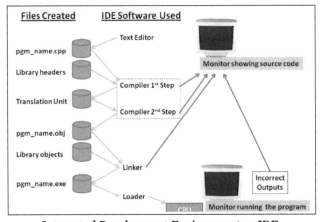

Integrated Development Environment or IDE.

Upon starting the IDE software the programmer usually indicates the file he or she wants to open for editing as source code. As they make changes they might either do a "save as" or "save". When they have finished entering the source code, they usually direct the IDE to "compile & run" the program. The IDE does the following steps:

- If there are any unsaved changes to the source code file it has the test editor save the changes.

- The compiler opens the source code file and does its first step which is executing the pre-processor compiler directives and other steps needed to get the file ready for the second step. The #include will insert header files into the code at this point. If it encounters an error, it stops the process and returns the user to the source code file within the text editor with an error message. If no problems encountered it saves the source code to a temporary file called a translation unit.

- The compiler opens the translation unit file and does its second step which is converting the programming language code to machine instructions for the CPU, a data area, and a list of items to be resolved by the linker. Any problems encountered (usually a syntax or violation of the programming language rules) stops the process and returns the user to the source code file within the text editor with an error message. If no problems encountered it saves the machine instructions, data area, and linker resolution list as an object file.

- The linker opens the program object file and links it with the library object files as needed. Unless all linker items are resolved, the process stops and returns the user to the source code file within the text editor with an error message. If no problems encountered it saves the linked objects as an executable file.

- The IDE directs the operating system's program called the loader to load the executable file into the computer's memory and have the Central Processing Unit (CPU) start processing the instructions. As the user interacts with the program, entering test data, he or she might discover that the outputs are not correct. These types of errors are called logic errors and would require the user to return to the source code to change the algorithm.

GNU Binutils

The GNU Binutils are a collection of binary tools. The main ones are:

- ld - the GNU linker.

- as - the GNU assembler.

But they also include:

- addr2line - Converts addresses into filenames and line numbers.

- ar - A utility for creating, modifying and extracting from archives.

- c++filt - Filter to demangle encoded C++ symbols.

- dlltool - Creates files for building and using DLLs.

- gold - A new, faster, ELF only linker, still in beta test.

- gprof - Displays profiling information.

- nlmconv - Converts object code into an NLM.

- nm - Lists symbols from object files.

- objcopy - Copies and translates object files.

- objdump - Displays information from object files.

- ranlib - Generates an index to the contents of an archive.

- readelf - Displays information from any ELF format object file.

- size - Lists the section sizes of an object or archive file.

- strings - Lists printable strings from files.

- strip - Discards symbols.

- windmc - A Windows compatible message compiler.

- windres - A compiler for Windows resource files.

Most of these programs use BFD, the Binary File Descriptor library, to do low-level manipulation. Many of them also use the opcodes library to assemble and disassemble machine instructions.

The binutils have been ported to most major Unix variants as well as Wintel systems, and their main reason for existence is to give the GNU system (and GNU/Linux) the facility to compile and link programs.

Obtaining Binutils

The latest release of GNU binutils is 2.35.1. The various NEWS files (binutils, gas, and ld) have details of what has changed in this release.

```
git clone git://sourceware.org/git/binutils-gdb.git
```

Alternatively, you can use the gitweb interface, or the source snapshots, available as bzipped tar files via anonymous FTP from ftp://sourceware.org/pub/binutils/snapshots.

Bug Reports

There is a bug-tracking system at https://sourceware.org/bugzilla/.

Mailing Lists

There are three binutils mailing lists:

```
<bug-binutils@gnu.org> (archives)
```

For reporting bugs:

```
<binutils@sourceware.org> (archives)
```

For discussing binutils issues:

```
binutils-cvs (archives)
```

A read-only mailing list containing the notes from checkins to the binutils git repository.

Essential GNU Binutils Tools

Imagine not having access to a software's source code but still being able to understand how the software is implemented, find vulnerabilities in it, and—better yet—fix the bugs. All of this in binary form. It sounds like having superpowers, doesn't it?

You, too, can possess such superpowers, and the GNU binary utilities (binutils) are a good starting point. The GNU binutils are a collection of binary tools that are installed by default on all Linux distributions.

Binary analysis is the most underestimated skill in the computer industry. It is mostly utilized by malware analysts, reverse engineers, and people working on low-level software.

```
[~]# cat /etc/redhat-release
Red Hat Enterprise Linux Server release 7.6 (Maipo)
[~]#
[~]# uname -r
3.10.0-957.el7.x86_64
[~]#
```

Note that some packaging commands (like rpm) might not be available on Debian-based distributions, so use the equivalent dpkg command where applicable.

Software Development 101

In the open source world, many of us are focused on software in source form; when the software's source code is readily available, it is easy to simply get a copy of the source code, open your favorite editor, get a cup of coffee, and start exploring.

But the source code is not what is executed on the CPU; it is the binary or machine language instructions that are executed on the CPU. The binary or executable file is what you get when you compile the source code. People skilled in debugging often get their edge by understanding this difference.

Compilation 101

Before digging into the binutils package itself, it's good to understand the basics of compilation.

Compilation is the process of converting a program from its source or text form in a certain programming language (C/C++) into machine code.

Machine code is the sequence of 1's and 0's that are understood by a CPU (or hardware in general) and therefore can be executed or run by the CPU. This machine code is saved to a file in a specific format that is often referred to as an executable file or a binary file. On Linux (and BSD, when using Linux Binary Compatibility), this is called ELF (Executable and Linkable Format).

The compilation process goes through a series of complicated steps before it presents an executable or binary file for a given source file. Consider this source program (C code) as an example. Open your favorite editor and type out this program:

```
#include <stdio.h>

int main(void)
{
printf("Hello World\n");
return 0;
}
```

Step 1: Preprocessing with cpp

The C preprocessor (cpp) is used to expand all macros and include the header files. In this example, the header file stdio.h will be included in the source code. stdio.h is a header file that contains information on a printf function that is used within the program. cpp runs on the source code, and the resulting instructions are saved in a file called hello.i. Open the file with a text editor to see its contents. The source code for printing hello world is at the bottom of the file.

```
[testdir]# cat hello.c
#include <stdio.h>
```

```
int main(void)
{
printf("Hello World\n");
return 0;
}
[testdir]#
[testdir]# cpp hello.c > hello.i
[testdir]#
[testdir]# ls -lrt
total 24
-rw-r--r--. 1 root root 76 Sep 13 03:20 hello.c
-rw-r--r--. 1 root root 16877 Sep 13 03:22 hello.i
[testdir]#
```

Step 2: Compilation with gcc

This is the stage where preprocessed source code from Step 1 is converted to assembly language instructions without creating an object file. It uses the GNU Compiler Collection (gcc). After running the gcc command with the -S option on the hello.i file, it creates a new file called hello.s. This file contains the assembly language instructions for the C program.

You can view the contents using any editor or the cat command.

```
[testdir]#
[testdir]# gcc -Wall -S hello.i
[testdir]#
[testdir]# ls -l
total 28
-rw-r--r--. 1 root root 76 Sep 13 03:20 hello.c
-rw-r--r--. 1 root root 16877 Sep 13 03:22 hello.i
-rw-r--r--. 1 root root 448 Sep 13 03:25 hello.s
[testdir]#
[testdir]# cat hello.s
.file "hello.c"
.section .rodata
.LC0:
.string "Hello World"
.text
.globl main
.type main, @function
main:
.LFB0:
.cfi_startproc
```

```
pushq %rbp
.cfi_def_cfa_offset 16
.cfi_offset 6, -16
movq %rsp, %rbp
.cfi_def_cfa_register 6
movl $.LC0, %edi
call puts
movl $0, %eax
popq %rbp
.cfi_def_cfa 7, 8
ret
.cfi_endproc
.LFE0:
.size main, .-main
.ident "GCC: (GNU) 4.8.5 20150623 (Red Hat 4.8.5-36)"
.section .note.GNU-stack,"",@progbits
[testdir]#
```

Step 3: Assembling with as

The purpose of an assembler is to convert assembly language instructions into machine language code and generate an object file that has a .o extension. Use the GNU assembler as that is available by default on all Linux platforms.

```
[testdir]# as hello.s -o hello.o
[testdir]#
[testdir]# ls -l
total 32
-rw-r--r--. 1 root root 76 Sep 13 03:20 hello.c
-rw-r--r--. 1 root root 16877 Sep 13 03:22 hello.i
-rw-r--r--. 1 root root 1496 Sep 13 03:39 hello.o
-rw-r--r--. 1 root root 448 Sep 13 03:25 hello.s
[testdir]#
```

You now have your first file in the ELF format; however, you cannot execute it yet. Later, you will see the difference between an object file and an executable file.

```
[testdir]# file hello.o
hello.o: ELF 64-bit LSB relocatable, x86-64, version 1 (SYSV),
not stripped
```

Step 4: Linking with ld

This is the final stage of compilation, when the object files are linked to create an executable. An executable usually requires external functions that often come from system libraries (libc).

You can directly invoke the linker with the ld command; however, this command is somewhat complicated. Instead, you can use the gcc compiler with the -v (verbose) flag to understand how linking happens. (Using the ld command for linking is an exercise left for you to explore.)

```
[testdir]# gcc -v hello.o
Using built-in specs.
COLLECT_GCC=gcc
COLLECT_LTO_WRAPPER=/usr/libexec/gcc/x86_64-redhat-linux/4.8.5/
lto-wrapper
Target: x86_64-redhat-linux
Configured with: ../configure --prefix=/usr --mandir=/usr/share/
man [...] --build=x86_64-redhat-linux
Thread model: posix
gcc version 4.8.5 20150623 (Red Hat 4.8.5-36) (GCC)
COMPILER_PATH=/usr/libexec/gcc/x86_64-redhat-linux/4.8.5/:/
usr/libexec/gcc/x86_64-redhat-linux/4.8.5/:[...]:/usr/lib/gcc/
x86_64-redhat-linux/
LIBRARY_PATH=/usr/lib/gcc/x86_64-redhat-linux/4.8.5/:/usr/
lib/gcc/x86_64-redhat-linux/4.8.5/../../../../lib64/:/lib/../
lib64/:/usr/lib/../lib64/:/usr/lib/gcc/x86_64-redhat-li-
nux/4.8.5/../../../:/lib/:/usr/lib/
COLLECT_GCC_OPTIONS='-v' '-mtune=generic' '-march=x86-64'
/usr/libexec/gcc/x86_64-redhat-linux/4.8.5/collect2
--build-id --no-add-needed --eh-frame-hdr --hash-style=gnu
[...]/../../../../lib64/crtn.o
[testdir]#
```

After running this command, you should see an executable file named a.out:

```
[testdir]# ls -l
total 44
-rwxr-xr-x. 1 root root 8440 Sep 13 03:45 a.out
-rw-r--r--. 1 root root 76 Sep 13 03:20 hello.c
-rw-r--r--. 1 root root 16877 Sep 13 03:22 hello.i
-rw-r--r--. 1 root root 1496 Sep 13 03:39 hello.o
-rw-r--r--. 1 root root 448 Sep 13 03:25 hello.s
```

Running the file command on a.out shows that it is indeed an ELF executable:

```
[testdir]# file a.out
a.out: ELF 64-bit LSB executable, x86-64, version 1 (SYSV),
dynamically linked (uses shared libs), for GNU/Linux 2.6.32,
```

```
BuildID[sha1]=48e4c11901d54d4bf1b6e3826baf18215e4255e5, not
stripped
```

Run your executable file to see if it does as the source code instructs:

```
[testdir]# ./a.out
Hello World
```

It does! So much happens behind the scenes just to print Hello World on the screen. Imagine what happens in more complicated programs.

Explore the Binutils Tools

This exercise provided a good background for utilizing the tools that are in the binutils package.

```
[~]# rpm -qa | grep binutils
binutils-2.27-34.base.el7.x86_64
```

The following tools are available in the binutils packages:

```
[~]# rpm -ql binutils-2.27-34.base.el7.x86_64 | grep bin/
/usr/bin/addr2line
/usr/bin/ar
/usr/bin/as
/usr/bin/c++filt
/usr/bin/dwp
/usr/bin/elfedit
/usr/bin/gprof
/usr/bin/ld
/usr/bin/ld.bfd
/usr/bin/ld.gold
/usr/bin/nm
/usr/bin/objcopy
/usr/bin/objdump
/usr/bin/ranlib
/usr/bin/readelf
/usr/bin/size
/usr/bin/strings
/usr/bin/strip
```

The compilation exercise above already explored two of these tools: the as command was used as an assembler, and the ld command was used as a linker.

readelf: Displays Information about ELF Files

The exercise above mentioned the terms object file and executable file. Using the files from that exercise, enter readelf using the -h (header) option to dump the files' ELF header on your screen. Notice that the object file ending with the .o extension is shown as Type: REL (Relocatable file):

```
[testdir]# readelf -h hello.o
ELF Header:
Magic: 7f 45 4c 46 02 01 01 00 [...]
[...]
Type: REL (Relocatable file)
[...]
```

If you try to execute this file, you will get an error saying it cannot be executed. This simply means that it doesn't yet have the information that is required for it to be executed on the CPU.

Remember, you need to add the x or executable bit on the object file first using the chmod command or else you will get a Permission denied error.

```
[testdir]# ./hello.o
bash: ./hello.o: Permission denied
[testdir]# chmod +x ./hello.o
[testdir]#
[testdir]# ./hello.o
bash: ./hello.o: cannot execute binary file
```

If you try the same command on the a.out file, you see that its type is an EXEC (Executable file).

```
[testdir]# readelf -h a.out
ELF Header:
Magic: 7f 45 4c 46 02 01 01 00 00 00 00 00 00 00 00 00
Class: ELF64
[...] Type: EXEC (Executable file)
```

As seen before, this file can directly be executed by the CPU:

```
[testdir]# ./a.out
Hello World
```

The readelf command gives a wealth of information about a binary. Here, it tells you that it is in ELF64-bit format, which means it can be executed only on a 64-bit CPU and won't work on a 32-bit CPU. It also tells you that it is meant to be executed on X86-64 (Intel/AMD) architecture. The entry point into the binary is at address 0x400430, which is just the address of the main function within the C source program.

Try the readelf command on the other system binaries you know, like ls. Note that your output (especially Type:) might differ on RHEL 8 or Fedora 30 systems and above due to position independent executable (PIE) changes made for security reasons.

```
[testdir]# readelf -h /bin/ls
ELF Header:
Magic: 7f 45 4c 46 02 01 01 00 00 00 00 00 00 00 00 00
Class: ELF64
Data: 2's complement, little endian
Version: 1 (current)
OS/ABI: UNIX - System V
ABI Version: 0
Type: EXEC (Executable file)
```

Learn what system libraries the ls command is dependent on using the ldd command, as follows:

```
[testdir]# ldd /bin/ls
linux-vdso.so.1 => (0x00007ffd7d746000)
libselinux.so.1 => /lib64/libselinux.so.1 (0x00007f060daca000)
libcap.so.2 => /lib64/libcap.so.2 (0x00007f060d8c5000)
libacl.so.1 => /lib64/libacl.so.1 (0x00007f060d6bc000)
libc.so.6 => /lib64/libc.so.6 (0x00007f060d2ef000)
libpcre.so.1 => /lib64/libpcre.so.1 (0x00007f060d08d000)
libdl.so.2 => /lib64/libdl.so.2 (0x00007f060ce89000)
/lib64/ld-linux-x86-64.so.2 (0x00007f060dcf1000)
libattr.so.1 => /lib64/libattr.so.1 (0x00007f060cc84000)
libpthread.so.0 => /lib64/libpthread.so.0 (0x00007f060ca68000)
```

Run readelf on the libc library file to see what kind of file it is. As it points out, it is a DYN (Shared object file), which means it can't be directly executed on its own; it must be used by an executable file that internally uses any functions made available by the library.

```
[testdir]# readelf -h /lib64/libc.so.6
ELF Header:
Magic: 7f 45 4c 46 02 01 01 03 00 00 00 00 00 00 00 00
Class: ELF64
Data: 2's complement, little endian
Version: 1 (current)
OS/ABI: UNIX - GNU
ABI Version: 0
Type: DYN (Shared object file)
```

size: Lists Section Sizes and the Total Size

The size command works only on object and executable files, so if you try running it on a simple ASCII file, it will throw an error saying File format not recognized.

```
[testdir]# echo "test" > file1
[testdir]# cat file1
test
[testdir]# file file1
file1: ASCII text
[testdir]# size file1
size: file1: File format not recognized
```

Now, run size on the object file and the executable file from the exercise above. Notice that the executable file (a.out) has considerably more information than the object file (hello.o), based on the output of size command:

```
[testdir]# size hello.o
text data bss dec hex filename
89 0 0 89 59 hello.o
[testdir]# size a.out
text data bss dec hex filename
1194 540 4 1738 6ca a.out
```

But what do the text, data, and bss sections mean?

The text sections refer to the code section of the binary, which has all the executable instructions. The data sections are where all the initialized data is, and bss is where all the uninitialized data is stored.

Compare size with some of the other available system binaries.

For the ls command:

```
[testdir]# size /bin/ls
text data bss dec hex filename
103119 4768 3360 111247 1b28f /bin/ls
```

You can see that gcc and gdb are far bigger programs than ls just by looking at the output of the size command:

```
[testdir]# size /bin/gcc
text data bss dec hex filename
755549 8464 81856 845869 ce82d /bin/gcc
[testdir]# size /bin/gdb
text data bss dec hex filename
6650433 90842 152280 6893555 692ff3 /bin/gdb
```

strings: Prints the Strings of Printable Characters in Files

It is often useful to add the -d flag to the strings command to show only the printable characters from the data section.

hello.o is an object file that contains instructions to print out the text Hello World. Hence, the only output from the strings command is Hello World.

```
[testdir]# strings -d hello.o
Hello World
```

Running strings on a.out (an executable), on the other hand, shows additional information that was included in the binary during the linking phase:

```
[testdir]# strings -d a.out
/lib64/ld-linux-x86-64.so.2
!^BU
libc.so.6
puts
__libc_start_main
__gmon_start__
GLIBC_2.2.5
UH-0
UH-0
=(
[]A\A]A^A_
Hello World
;*3$"
```

Recall that compilation is the process of converting source code instructions into machine code. Machine code consists of only 1's and 0's and is difficult for humans to read. Therefore, it helps to present machine code as assembly language instructions. What do assembly languages look like? Remember that assembly language is architecture-specific; since I am using Intel or x86-64 architecture, the instructions will be different if you're using ARM architecture to compile the same programs.

objdump: Displays Information from Object Files

Another binutils tool that can dump the machine language instructions from the binary is called objdump.

Use the -d option, which disassembles all assembly instructions from the binary.

```
[testdir]# objdump -d hello.o
hello.o: file format elf64-x86-64
Disassembly of section .text:
```

```
0000000000000000:
0: 55 push %rbp
1: 48 89 e5 mov %rsp,%rbp
4: bf 00 00 00 00 mov $0x0,%edi
9: e8 00 00 00 00 callq e
e: b8 00 00 00 00 mov $0x0,%eax
13: 5d pop %rbp
14: c3 retq
```

This output seems intimidating at first, but take a moment to understand it before moving ahead. Recall that the .text section has all the machine code instructions. The assembly instructions can be seen in the fourth column (i.e., push, mov, callq, pop, retq). These instructions act on registers, which are memory locations built into the CPU. The registers in this example are rbp, rsp, edi, eax, etc., and each register has a special meaning.

Now run objdump on the executable file (a.out) and see what you get. The output of objdump on the executable can be large, so I've narrowed it down to the main function using the grep command:

```
[testdir]# objdump -d a.out | grep -A 9 main\>
000000000040051d:
40051d: 55 push %rbp
40051e: 48 89 e5 mov %rsp,%rbp
400521: bf d0 05 40 00 mov $0x4005d0,%edi
400526: e8 d5 fe ff ff callq 400400
40052b: b8 00 00 00 00 mov $0x0,%eax
400530: 5d pop %rbp
400531: c3 retq
```

Notice that the instructions are similar to the object file hello.o, but they have some additional information in them:

- The object file hello.o has the following instruction: callq e.

- The executable a.out consists of the following instruction with an address and a function:callq 400400 <puts@plt>.

The above assembly instruction is calling a puts function. Remember that you used a printf function in the source code. The compiler inserted a call to the puts library function to output Hello World to the screen.

Look at the instruction for a line above puts:

- The object file hello.o has the instruction mov:mov $0x0,%edi.

- The instruction mov for the executable a.out has an actual address ($0x4005d0) instead of $0x0:mov $0x4005d0,%edi.

This instruction moves whatever is present at address $0x4005d0 within the binary to the register named edi.

What else could be in the contents of that memory location? Yes, you guessed it right: it is nothing but the text Hello, World. How can you be sure?

The readelf command enables you to dump any section of the binary file (a.out) onto the screen. The following asks it to dump the .rodata, which is read-only data, onto the screen:

```
[testdir]# readelf -x .rodata a.out

Hex dump of section '.rodata':
0x004005c0 01000200 00000000 00000000 00000000 ....
0x004005d0 48656c6c 6f20576f 726c6400 Hello World.
```

You can see the text Hello World on the right-hand side and its address in binary on the left-hand side. Does it match the address you saw in the mov instruction above? Yes, it does.

strip: Discards Symbols from Object Files

This command is often used to reduce the size of the binary before shipping it to customers.

Remember that it hinders the process of debugging since vital information is removed from the binary; nonetheless, the binary executes flawlessly.

Run it on your a.out executable and notice what happens. First, ensure the binary is not stripped by running the following command:

```
[testdir]# file a.out
a.out: ELF 64-bit LSB executable, x86-64, [......] not stripped
```

Also, keep track of the number of bytes originally in the binary before running the strip command:

```
[testdir]# du -b a.out
8440 a.out
```

Now run the strip command on your executable and ensure it worked using the file command:

```
[testdir]# strip a.out
```

```
[testdir]# file a.out a.out: ELF 64-bit LSB executable, x86-64,
[......] stripped
```

After stripping the binary, its size went down to 6296 from the previous 8440 bytes for this small program. With this much savings for a tiny program, no wonder large programs often are stripped.

```
[testdir]# du -b a.out
6296 a.out
```

addr2line: Converts Addresses into File Names and Line Numbers

The addr2line tool simply looks up addresses in the binary file and matches them up with lines in the C source code program. Pretty cool, isn't it?

Write another test program for this; only this time ensure you compile it with the -g flag for gcc, which adds additional debugging information for the binary and also helps by including the line numbers (provided in the source code here):

```
[testdir]# cat -n atest.c
1 #include <stdio.h>
2
3 int globalvar = 100;
4
5 int function1(void)
6 {
7 printf("Within function1\n");
8 return 0;
9 }
10
11 int function2(void)
12 {
13 printf("Within function2\n");
14 return 0;
15 }
16
17 int main(void)
18 {
19 function1();
20 function2();
21 printf("Within main\n");
22 return 0;
23 }
```

Compile with the -g flag and execute it.

```
[testdir]# gcc -g atest.c
[testdir]# ./a.out
Within function1
Within function2
Within main
```

Now use objdump to identify memory addresses where your functions begin. You can use the grep command to filter out specific lines that you want. The addresses for your functions are highlighted below:

```
[testdir]# objdump -d a.out | grep -A 2 -E 'main>:|func-
tion1>:|function2>:'
000000000040051d :
40051d: 55 push %rbp
40051e: 48 89 e5 mov %rsp,%rbp
--
0000000000400532 :
400532: 55 push %rbp
400533: 48 89 e5 mov %rsp,%rbp
--
0000000000400547:
400547: 55 push %rbp
400548: 48 89 e5 mov %rsp,%rbp
```

Now use the addr2line tool to map these addresses from the binary to match those of the C source code:

```
[testdir]# addr2line -e a.out 40051d
/tmp/testdir/atest.c:6
[testdir]#
[testdir]# addr2line -e a.out 400532
/tmp/testdir/atest.c:12
[testdir]#
[testdir]# addr2line -e a.out 400547
/tmp/testdir/atest.c:18
```

It says that 40051d starts on line number 6 in the source file atest.c, which is the line where the starting brace ({) for function1 starts. Match the output for function2 and main.

nm: Lists Symbols from Object Files

Use the C program above to test the nm tool. Compile it quickly using gcc and execute it.

```
[testdir]# gcc atest.c
[testdir]# ./a.out
Within function1
Within function2
Within main
```

Now run nm and grep for information on your functions and variables:

```
[testdir]# nm a.out | grep -Ei 'function|main|globalvar'
000000000040051d T function1
0000000000400532 T function2
000000000060102c D globalvar
U    __libc_start_main@@GLIBC_2.2.5
0000000000400547 T main
```

You can see that the functions are marked T, which stands for symbols in the text section, whereas variables are marked as D, which stands for symbols in the initialized data section.

Imagine how useful it will be to run this command on binaries where you do not have source code? This allows you to peek inside and understand which functions and variables are used. Unless, of course, the binaries have been stripped, in which case they contain no symbols, and therefore the nm command wouldn't be very helpful, as you can see here:

```
[testdir]# strip a.out
[testdir]# nm a.out | grep -Ei 'function|main|globalvar'
nm: a.out: no symbols
```

Parser Generators

A parser generator is a good tool that you should make part of your toolbox. A parser generator takes a grammar as input and automatically generates source code that can parse streams of characters using the grammar.

The generated code is a parser, which takes a sequence of characters and tries to match the sequence against the grammar. The parser typically produces a parse tree, which shows how grammar productions are expanded into a sentence that matches the character sequence. The root of the parse tree is the starting nonterminal of the grammar. Each node of the parse tree expands into one production of the grammar.

The final step of parsing is to do something useful with this parse tree. Recursive abstract data types are often used to represent an expression in a language, like HTML, or Markdown, or Java, or algebraic expressions. A recursive abstract data type that represents a language expression is called an abstract syntax tree (AST).

Antlr is a mature and widely-used parser generator for Java, and other languages as well. The remainder of this reading will get you started with Antlr.

An Antlr Grammar

The code for the examples that follow can be found on Github as fa15-ex18-parser-generators.

Here is what our HTML grammar looks like as an Antlr source file:

```
grammar Html;


root : html EOF;

html : ( italic | normal ) *;

italic : '<i>' html '</i>';

normal : TEXT;

TEXT : ~[<>]+;  /* represents a string of one or more charac-
ters that are not < or >
```

Let's break it down.

Each Antlr rule consists of a name, followed by a colon, followed by its definition, terminated by a semicolon.

Nonterminals in Antlr have to be lowercase: root, html, normal, italic. Terminals are either quoted strings, like `'<i>'`, or capitalized names, like EOF and TEXT.

```
root : html EOF;
```

root is the entry point of the grammar. This is the nonterminal that the whole input needs to match. We don't have to call it root. The entry point can be any nonterminal.

EOF is a special terminal, defined by Antlr, that means the end of the input. It stands for end of file, though your input may also come from a string or a network connection rather than just a file.

```
html : ( normal | italic ) *;
```

This rule shows that Antlr rules can have the alternation operator |, the repetition operators * and +, and parentheses for grouping, in the same way we've been using in the grammars reading. Optional parts can be marked with ?, just like we did earlier, but this particular grammar doesn't use ?

```
italic : '<i>' html '</i>';

normal : TEXT;

TEXT : ~[<>]+;
```

TEXT is a terminal matching sequences of characters that are neither < nor >. In the more conventional regular expression syntax used earlier in this reading, we would write [^<>] to represent all characters except < and >. Antlr uses a slightly different syntax – ~ means not, and it is put in front of the square brackets instead of inside them, so ~[<>] matches any character except < and >.

In Antlr, terminals can be defined using regular expressions, not just fixed strings. For example, here are some other terminal patterns we used in the URL grammar earlier in the reading, now written in Antlr syntax and with Antlr's required naming convention:

```
IDENTIFIER : [a-z]+;

INTEGER : [0-9]+;
```

Generating the Parser

The rest of this reading will focus on the Sum grammar used in the exercise above, which we'll store in a file called Sum.g4. Antlr 4 grammar files end with .g4 by convention.

The Antlr parser generator tool converts a grammar source file like Sum.g4 into Java classes that implement a parser. To do that, you need to go to a command prompt (Terminal or Command Prompt) and run a command like this:

```
java -jar antlr.jar Sum.g4
```

You'll need to make sure you're in the right folder (where Sum.g4 is) and that antlr. jar is in there too (or refer to it where it is in your project folder structure – it may be a relative path like ../../lib/antlr.jar).

Assuming you don't have any syntax errors in your grammar file, the parser generator will produce new Java source files in the current folder.The generated code is divided into several cooperating modules:

- The lexer takes a stream of characters as input, and produces a stream of terminals as output, like NUMBER, +, and (. For Sum.g4, the generated lexer is called SumLexer.java.

- The parser takes the stream of terminals produced by the lexer and produces a parse tree. The generated parser is called SumParser.java.

- The tree walker lets you write code that walks over the parse tree produced by the parser, as explained below. The generated tree walker files are the interface SumListener.java, and an empty implementation of the interface, SumBaseListener.java.

Antlr also generates two text files, Sum.tokens and SumLexer.tokens, that list the terminals that Antlr found in your grammar. These aren't needed for a simple parser, but they're needed when you include grammars inside other grammars.

- Never edit the files generated by Antlr. The right way to change your parser is to edit the grammar source file, Sum.g4, and then regenerate the Java classes.

- Regenerate the files whenever you edit the grammar file. This is easy to forget when Eclipse is compiling all your Java source files automatically. Eclipse does not regenerate your parser automatically. Make sure you rerun the java -jar ... command whenever you change your .g4 file.

- Refresh your project in Eclipse each time you regenerate the files. You can do this by clicking on your project in Eclipse and pressing F5, or right-clicking and choosing Refresh. The reason is that Eclipse sometimes uses older versions of files already part of the source, even if they have been modified on your filesystem.

Calling the Parser

Now that you've generated the Java classes for your parser, you'll want to use them from your own code.

First we need to make a stream of characters to feed to the lexer. Antlr has a class ANTLRInputStream that makes this easy. It can take a String, or a Reader, or an InputStream as input. Here we are using a string:

```
CharStream stream = new ANTLRInputStream("54+(2+89)");
```

Next, we create an instance of the lexer class that our grammar file generated, and pass it the character stream:

```
SumLexer lexer = new SumLexer(stream);

TokenStream tokens = new CommonTokenStream(lexer);
```

The result is a stream of terminals, which we can then feed to the parser:

```
SumParser parser = new SumParser(tokens);
```

To actually do the parsing, we call a particular nonterminal on the parser. The generated parser has one method for every nonterminal in our grammar, including root(), sum(), and addend(). We want to call the nonterminal that represents the set of strings that we want to match – in this case, root(). the parse tree produced by parsing the sum expression.

Calling it produces a parse tree:

```
SumParser parser = new SumParser(tokens);
```

For debugging, we can then print this tree out:

```
System.err.println(tree.toStringTree(parser));
```

Or we can display it in a handy graphical form:

```
Trees.inspect(tree, parser);
```

which pops up a window with the parse tree shown on the right.

Traversing the Parse Tree

So we've used the parser to turn a stream of characters into a parse tree, which shows how the grammar matches the stream. Now we need to do something with this parse tree. We're going to translate it into a value of a recursive abstract data type.

The first step is to learn how to traverse the parse tree. To do this, we use a ParseTree-Walker, which is an Antlr class that walks over a parse tree, visiting every node in order, top-to-bottom, left-to-right. As it visits each node in the tree, the walker calls methods on a listener object that we provide, which implements SumListener interface.

Just to warm up, here's a simple implementation of SumListener that just prints a message every time the walker calls us, so we can see how it gets used:

```
class PrintEverything implements SumListener {

    @Override public void enterRoot(SumParser.RootContext con-
text) {

        System.err.println("entering root");

    }

    @Override public void exitRoot(SumParser.RootContext con-
text) {

        System.err.println("exiting root");

    }


    @Override public void enterSum(SumParser.SumContext con-
```

```
text) {

        System.err.println("entering sum");

    }

    @Override public void exitSum(SumParser.SumContext context)
{

        System.err.println("exiting sum");

    }


    @Override public void enterAddend(SumParser.AddendContext
context) {

        System.err.println("entering addend");

    }

    @Override public void exitAddend(SumParser.AddendContext
context) {

        System.err.println("exiting addend");

    }


    @Override public void visitTerminal(TerminalNode terminal)
{

        System.err.println("terminal " + terminal.getText());

    }


    // don't need these here, so just make them empty implemen-
tations
    @Override public void enterEveryRule(ParserRuleContext con-
text) { }
    @Override public void exitEveryRule(ParserRuleContext con-
text) { }
    @Override public void visitErrorNode(ErrorNode node) { }

}
```

Notice that every nonterminal N in the grammar has corresponding enterN() and exitN() methods in the listener interface, which are called when the tree walk enters and exits a parse tree node for nonterminal N, respectively. There is also a visitTerminal() that is called when the walk reaches a leaf of the parse tree. Each of these methods has a parameter that provides information about the nonterminal or terminal node that the walk is currently visiting.

The listener interface also has some methods that we don't need. The methods enterEveryRule() and exitEveryRule() are called on entering and exiting any nonterminal node, in case we want some generic behavior. The method visitErrorNode() is called if the input contained a syntax error that produced an error node in the parse tree. In the parser we're writing, however, a syntax error causes an exception to be thrown, so we won't see any parse trees with error nodes in them. The interface requires us to implement these methods, but we can just leave their method bodies empty.

```
ParseTreeWalker walker = new ParseTreeWalker();

SumListener listener = new PrintEverything();

walker.walk(listener, tree);
```

If we walk over the parse tree with this listener, then we see the following output:

```
entering root

entering sum

entering addend

terminal 54

exiting addend

terminal +

entering addend

terminal (

entering sum

entering addend

terminal 2

exiting addend

terminal +

entering addend

terminal 89
```

```
exiting addend

exiting sum

terminal )

exiting addend

exiting sum

terminal <EOF>

exiting root
```

Compare this printout with the parse tree shown at the right, and you'll see that the ParseTreeWalker is stepping through the nodes of the tree in order, from parents to children, and from left to right through the siblings.

References

- Hens, Stefan; Monperrus, Martin; Mezini, Mira (2012). "Semi-automatically extracting FAQs to improve accessibility of software development knowledge". arXiv:1203.5188. doi:10.1109/ICSE.2012.6227139

- "Launches SAS JMP 8 for Mac and Linux". Ti Journal. April 11, 2009. Retrieved December 30, 2012

- Integrated-development-environment, programmingfundamentals: press.rebus.community, Retrieved 6 April, 2020

- Salkind, Neil (2010). Encyclopedia of Research Design Encyclopedia of research design. doi:10.4135/9781412961288. ISBN 9781412961271

Permissions

All chapters in this book are published with permission under the Creative Commons Attribution Share Alike License or equivalent. Every chapter published in this book has been scrutinized by our experts. Their significance has been extensively debated. The topics covered herein carry significant information for a comprehensive understanding. They may even be implemented as practical applications or may be referred to as a beginning point for further studies.

We would like to thank the editorial team for lending their expertise to make the book truly unique. They have played a crucial role in the development of this book. Without their invaluable contributions this book wouldn't have been possible. They have made vital efforts to compile up to date information on the varied aspects of this subject to make this book a valuable addition to the collection of many professionals and students.

This book was conceptualized with the vision of imparting up-to-date and integrated information in this field. To ensure the same, a matchless editorial board was set up. Every individual on the board went through rigorous rounds of assessment to prove their worth. After which they invested a large part of their time researching and compiling the most relevant data for our readers.

The editorial board has been involved in producing this book since its inception. They have spent rigorous hours researching and exploring the diverse topics which have resulted in the successful publishing of this book. They have passed on their knowledge of decades through this book. To expedite this challenging task, the publisher supported the team at every step. A small team of assistant editors was also appointed to further simplify the editing procedure and attain best results for the readers.

Apart from the editorial board, the designing team has also invested a significant amount of their time in understanding the subject and creating the most relevant covers. They scrutinized every image to scout for the most suitable representation of the subject and create an appropriate cover for the book.

The publishing team has been an ardent support to the editorial, designing and production team. Their endless efforts to recruit the best for this project, has resulted in the accomplishment of this book. They are a veteran in the field of academics and their pool of knowledge is as vast as their experience in printing. Their expertise and guidance has proved useful at every step. Their uncompromising quality standards have made this book an exceptional effort. Their encouragement from time to time has been an inspiration for everyone.

The publisher and the editorial board hope that this book will prove to be a valuable piece of knowledge for students, practitioners and scholars across the globe.

Index

CPSIA information can be obtained
at www.ICGtesting.com
Printed in the USA
LVHW060402010622
720214LV00003B/13